Licensed by Authority

Licensed by Authority

BEN JONSON AND
THE DISCOURSES
OF CENSORSHIP

Richard Burt

Cornell University Press

Ithaca and London

First published 1993 by Cornell University Press.

Library of Congress Cataloging-in-Publication Data

Burt, Richard, 1954–
  Licensed by authority : Ben Jonson and the discourses of censorship / Richard Burt.
    p.   ;   cm.
  Includes bibliographical references and index.
  ISBN 0-8014-2782-7
    1. Jonson, Ben, 1573?–1637—Censorship.   2. Theater—Censorship—England—History—17th century.   3. Drama—Censorship—England—History—17th century.   I. Title.
  PR2642.C4B87   1993
  822'.3—dc20   92-38020

In memory of my uncle

Alan M. Hollingsworth

Contents

Preface

This book has a twin focus: it provides an account of Ben Jonson and the politics of early Stuart theater, and it provides an account of censorship. Broadly speaking, I concentrate on Jonson and early modern England in order to contest a set of ahistorical assumptions about censorship which inform present accounts of the politics of the theater. As Renaissance critics and historians have debated whether the early Stuarts were barbarians who repressed radical drama or enlightened, sophisticated rulers who licensed dramatic criticism of the state, those on both sides of the debate have increasingly turned to licensing and censorship to prove their respective cases. Although these critics and historians have contested the politics of the theater, they have not contested the meaning of censorship itself, taking it to be repressive or consensual state control intended to inhibit or silence oppositional or radical voices. In my view, to account for Jonson's case, we must historicize censorship. If we adopt the traditional definition we cannot make sense of Jonson's writings, their reception, and the shape of his career. As a dramatist who was both censored by the court and in line to become the court censor, Jonson registers with great resonance and complexity the many paradoxes and contradictions that traversed what I take to be the complicated, uneven development of theater censorship. My focus on Jonson is thus strategic. Through a reading of the exemplary paradoxes of his complex career, a career that

spans an unusually wide spectrum of courts, literary practices, theatrical venues, and codes of judgment, I undertake to displace the
moralistic, monolithic, ahistorical definition of censorship which
has informed the present debate over the Renaissance theater with a
historically specific, epistemological definition.[1] Literary censorship was less a matter of denying liberty of speech than a legitimation or delegitimation of specific discursive practices.[2]

I should add that my focus on Jonson and early modern England
is also determined by my position as a cultural critic in the postmodern present. As I wrote the book, I became increasingly atten-
tive to a proliferation of censorship cases, particularly those concerning academic freedom, political criticism, and the fine arts, and
I became increasingly struck both by their complexity and by the
difficulty of using the traditional definition of censorship to explain
them. An understanding of early modern censorship was important
not because it marked the origin and foundation of present forms of
censorship but because contemporary debates over Renaissance
censorship were empowered by the traditional, ahistorical definition of censorship I was concerned to interrogate. Reconceptualiz-
ing censorship in the early modern past, developing a more nuanced
understanding of it, could show us how to reconceptualize censorship in the postmodern present. As I suggest at length in the Conclusion, it is not enough to employ the traditional definition. In
order to criticize the kinds of censorship practiced in the postmodern present we must understand both how they differ from other
practices (in this case, early modern practices) and why it is crucial
to differentiate between them.

My critical perspective is Foucauldian and post-Marxist.[3] Following Foucault, I historicize censorship in genealogical fashion,
differentiating forms of it in the early modern past and in the
postmodern present in order to provide a critique of both. In following this procedure I hope to shift our perspective on Jonson and
the early Stuart theater significantly, to demonstrate that Jonson and
others made sense of censorship through a different set of distinctions from those assumed by modern and postmodern critics of the
Renaissance. Censorship, in my account, pervaded early Stuart
theatrical culture: it was practiced and nurtured not only by the
court but also by playwrights, theatrical entrepreneurs, printers,
poets, courtiers, and critics. Thus, the broad questions critics have

regularly asked about the theater—Who was for or against censorship? Was this text oppositional or orthodox?—simply do not make sense. Though some dramatists defended "liberty of speech," that liberty always entailed some form of censorship. Dramatists and patrons did not group themselves in opposition to censorship, or in favor of it. Rather, they debated who should censor and who have liberty, for what ends and on what grounds, and their struggle was registered in a contest over the meanings of the words *liberty* and *censorship* themselves. *License* could mean liberty or licentiousness. Words such as *censure, censor,* and *censureship* could admit ambiguous meanings. The words *censor* and *critick* might be conflated or contrasted; *censure* might be used positively or negatively to legitimate or delegitimate certain speakers and certain discourses. The meaning of *censor* itself changed during the Renaissance, passing from its classical sense to its modern sense.[4]

The present book follows what I take to be a characteristically Jonsonian strategy of exaggerating the differences between my definition of censorship and the one I contest in order to avoid the problems we would otherwise inevitably face. In defining censorship as a differentiation between legitimate and illegitimate discourses, I wish to acknowledge at the outset that my critique of a traditional moralistic discourse about censorship necessarily reinscribes rather than absolutely breaks with its central assumptions and terms. Some version of a binary model of censorship, power, or ideology will always be in place in any account of early modern literary censorship. Similarly, my genealogical critique of a moral definition of censorship does not (indeed, cannot) entirely escape moral critical terrain (the genealogical critique being itself a highly moralistic one). My point is that existing binary models (whether explicitly moralistic or not) are complicated to the point of breakdown once censorship is historicized.

Beyond acknowledging that my critique of censorship paradoxically reinscribes what it seeks to displace, I wish to clarify my use of two central critical terms throughout the book, namely, *neurosis* and *censorship* itself. I use *neurotic* to characterize Jonson's decentered subjectivity, to register a contradiction between Jonson's desire to censor himself in order to legitimate himself and his equally powerful desire to express the censored material in a different (sometimes in the same) context. By characterizing Jonson as a neurotic I wish to account for what I would call Jonson's "irregularity" as a consuming censor/critic and producing censor/author, not to denigrate him. I aim to elaborate and complicate recent antihumanist, post-Freudian symptomatic readings of the political unconscious of Jonsonian textuality. In order to recover Jonson from his earlier marginalization, modern and postmodern political critics have in turn (too quickly, in my view) marginalized critics such as Edmund Wilson (1938), who were central to Jonson's marginalization. Consequently, they have often domesticated Jonson, assimilating him to a psychological and cultural norm that leaves out of account those contradictory features that constitute a specifically neurotic Jonsonian subjectivity. Furthermore, in marginalizing Wilson, critics have indirectly adopted a model of repression that relies on an opposition between conscious intentions and unconscious forces and that has also, insofar as it has equated these terms with the censored and uncensored, displaced censorship as an object of study (repression substitutes for censorship). By refusing a stable opposition between unconscious forces and conscious intentions, between what is repressed and what is liberated, the term *neurosis* not only puts censorship on the front burner of political criticism but makes it possible to recognize how Jonson's textual strategies, such as revision and editing, or his own codes of criticism are also diverse forms of censorship.[5]

My adoption of a different, much more encompassing definition of censorship, which includes not only Jonson's textual practices but the institutional foundations of poetic production, licensing, and even literary criticism, may seem to put the term *censorship* in danger of being overwhelmed. Indeed, some readers might wonder why it should be retained at all when I assign it a positive legitimating function and insist that it cannot be decisively separated from criticism. Foucault himself treated censorship as a relic of what he called the repressive hypothesis, left behind by postmodernism. More recently Andrew Ross (1990) has suggested that *regulation* ought to be substituted for *censorship* in discussions of the National Endowment for the Arts (NEA) funding controversy.

I have retained the term for two reasons, both of which derive from my interest in accounting for the continued appeal of censorship as a tool in cultural criticism. First, by expanding the meaning of censorship to include productive as well as repressive regulatory practices, I aim to expand the critique of these practices as well, drawing attention to forms of censorship that would otherwise have remained invisible. Second, as much as I wish to achieve a fuller understanding of censorship by recognizing the diversity of its forms, I wish to foreground the difficulty and complexity of recognizing them as forms of censorship. That is, my aim is not simply to arrive at an exhaustive definition of early modern censorship but to examine the nuances, complexity, even elusiveness of this contested term. In my view, the very drive to define censorship, to pin down its meaning and determine what does or does not count as censorship, to assess which forms are more significant than others, serves to regulate (one might even say, police) its proper, legitimate use within contemporary cultural criticism.[6] The very escalation of controversy over the meaning of the term demands attention, as does the similar contest over terms to which *censorship* is often opposed: among others, one could list *criticism, diversity, debate,* and *dialogue*.

Apart from these reasons, my use of the term *censorship* is determined by the larger theoretical ambition of this book. I use it to contest the two dominant accounts of domination, so to speak, now widely in circulation. In modern accounts, repression is defined negatively as whatever keeps one from speaking. In more sophisticated versions of discourse ethics, a variety of impediments to ethical communication are acknowledged, but censorship is not generally defined as one of them (censorship supposedly having disappeared or existing only elsewhere). By contrast, postmodern accounts (ideology critique and discourse theory) acknowledge that power operates negatively but focus on more indirect discursive forms of domination, which are thought to be all the more effective for not being recognized as domination. While I side with the postmodern account of domination, I nevertheless keep one foot firmly planted in both camps. As a theoretical "payoff," the book offers a deeper sense of censorship as a problematic, not, as in more predictable postmodern critiques, a more stable notion of oppositional criticism: without giving up the traditional definition of censorship as brute repression, we can begin to see that censorship includes as well a set of paradoxical and often contradictory strategies for the administration of aesthetics and for the regulation of literary criticism.

By expanding the meaning of censorship, I aim to disturb assumptions about the court's monopoly on the benefits and evils of censorship which have informed and empowered recent work on the Renaissance and to complicate the usual response to contemporary right-wing censorial practices and the often knee-jerk, defensive reactions to neoconservative critiques of political criticism as a censorious politically correct practice. My aim is not to neutralize a critique of censorship by deconstructing a distinction between censorship and criticism which is central to many avowedly political critics. Although I am critical of a traditional account of censorship and the arguments about subversive theatrical politics which follow from it, I seek to rethink the dynamics of censorship and call attention to the ways its various forms sustain the purposes of cultural legitimation, not to replace a traditional criticism of censorship with a defense of it. To collapse criticism into censorship would be simply to replace one monolithic model of censorship with another.[7] Furthermore, in arguing that the importance of various kinds of censors (such as the court and the market) is relative, that it cannot be decided apart from local cases, I nevertheless want to keep their differences clear. State censorship is repressive in ways that market censorship, for example, is not: the threat of torturing an author's body (or of burning his or her books) is not the same as the threat of penury resulting from lack of literary patronage; a death threat is not the same thing as being denied funding by the NEA. Yet if there are differences between forms of censorship, there is not, in my view, a stable binary opposition between criticism and censorship (each regarded as a self-identical, unified term), nor does one form of censorship always take priority over another; rather, the relationship between criticism and censorship is a contradictory one in which criticism can also serve as a form of censorship and censorship can also serve as a form of criticism.[8]

In interrogating the meaning of censorship and calling for a broader reflection on the historical role of criticism as a legitimating and delegitimating activity, this book speaks both to its primary intended audience of Renaissance critics and to a broad spectrum of critics and historians studying censorship in other periods or disciplines. My sense of early Stuart theater censorship as multiple and paradoxical bears importantly, I think, on a now widely shared assumption that literary criticism and literature are always institutionally constrained and on recent debates within the profession over the implications of that constraint, conducted between critics who wish to politicize literary criticism and critics who wish to salvage through discourse ethics some notion of literary criticism based on consensus, community, and the public sphere.

Some of the book has already seen print. Parts of the Introduction were published in " ' 'Tis Writ by Me': Massinger's *The Roman Actor* and the Politics of Reception in the Renaissance Theatre," *Theatre Journal* (Fall 1988): 332–46, and parts of the second and third chapters were published as " 'Licensed by Authority': Ben Jonson and the Politics of Early Stuart Theater," *English Literary History* (Fall 1987): 529–60. I am grateful to the Johns Hopkins University Press for permission to publish revisions of the material.

In helping me to develop the argument and focus of this book, Leonard Tennenhouse provided invaluable support and direction. Timothy Murray and Christopher Pye, the readers for Cornell University Press, gave the manuscript especially detailed, thoughtful, and illuminating readings. I am also deeply indebted to Stephen Greenblatt, whose dazzling undergraduate and graduate courses on Renaissance literature and Marxism and literature, and whose direction of my dissertation on Shakespearean comedy, made it possible to write this book. I have been fortunate to exchange work with and to receive extremely useful readings from John Archer, Lee Beier, Mark Breitenberg, Lynda Boose, Martin Butler, Stephen Clingman, Stuart Culver, Jonathan Dollimore, Ian Donaldson, Richard Dutton, Lee Edwards, Philip Finkelpearl, Jonathan Goldberg, Judith Haber, Alexandra Halasz, Don Hedrick, Jim Holstun, Lindsay Kaplan, Wally Kerrigan, Randall Knopper, Joseph Loewenstein, Cristina Malcolmson, Leah Marcus, Katharine Maus, Ron McDonald, Louis Montrose, David Norbrook, Stephen Orgel, Dennis Porter, Alan Sinfield, Michael Schoenfeldt, Peter Stallybrass, Lawrence Venuti, Jeffrey Wallen, and Rob Wilson. Richard Dutton first got me thinking about Jonson and literary criticism. In addition to correcting an embarrassing number of errors, Martin Butler helped sharpen my focus on Jonson's later career.

Critics with whom I am often in serious disagreement have been extremely generous in responding to my criticisms of their work. Conversations about my views on censorship with John Archer,

Hussein Ibish, Amy Kaplan, Tim Murray, Mary Russo, Jeff Wallen, and George Yudice have been invaluable. I have also benefited from presenting parts of the book to my department, to the Five College Faculty Seminar on the Renaissance, the Columbia Seminar on the Renaissance, and at annual meetings of the Modern Language Association, the Shakespeare Association of America, the Renaissance Society of America, and various international conferences held in England and Scotland. I thank the American Council of Learned Societies and the graduate school of the University of Massachusetts for travel grants that got me to these conferences. I am grateful also to the Institute for the Advanced Study of the Humanities for making me a fellow and for providing me with the opportunity to teach a faculty seminar on censorship, political criticism, and the public sphere. My thanks to Jacqueline Le Blanc and Roger Stritmatter for proofreading the manuscript. I record here the debts I owe three friends, Rochelle Slamovich, Charles K. Smith, and Murray Cohen. Finally, I acknowledge with pleasure that this book would not have been completed without the sustaining love of my baby daughter, Nora, herself a terrific taster of books.

RICHARD BURT

Amherst, Massachusetts

Abbreviations

H & S   *Ben Jonson*. Edited by C. H. Herford, Evelyn Simpson, and Percy Simpson. 11 vols. Oxford: Clarendon Press, 1925–52.

ES   *The Elizabethan Stage*. Edited by E. K. Chambers. 4 vols. Oxford: Clarendon Press, 1923–31.

JCS   *The Jacobean and Caroline Stage*. Edited by G. E. Bentley. 7 vols. Oxford: Clarendon Press, 1941–68.

Unless otherwise indicated, all citations of Jonson's plays are to *The Complete Plays of Ben Jonson*, ed. G. A. Wilkes, 4 vols. (Oxford: Clarendon Press, 1982); all citations of *Discoveries* are to *Ben Jonson: The Complete Poems*, ed. Robert Hunter (New Haven: Yale University Press, 1975); all citations of the poems are to *Ben Jonson: Poems*, ed. Ian Donaldson (London: Oxford University Press, 1975); all citations of the masques are to *Ben Jonson: The Complete Masques*, ed. Stephen Orgel (New Haven: Yale University Press, 1969). All citations of Shakespeare's plays are to *The Complete Works of Shakespeare*, ed. David Bevington, 3d ed. (Glendale, Ill.: Scott, Foresman, 1980). Citations of James Shirley, *The Bird in a Cage*, are to *James Shirley's "The Bird in a Cage": A Critical Edition*, ed. Frances Senescu (New York: Garland, 1980).

Licensed by Authority

Ben Jonson and the
Discourses of Censorship

Writing about theater censorship in the Renaissance, critics have often relied on images of the cropped ears of William
Prynne and severed hand of John Stubbes, of book burnings, imprisoned authors, and shattered printing presses. These images
have a particular resonance given the recent death threat against
Salman Rushdie and the public burnings of his novel *The Satanic
Verses,* and the resurgence of a broad range of attempts to censor the
fine arts and mass culture makes it all the more important that we
understand the meaning of these images of Renaissance censorship.[1] Yet their very seriousness has often led critics to regard
censorship in monolithic, narrow terms, defining it exclusively as a
negative exercise of power centered in the court. In her influential
account of Renaissance censorship, for example, Annabel Patterson
maintains that court censorship was the "only kind that really
counted" (1984, 17). Although political critics have historicized
Renaissance literature by examining censorship as a (in some cases,
as *the*) constituent historical determinant of literature, they have not
historicized censorship itself. Their univocal (if often complex and
highly nuanced) definition of censorship has tended to reduce both
poetic liberty and censorship to abstract, consistent, univocal, and
ahistorical values.[2]

The readings of plays by a writer such as Ben Jonson and the
accounts of the theater as a social institution enabled by this es-

sentially anachronistic and ahistorical court-centered definition of censorship have thus far been played out in terms of the all too familiar debate over whether the theater subverted power or defused resistance by containing it. In one account, authors under capitalism always resist a repressive censorship and are always on the side of liberty and freedom. Ambiguity, equivocation, irony, disavowal, and other forms of semantic polysemy and indeterminacy are always to be read as evidence of a conscious or unconscious revolutionary critique of the court.[3] Others have argued in an opposing account that critique is always already contained: the court licensed reformist, even rebellious critiques of the court, giving poets (whose loyalty was unquestioned) the liberty to criticize the court's policies or alert the court to corrupting agents and forces. Against an earlier Whig view of the early Stuart court as uniform, repressive, and decadent, seeking escapist entertainment in the elite theaters of a coterie, revisionist and New Historicist critics have emphasized the diversity of the court and the sophistication and seriousness of its theatrical tastes. Court censorship, according to these critics, was remarkably tolerant and lenient.[4]

Despite their differences, both accounts share the same court-centered definition of censorship. The court and dramatists can be judged by the same moral criteria: if court censorship is regarded as repressive, dramatists are ranked according to whether they collaborated or resisted; if, by contrast, the court is regarded as having licensed an enlightened critique, dramatists are shown to have engaged in morally serious, sophisticated criticism. In contrast to these critics, I wish to historicize early Stuart theater censorship in order to make available a fuller understanding of its contradictions and the multiplicity of its forms and agents. Historicizing censorship will involve a critique of four interlocking assumptions that accompany the definition of censorship presently adopted by political critics. First, censorship is thought to have been confined to the court. Second, authors and critics are always assumed to have desired to evade court censorship, never to have been its agents. Progressive authors, it is said, smuggled secret meanings into their texts, which critics could in turn decipher.[5] Third, mutilation or torture of the author's body is a measure of the repressiveness of a given form of censorship. Finally, and perhaps most crucial, critics have assumed that there was an alternative to censorship, that authors and printers would have preferred to write and print without it.

In questioning these assumptions, I do not mean to deny that court censorship could be brutally repressive, nor do I wish to rule out a critique of such repression. Yet when we look at Jonson we see a complexity—by no means idiosyncratic—that challenges the validity of the assumptions that follow from the present way of defining censorship as a negative exercise of power over which the court had a monopoly.[6] Consider first the range of censors Jonson faced. His plays were regularly censored by both the court and the market. The *Isle of Dogs,* the epilogue to *Poetaster* (cut in 1602), *Eastward Ho!, Sejanus, Epicoene, The Devil Is an Ass, The Magnetic Lady,* and *A Tale of a Tub* all suffered some measure of censorship. And at least one masque, *Neptune's Triumph for the Return of Albion,* was censored by James I himself.[7] Jonson suffered imprisonment and interrogation. Along with George Chapman, he was imprisoned as coauthor of *Eastward Ho!* Both were charged with seditious libel, and the report, according to William Drummond, was that "they should then have their ears cut and noses" (H & S, 1:273). Earlier, Jonson had been imprisoned for the "seditious and slanderous" *Isle of Dogs,* and for *Sejanus* "he was called before the [Privy Council] . . . and accused both of popery and treason" (H & S, 1:217–18). Jonson was censored by his popular audiences as well. The market-based audiences of the public theater were composed of what he termed "envious censors" (Induction, *Every Man out of His Humour,* 62). One such, Alexander Gill, attacked Jonson's failed *Magnetic Lady.* Gill repeats a charge leveled by the Court of High Commission, namely, that the play contained oaths that violated the 1606 statute regarding blasphemy on the stage: "Foh! how it stinks! What general offense / Gives thy prophanes, and gross impudence! / And yet thou crazily art confident / Belching out foul mouthed oaths with foul intent" (H & S, 11:347). Gill assumes Jonson would print his play to make it available to a competent readership as he had done for the failed *New Inn.* Instead, he insists, "to vindicate thy fame, / Th'hadst better give thy pamphlet to the flame" (H & S, 11:348).[8]

Jonson's case also shows quite clearly that authorship and literary criticism were not necessarily opposed to either form of censorship; rather, authors and critics could be agents of censorship as well as its victims. In 1624 Jonson himself stood in succession to become the official court censor when he was granted a warrant for the reversion of the Office of the Master of the Revels. As an author and critic, Jonson undertook to reform the public theaters by aligning himself with the court censor, internalizing its interpretive categories and practices. Far from evading or dismantling court censorship of his own works, Jonson often invited it, as when in the epistle to *Volpone* he asserts that his works have been "read" (54) and "allowed" (54) by the censor. Indeed, in this epistle Jonson establishes the distinctions that legitimize his poetic liberty. Addressing himself to the "learned and charitable critic" (111), he maintains he will police the stage to purge it of offenses and defend it against the frequent charge by Puritan critics "that now, especially in dramatic, or, as they term it, stage poetry, nothing but ribaldry, profanation, blasphemy, all license of offense to God and man is practised" (34–36). In contrast to most of his dramatic contemporaries, Jonson eschews the "use of such foul and unwashed bawdry" and condemns "the increase of lust in liberty, together with the present trade of the stage, in their mis'line interludes" (82–84). Jonson's categories are exactly those of the court censor.[9] Speaking of his censorship of John Fletcher's *Tamer Tamed,* for example, Sir Henry Herbert, Master of the Revels, nearly repeats the categories of the epistle to *Volpone,* saying, "I have done God good service, and the quality no wrong; who hath no greater enemies than oaths, profaneness, and public ribaldry, which for the future I absolutely forbid to be presented to me in any playbook, as you will answer at your peril" (Adams 1917, 21).

Moreover, Jonson took over the functions of the court censor, symbolically enacting the penalties for libel on the bodies and books of other authors and critics. Sir Henry Herbert threatened transgressive stage poets with "public punishment" and occasionally burned scripts he declined to allow, noting in one instance, "received of Mr. Kirke, for a new play which I burnte for the ribaldry and offense that was in it" (Adams 1917, 23). In his own theater of punishment, Jonson symbolically branded, beat, or purged the bodies of poetasters and censurers, invoked a muse of fire to torch the writing of libelous informers and seditious slanderers, from whom he could distinguish himself as a loyal servant of the court. He concludes the epistle to *Volpone,* for example, by saying he will brand licentious poetasters: "[Poetry] shall out of just rage incite her servants (who are *genus irritabile*) to spout ink in [the] faces [of its abusers] that shall eat, farther than their marrow, into their fames, and not Cinnamus the barber with his art shall be able to take out the brands, but they shall live, and be read, till the wretches die, as things worth deserving of themselves in chief, and then of all mankind" (132–36). At the end of *Every Man in His Humour,* Jonson stages a moment of censorship as Justice Clement burns Bobadill's verses: "Bring me a torch; lay it together, and give fire. Cleanse the air. Here was enough to have infected the whole city, if it had not been taken in time! See, see, how our poet's glory shines" (5.4.26–29). Jonson threatens to perform a similar function in the "Apologetical Dialogue" of *Poetaster:*

> what they write 'gainst me,
> Shall like a figure, drawn in water, fleet,
> And the poor wretched papers be employed
> To cloth tobacco, or some cheaper drug.
> (167–70)

In these instances and elsewhere, Jonson attempted to legitimate a realm of poetic liberty, at once purging poetasters and purifying poetry in a theater of punishment.

Jonson's position as a man of letters similarly complicates any straightforward opposition between an author's body and his writings which would allow one to use the body as a measure of the repressiveness of a given regime. For the murder of his fellow actor Gabriel Spencer, Jonson was branded with a "T" on his thumb rather than hanged at Tyburn because he was literate (his ability to read a "neck-verse" of Latin saved him from execution); his literacy in turn enabled him, as legitimate poet and man of letters, to perform the role of censor, discursively branding the bodies of transgressors and symbolically burning their writings while imagining himself as a "monarch of letters" (*Underwood* 14.165) who could canonize his writings by printing them and thereby establish a unified corpus. If letters were an entry into a position of authority, enabling the stepson of a bricklayer to speak to monarchs, they were also a dangerous institution, putting an author's body at risk of being branded—SL for "seditious libeller" or SS for "sower of sedition"—and one's books of being "dismembered" (as George Chapman put it when lamenting the extensive censorship of his *Byron* plays) either by the court censor or by the market censor.

Whether circulating as printed commodities or as manuscripts, "letters" were inevitably subject to decontextualization and misinterpretation by these authorities. Hence, Jonson's corpus (in both senses of the word) might be harmed: his plays or verses might be censored by the court censor or the monarch, and his body might be subjected to the searing disciplinary instruments of early Stuart torture. Thus, letters signified Jonson's subjection to power and his entry into power, legitimating him as a censoring author/critic.

How Jonson's experience, in challenging the commonly held assumptions about censorship, implicitly challenges the assumption that there was an alternative to censorship is perhaps already apparent. He did not seek to escape from censorship but negotiated between different kinds of censors with different kinds of authority. To be sure, Jonson did criticize some forms of censorship. Indeed, he never entirely identified with court censorship and often resisted it. For example, he sometimes restored passages cut by the Master of the Revels. In *Poetaster,* Jonson quotes (1.1.43–84, 5.3.241–58), with only minimal changes, from Christopher Marlowe's *Elegies* (1.15) and from John Marston's *Scourge of Villainy* and *Pygmalion's Image* (all of which were banned by the bishops in 1599 and burned at Stationers' Hall). The Master of the Revels ordered Jonson to cut the satirical references to Inigo Jones in *A Tale of a Tub* and the concluding scene of a tub in motion, a parody of Jones's masque technology. Jonson cut the satirical character reference to Jones as Vitruvius Hoop but inserted the character In-and-In Medley, who, as masquer, is an equally unmistakable representation of Jones; moreover, he left in the concluding scene. In addition, he called attention to the inclusion of an unlicensed scene, which he titled the "scene interloping," *interloping* meaning not "irregular" but, as Martin Butler points out, "unauthorized." Similarly, in the 1616 folio of his collected works, Jonson restored the "Apologetical Dialogue" of *Poetaster,* which had been struck from the 1602 quarto. He also included other passages apparently struck from the quarto by the censor (Clare 1990, 86–88). And in that quarto, he informed his readers that the dialogue had been censored: "HERE (Reader) in place of the Epilogue, was meant to thee an Apology from the Author, with his reasons for the publishing of this booke; but (since he is no lesse restrained, then thou depriv'd of it, by Authoritie) hee praies thee think charitably of what thou hast read, till thou maist

heare him speake what he hath written." "Authoritie" is paren-
thetically faulted for depriving the public and for restraining Jonson, who implies that he will go over the court censor's head: the
defense will be spoken on stage. Furthermore, Jonson painstakingly
restored the censored passages (the obscene ones) of his friend,
Thomas Farnaby's expurgated edition of Martial's *Epigrams,* which
Jonson referred to as *Jesuitaru castratus.*

Yet if Jonson criticized court censorship on behalf of dramatic
liberty, as when he appealed to Suffolk to secure his "liberty" when
imprisoned for his shared authorship of *Eastward Ho!,* any defense
of liberty he made involved submission to an authority—"To you I
submit myself and my work" ("To the Reader Extraordinary")—
and often produced a countereffort to limit that authority. In *Every
Man out of His Humour,* for example, Asper addresses the "gracious
and kind spectators" (52) and submits himself to the severest censors of the audience:

> Yet here, mistake me not, judicious friends.
> I do not this to beg your patience,
> Or servilely to fawn on your applause,
> Like some dry brain, despairing in his merit:
> Let me be censured by the auster'st brow,
> Where I want art, or judgement, tax me freely:
> Let envious censors, with their broadest eyes,
> Look through and through me.
> (Second sounding, 56–63)

Yet after saying he will submit to censure, Asper appoints his own
censors on stage:

> I leave you two as censors, to sit here:
> Observe what I present, and liberally
> Speak your opinions, upon every scene,
> As it shall pass the view of these spectators.
> (Second sounding, 153–56)

Though Jonson offers his audience the liberty to censor his play, he
immediately modifies that offer and restricts the exercise of that
liberty to his own characters, who may "liberally speak [their]
opinions."

When such contradictory attempts to license and limit his audience's liberty failed to control the reception of his writings, Jonson did not seek to escape censorship but generally displaced the contradiction, both submitting to a particular form of censorship and appealing to an alternative authority, typically setting the reader above the spectator, the court above both. Consider, for example, Jonson's contradictory response to the audience's censure of the ending of *Every Man out of His Humour,* in which Queen Elizabeth was impersonated by an actor on stage. On the one hand, Jonson revised the ending to avoid censure. On the other, he defiantly justified the original ending in the quarto edition of the play: "It had another *Catastrophe,* or Conclusion, at the first Playing: which . . . many seem'd not to rellish it; and therefore 'twas since alter'd: yet that a right-ei'd and solide *Reader* may perceiue it was not so great a part of the Heauen awry, as they would make it; we request him but to looke downe vpon these following Reasons" (H & S, 3:602).

To limit the authority of censors other than the court, Jonson in turn subjected them to the court's authority, producing in the process a critique of market censorship. After *The New Inn* failed, presumably because of some perceived topical meaning in the chambermaid's name, Cis (H & S, 9:252), Jonson printed the play, asserting on the title page that its value would be recognized if readers were given the liberty to read it: "As it was never acted, but most negligently played, by some, the Kings servants. And squeamishly beheld, and censured by others. 1629. Now, at last, set at liberty to the readers, his Majesties servants, and Subjects, to be judged." Jonson makes a more direct appeal to the court in the second epilogue (written, we are told, because the play "liv'd not in opinion to have it spoken"). He notes that he has changed the chambermaid's name from Cis to Pru but insists that the court would have found the revision unnecessary. The purpose of his play has been

> To give the King and Queen and Court delight:
> But then we mean the Court above the stairs,
> And past the guard; men that have more of ears
> Than eyes to judge us: such as will not hiss
> Because the chambermaid was named Cis.

> We think it would have served our scene as true,
> If, as it is, at first we had called her Pru.
>
> (4–10)

Jonson never criticized either court or market censors, then, on behalf of a conception of poetic liberty or freedom that was opposed to all forms of censorship: poetic liberty was by definition licensed poetry.

This point may be buttressed by briefly examining Jonson's panegyric nondramatic poetry and masques and his editing and publication practices. It might be thought that censorship was genre specific, confined to satire, that Jonson could escape the constraints of the court censor or the public theaters by winning the patronage of aristocrats. Richard Dutton argues that court patronage freed Jonson from the oppressiveness of the public theaters: "The regular masque commissions were well rewarded and helped Jonson to escape the treadmill of hack writing for the likes of Henslowe in a way that writers like Dekker, Webster, and Heywood never managed" (1983, 8). And some critics have contrasted the country house poem to the court masque and the drama. Peggy Knapp, for example, declares: "To find Jonson's ideal social world described fully and without irony, we might try the non-dramatic poetry. In 'To Penshurst' Jonson could write with more candor than he could for either the public theater with its crowds to please or the private audiences with their demand for courtly tact" (1979, 234).

Yet even if aristocrats did not directly censor his panegyrics (they didn't license his poetry, though they often did pay him for it), to obtain or keep their favor Jonson sometimes found it necessary to edit his manuscripts to avoid either embarrassing them or being embarrassed by them (see Lindley 1986). And whereas editing is not necessarily a form of censorship, these revisions do involve suppression, and it is worth noting that *to edit* originally meant to decide the fate of a defeated gladiator (showing the thumbs up or not). There are several examples of Jonson's editing of his panegyrics in the 1616 folio. Jonson omitted all reference to the occasion of *Hymnaei,* for example, subtitling it only "The solemnities of Masques and Barriers at a Marriage," and did the same for *The Irish Masque at Court,* part of the wedding festivities for Lady Frances

Howard's marriage to Robert Carr. In 1613 Howard had sued for divorce on grounds that her husband, Essex, was impotent and that the marriage had never been consummated. In 1615 she and her second husband, Carr, were revealed to be implicated in the murder of Thomas Overbury.

What concerns me is the significance of this suppression and revision. Modern readers are often embarrassed by panegyrics that uncritically flattered aristocrats whose behavior was rather sordid, and they have tended to deal with the potential embarrassment of Jonson's panegyrics in two ways. They assume either that Jonson was free at court or in a country house to criticize while complimenting or that Jonson wanted to "fit in," neither embarrass his patrons nor be embarrassed by them, and that he therefore chose to edit his writings, making the changes illegible to most of his readers. (Only those who had attended the performances of these masques or who had heard about them would have been able to notice Jonson's alterations or omissions, though Jonson did inform Drummond that the unnamed masque in his first folio was performed for the Essex marriage.) Both of these strategies for managing embarrassment felt by modern critics rely on a notion of tact which can be opposed (as a form of criticism) to censorship.

Yet Jonson's tact, I would argue, is less a resolution of the problem of censorship than a subjection to another version of it. He was not always happy about submitting to his aristocratic patrons. To his dismay, the concluding stanzas of *Hymnaei* were not performed at the wedding of Howard and Essex (she was thirteen and he was fifteen). The "Epistle to the Countess of Rutland" (*Forest,* 12), celebrating her marriage, more clearly complicates modern views of Jonson's tactful relation to his patrons. In the original ending Jonson hoped that the countess would "bear a son" (100). The last lines were canceled in the folio version, however, which ends abruptly:

> Moods which the god-like Sidney oft did prove,
> And your brave friend and mine so well did love.
> Who whereso'er he be . . . .
> *The rest is lost*

C. H. Herford and Percy and Evelyn Simpson note:

> The Folio version breaks off at line 93, with a note "*The rest is lost.*" It was not lost, but tactfully cancelled. The poem was written in the first year of the marriage, 1599, and ended with the hope that, before the year was out, the Countess would bear a son. The Earl was impotent, if not at the time of the marriage, at any rate shortly after it. The impotence was current gossip long before the Folio appeared, and the original conclusion would have excited derision in Court circles, apart from the pain it would have given the Countess. (H & S, 8:10)

Yet Jonson's omission of the concluding lines is more paradoxical than Herford and Simpson allow. For Jonson's revision is tactlessly tactful. If he canceled the original ending out of deference to the countess, he also gracelessly calls attention (albeit in a way no one without access to earlier versions could understand) to his own suppression of the original ending, stopping abruptly in midsentence and leaving a note rather than replacing it with a revised version that would efface the cancelation altogether. Panegyric (and editing panegyric) involves neither willing submission to courtly tact nor open defiance of it but a mixture of both, what psychoanalytic critics might call a neurotic compromise between the desire to fit in and the desire to express the censored material. Whereas tact is not identical to other forms of censorship to which Jonson was subjected, its pressure is, if anything, registered even more intensely in the contradictions in his writings (both panegyric and satiric) and in his career as a dramatist and court poet in the public and court theaters.

This brief review of Jonson's contradictory relation to court and market censorship is sufficient, I hope, to make clear that his case raises questions that can hardly be answered if one defines censorship in ahistorical, moralistic terms. One would be restricted to making arguments that Jonson's case radically complicates: either he was critical (intentionally or unintentionally) of a repressive court, or a tolerant, enlightened court licensed his critique. As a victim and agent of court and market censorship, Jonson strikingly falls on both sides of the division—legitimation and critique, authority and subversion, opposition and orthodoxy—over which the politics of his writings have hitherto been constructed. How could Jonson, the victim of censorship, have come to think of himself as the court censor? Indeed, how could a poet who had been repeatedly censored not only gain preferment (*Eastward Ho!* and Jonson's first masque were written within a year of each other) as the leading court poet but come to be thought of as an appropriate person to fill the office of court censor? If Jonson was a loyal critic of the court, why did his critique take a transgressive form even during James's reign when Jonson's position at court was more secure than at any other time in his career? If the court licensed a reformist theatrical critique, why did it so regularly regard it as transgressive? If Jonson's works constitute a critique of the court, why did Jonson subject himself to a court he so often (sometimes transgressively) criticized? Why did he not simply pursue a career in the theater rather than write entertainments and poems for aristocrats and monarchs he apparently held in contempt? And if he sought to place himself above the vulgar, censorious patronage of the literary marketplace, why did he continue to write for the popular theaters well after he secured court patronage?

I do not want to accuse Jonson of acting as an agent of censorship in order to dismiss him, in Whiggish fashion, as a sycophant, a poacher turned gamekeeper who "sold out" to a decadent, barbaric court.[10] I want, rather, to account for the contradictions of his case and his problems of reception in terms of a historically specific definition of censorship. To read Jonson's writings and their reception exclusively according to a determination of what the authorities censored and tolerated or what authors got away with, how audiences read, what they did or did not understand is, in my view, to miss the very multiplicity and complexities of censorship and to misunderstand the consequent hermeneutic problems of reception involving specific technologies of textual reproduction, circulation, and transmission to which Jonson's contradictory case calls our attention.

I propose instead that we think of censorship broadly as a mechanism for legitimating and delegitimating access to discourse. Censorship in its usual sense—the repression of sedition, libel, or blasphemy—was only one mechanism for regulating the circulation of discourses, exchanges of power between institutions, transfers of status markers from one institution to another, and so on which marked the emergence of a licensed and relatively autonomous aesthetic domain.[11] To define literary censorship as an activity that

legitimates and delegitimates discourses and their modes of circulation means broadening the term, so that its negative, repressive
function is seen as only one of many regulatory mechanisms.[12]

What I am calling an aesthetic domain was both internally differentiated in terms of superior and inferior licensed practices and
externally differentiated in terms of licensed and unlicensed aesthetic practices, and it involved the encoding of legitimating distinctions between literary and nonliterary discourses and between
licensed literary producers and licensing consumers as well. Censorship, whether repressive or lenient, was legitimated through the
codification of literary "taste." Distinctions between the audiences
that consumed plays could thereby be put in place; audiences could
be arranged hierarchically according to their ability to judge—
either license or censure—literary works. For theatrical producers,
licensing authorized a given company and its plays by distinguishing producers as legitimate professionals both from unlicensed entertainers and from other, more or less prestigious licensed companies. As Jonathan Goldberg writes, "The difference between
[public and private theaters] was a matter of privilege, power,
prestige and class. Public and private as kinds of theaters distinguish
public categories of power. The court established itself as the crown
and pinnacle of these differences" (1983a, 151). The poet laureate is
at the pinnacle of literary production. His authority, as Richard
Helgerson (1983) argues, derives from a differential system wherein
the laureate distinguishes himself both from the gentleman amateur
and from the professional. And in terms of consumers, theatrical
patronage was a means by which an audience conferred distinction
and authority on a particular acting company or dramatist. Support
for a given play might be taken as evidence of "the elevation of [the
audience's] wit," in Thomas Carew's words (Davenant 1872, 1:206)
and attendance at a given theater was coded the same way. The Red
Bull audience, for example, was said regularly to include undiscriminating spectators. At issue was telling the difference between
legitimate poetry and illegitimate libel, between a legitimate censor
and a mere censurer, between license and liberty.

Yet the equivocal meaning of *license* (both liberty and licentiousness) indicates the difficulty in maintaining a distinction between
legitimate poetic liberty and libel or blasphemy. The multiple licensing authorities of court and market alternately affirmed and

dissolved the distinctions by which a text was receiveable as legitimate and poetic or transgressive and nonpoetic, thereby contributing to what I will call a theatrical legitimation crisis in early Stuart England.

Consider the court. The early Stuart courts made efforts to reinforce the boundaries and distinctions between the licensed theater and unlicensed theatrical practices. The authority of the Masters of the Revels was greatly increased over commercial forms of popular culture. By 1606 the Office of the Revels combined duties that had hitherto been divided, censoring both the printing and the performance of plays. Similarly, the Stuart monarchs increased their own authority. After his accession in 1603, James I placed all the major London dramatic companies exclusively under royal patronage. And both James I in 1617 and Charles I in 1633 defended the license of traditional, rural pastimes by issuing the *Book of Sports* (see Marcus 1986b). The practice of licensing players may be seen as an enfranchisement of the professional, a monopoly awarded to the licensed player over the unlicensed rogue.

Yet the inconsistency of the early Stuart court's licensing practices called its model of theatrical legitimation into question. Though in an earlier Whiggish account the court was thought to have invaded the theater, Leeds Barroll (1988) and Philip Finkelpearl (1986) have shown that the court did not in fact take a consistent interest in the theater. And as Martin Butler (1984), Malcolm Smuts (1987; 1991), and Kevin Sharpe (1987) have shown, the court circulated among theaters of varying degrees of status and of varied repertoires. The court's tastes were diverse, not uniform.

I would argue, however, that the court's heterogeneity cannot be recuperated in terms of a politics of cultural diversity and tolerance, as some critics have maintained (see Smuts 1987; 1991; Sharpe 1987), for the court's model of theatrical legitimation was contradictory to the point of incoherence. The court was only intermittently interested in maintaining the division between licensed and unlicensed theaters, between poetic liberty and libel. James shut down acting companies and then allowed them to reopen. Similarly, though the censorship apparatus became increasingly centralized and the powers of the Master of the Revels more extensive, theater censorship by the court was erratic, even contradictory. As

Stephen Greenblatt points out, "The Tudor and Stuart regulations governing the public stage were confused, inconsistent, and haphazard, the products neither of a traditional, collective understanding nor of a coherent, rational attempt to regularize and define a new cultural practice. They were instead a jumble of traditional rules and offices designed to govern older, very different theatrical practices and a set of ordinances drawn up very hastily in response to particular and local pressures" (1988, 16).

Jonson's case was hardly exceptional in this regard: he and other dramatists were regularly both licensed and censored.[13] Perhaps the most notable feature of court censorship is that virtually all censored plays had previously been licensed by the Master of the Revels. The office was part of a patronage network and was desirable less for the cash it provided the Master than for the power and prestige it conferred. Yet, as I will later show in detail, the office itself became increasingly lucrative as the fees charged to license plays rose, in part accounting for the fact that the Master licensed performances that were later deemed seditious. Since licensing plays, players, and playhouses was a profitable business, it was in the interest of the Master to develop his authority as extensively as possible, not only over the players, plays, and playhouses but over all kinds of variety shows, exhibitions, and entertainments regardless of their didactic purpose or political effect. And though the Master of the Revels or the monarch might threaten dramatists with "public punishment," no dramatist, as Philip Finkelpearl (1986, 124) points out, was ever convicted of libel.

In other ways as well the court's licensing practices violated the legitimating distinctions they were ostensibly designed to uphold. Although the statute of 1599 granted only two licenses, in practice, the number of theaters was limited only by the number of paying audiences. Similarly, though the court differentiated between court and public theaters, assigning speaking parts in court masques to professional actors, theatrical practices circulated in ways that dissolved this difference: court performances were drawn from the public repertory, as Jonathan Goldberg (1983a, 231) notes, while plays in the public theaters used theatrical devices from court masques. Instead of consistently applying a "court standard" for liberty or manifesting a coherent diversity of theatrical tastes, the court alternated between moments when it cared deeply about distinctions between poetic liberty and libel and others when it didn't care about them at all.

The court's ability to uphold its model of theatrical legitimation was further compromised by the decentralization of patronage (see Smuts 1987, 16–18; Bergeron 1988) and by the fact that in licensing the theater, the court authorized an institution that was connected to other kinds of liberty over which it had little or no control. One kind of liberty was connected to guilds and monopolies. These organizations secured for their members "liberty," meaning the exclusive right or privilege to practice a craft or engage in a trade. This liberty was assumed to be aligned with the court rather than opposed to it. The charter to the Stationers' Company, for example, gave the company exclusive printing privileges on the condition that it brought "order" into the trade by policing its own members as well as unlicensed printers. Theater companies were similarly assumed to be self-policing, performing the licensed playbooks without further revision. Yet this way of securing liberty through self-censorship was less than consistently successful. Licensed acting companies circumvented the licenser; fraudulent licenses were sold to vagabonds; actors sometimes inserted oaths or used props in ways that changed the meaning of the text licensed by the Master of the Revels; and licensed printers printed and sold censored texts.[14] The court had virtually no control over the "liberties," or suburbs, of London in which many of the popular theaters were located (see Mullaney 1987).

As a consequence of this inconsistency and the alienation and dispersal of its licensing authority, the court and its delegated officials were compelled to intervene, restrain, or disavow, sometimes at cross-purposes, the "licentiousness" of the very entertainers and entertainments they themselves licensed. The Lord Chamberlain, for example, felt compelled in 1622 to complain about licensed itinerant players and entertainers. Pembroke was aware, he wrote all mayors, sheriffs, and justices of the peace, "that there are many & very great disorders & abuses daily comitted by diverse & sundry Companyes of stage players Tumblers vaulters dauncers on the Ropes And also by such as goe about wth motions & shewes & other the like kind of psons" who, by virtue of the grants and "lycences" they have procured from the king, "do abusively claim to themselves a kinde of licentious fredome to travell as well to shew play & exercise . . . in this kingdom." The plays and shows these performers present are for the most part, he said, "full of scandal & offense both against the Church & State" (Murray 1963, 2:351). In other, similarly contradictory cases, theater managers, poets, printers, and players were all called to account for their "licentiousness."[15] These attempts to secure a semiotic difference between license and licentiousness, then, paradoxically register the court's own contribution to a theatrical legitimation crisis.

This crisis was intensified as well by a contradiction in market censorship. Though the court was at the pinnacle of semiotic differences, the court's authority as *the* determining consumer was complicated by the fact that theatrical production was actually geared toward a different consumer, the public market. The literary marketplace, though it opened up new, specifically poetic liberties that might be exercised by authors, also enabled a consuming public to exercise its own forms of censorship. Audiences sometimes acted out the threat staged by Francis Beaumont in *The Knight of the Burning Pestle.* In 1617 apprentices destroyed the Cockpit and some lives were lost after the manager, Christopher Beeston, moved the company's repertory from the far less expensive Red Bull (Gurr 1987, 171–72), thereby excluding its popular audience. Similarly, according to Edmund Gayton, an audience might insist on determining what the players performed:

> The players had been appointed, notwithstanding their bills to the contrary, to act what a major part of the company had a mind to. Sometimes *Tamerlane,* sometimes *Jugurtha,* sometimes the Jew of Malta, and sometimes all of these; and at last, none of these three taking, they were forced to undress and to put off their tragick habits, and conclude the day with the merry milkmaides. And unless this were done, and the popular humour satisfied, as sometimes it so fortun'd, that these players were refractory; the Benches, the tiles, the laths, the stones, Oranges, Apples, Nuts, flew about most liberally, and as there were Mechanicks of all professions, who fell every one to his owne trade, and dissolved a house in an instant, and made a ruin of a stately Fabrick. (*JCS,* 2:690–91)

Like court censorship, market censorship was multiple and dispersed. The theater was the site of competing modes of regulation and of legitimation and delegitimation. The literary critic, in contrast to a mere censurer, might allow or censure plays as he saw fit. Yet just who might legitimately occupy the position of critic was open to negotiation, as is suggested by the often contradictory relation of *critic* to such words as *censurer, censureship,* and *censor.* The relationship between the court and market censors was also contradictory, as we shall see shortly, with no clear alliance between the ruling elite and legitimate author/critics against illegitimate popular interests. Even though the court indirectly licensed these censors, its learned tastes were not always different from more "popular" tastes.[16]

In the chapters that follow, I read Jonson's writings from a Foucauldian, post-Marxist critical perspective as an acute instance of this theatrical legitimation crisis. My aim in these chapters is not to "cover" Jonson's canon or his career but to account for their contradictions in terms of my alternative definition of censorship. The paradoxes of Jonson's relation to the dynamics of censorship clarify precisely the need to redefine censorship in discursive rather than exclusively moral terms. Jonson could not, for example, distinguish envious censors in the theater audiences from the court censor (who had really repressive powers that audience censurers did not) and align himself with the former against the latter, because the legitimation of his writings usually involved the delegitimation of some members of his audience; that is, Jonson needed the critics in the audience (and codes of taste) as much as he needed the court censor (with the power to burn and brand) to legitimate his writings and to delegitimate would-be envious censors.

In ascribing equal importance to both censors, I am not denying that state censorship was repressive in ways that market censorship was not. I am saying that one was not necessarily a more serious threat than the other. The threat posed by the loss of literary patronage at court or in the public theaters is less economic penury than the loss of social prestige, the cultural capital attached to being, say, the leading court poet. Modern ways of measuring repressive censorship against supposedly more progressive forms of censure and criticism underestimate the degree to which they are pressures continuous with censorship rather than radically opposed to it. In a status-oriented society, saying something that is receivable and that won't get one's play censured by a theater audience may produce a form of self-censorship equal to (or even more intense than) any resulting from the fear of bodily mutilation.[17]

The first chapter focuses on Jonson's contribution to an emergent discourse of literary criticism which regulated the exercise of a relatively autonomous poetic liberty. Jonson desired a paradoxically "free rei(g)n" for his literary production and consumption, with other author/critics acting as legitimate censors. His use of somatic metaphors for production and consumption enabled him to authorize an ideal, unified, self-identical critical community (see Fish 1984). I read Jonson's idealization of this community against its material conditions of cultural production and consumption. To maintain his ideal, Jonson regularly appealed to the court to reform and purge the theater of poetasters and censurers. If the court affirmed cultural distinctions more clearly, Jonson and others argued, its authority could be used to reform and regulate undifferentiating playwrights and popular audiences. Jonson's own reformist critique of the court's licensing practices could be seen as performing a service to the state. The reinstitution of the monarch's authority allowed for a reform of popular audiences: audiences would be arranged hierarchically, and poetic liberty would then be decisively distinguished from license.

Yet any clear exchange of authority between the court and a licensed dramatist such as Jonson was complicated by the fact that writing for the theater involved submission to two kinds of censoring authority, the court's and the critic's, each with its specific pressure. Jonson contributed to the emergence of literary criticism in order to regulate the circulation of his writings on what he calls "the Exchange of letters" (*Miscellaneous Poems* 11.14), the literary marketplace. He contrasted the classical body to the grotesque body, using metaphors of taste to codify reception through an idealized notion of imitation, which would differentiate legitimate from illegitimate criticism. Yet the multiplicity of censors contributed to a legitimation crisis by opening up multiple forms of what Jürgen Habermas (1989) has termed the public sphere. Alternative censors competed to legitimate themselves as critics and to delegitimate others as mere censurers. Jonson's neurotic relation to different kinds of censorship (evading them and embracing them) registers his pattern of circulating between competing public spheres with conflicting standards and criteria for legitimate criticism. In attempting to establish a discourse of legitimate literary criticism, Jonson was attempting to authorize himself to say in one place something he was not authorized to say in another and to censor others for engaging in criticism he could deem to be illegitimate.

The second and third chapters historicize Jonson's "antitheatricality" (Barish 1981) in relation to Shakespearean romance and to Jonson's Caroline contemporaries. Shakespeare and Jonson negotiated the court's contradictions from different, contradictory positions. In the second chapter, I argue that Jonson's critique of Shakespeare is at the same time a critique of the way the court's licensing practices produced the loss of distinction on which clear enunciation depended. The third chapter reconsiders Jonson's problems of reception late in his career in relation to his Caroline contemporaries. Far from envincing anything specific to Jonson, these problems were widely shared by major and minor Caroline playwrights. They register the incoherence of innovations in the Caroline theaters, particularly the representation of aristocratic women actors. Both chapters seek to explain why Jonson could neither straightforwardly identify his interests with the court's nor straightforwardly oppose them to those of his popular audiences. On the one hand, Jonson was increasingly identified with the court. He withdrew from the public stage in 1616 and turned to the court in order to uphold a reactionary assessment of licensed poetry (to secure the boundaries of a critical community, Jonson was willing effectively to censor everyone but himself). On the other hand, his eventual banishment from the court in 1631 registers his long-standing reservations about its contradictory licensing practices, the very practices that had driven him out of the public theaters and into the court in the first place.

Together, these three chapters place a local argument about Jonson's politics in the service of a larger argument about early Stuart theater censorship. Although Jonson's attempt to resolve the contradictions of the court in a reactionary direction was not the only possible way of responding to them, Jonson's case registers, I believe, a larger, unresolved contradiction between censorship and criticism (or poetic liberty). The theatrical reforms undertaken by Jonson and other Jacobean and Caroline poets and courts both reaffirmed and unsettled legitimating distinctions, producing a fierce dialectic between poetic liberty, on the one hand, and court and market censorship, on the other: the liberties of the court were elevated above the censorship of the market; the liberties of the market were elevated above the censorship of the court. In this respect, there was no alternative to censorship.[18] Instead of anticipating what Jürgen Habermas (1989) has termed a "public sphere" of enlightened criticism and debate, a sphere in which the state's power to censor no longer operated, the new forms of poetic liberty and literary criticism Jonson and others sought to legitimate entailed either introducing innovative forms of censorship or revamping and reinforcing older forms. The questions that formed the basis of a theatrical legitimation crisis were over what kinds of licensing and censorship should be authorized and exercised, who should exercise them, and to what ends.

My argument about Jonson will stand or fall on its own merits. In using him as an example to make a larger argument about early Stuart stage censorship, however, I raise questions about the force of this larger argument and about the pertinence of Jonson as an example, questions regarding historical method and the status of this argument as an intervention in present-day political criticism. I wish, therefore, to address these questions now and to clarify the force of the larger argument about censorship before I proceed to make the narrower argument about Jonson.

Weren't there other, more radical dramatists? some might ask. And what about Milton's *Areopagitica?* Isn't that tract a defense of liberty and "unlicensed printing," an attack on censorship? And what about unlicensed, noncanonical texts written by members of radical sects such as the Ranters? To take Jonson as an exemplary case, some political critics might argue, is to engage in a premature totalization of early Stuart theater which would foreclose the possibility of a radical critique of censorship. Furthermore, in saying that there was no alternative to censorship I may appear to have adopted the same monolithic definition of censorship I am criticizing, closing off critique (and thus the possibility of social change) both by imposing a universalist and ahistorical definition of censorship and by drawing on an insufficient data base. A definition of critique which does not include a critique of all forms of censorship is hardly a significant definition. My argument is apparently congruent with a familiar Foucauldian position about the pervasiveness of power, often identified with the New Historicism, which avowedly political critics have faulted largely on the grounds that it closes off critique in the past and in the present.[19] From this perspective my argument might even be thought to be a reactionary one.

These questions and conclusions follow from the very assumptions about censorship which I have already begun to interrogate by attending to Jonson. Critics on either side of the dominant theoretical debates over historicist critical practice—who debate whether power is monolithic or multiply determined and dispersed, whether texts are the products of authorial intention or of unconscious forces inscribed by History, whether subjects are unified or decentered— tend to share an interest in preserving a certain notion of critique and uncontained resistance.[20] For some critics, critique is located outside the court, in unified subjects or divided subjectivities, in the theater's overdetermination, or in the audience's diversity.[21] For others, it lies in the court's own sophisticated diversity or the consensual achievement of a court standard of poetic liberty (Finkelpearl 1986; Sharpe 1987; Dutton 1990). In one case, criticism is enabled as opposition; in another, it is enabled as licensed criticism. Thus Jonson has recently been read from a modern political perspective (which assigns authorial intention a privileged status) as a legitimate, serious moral poet who offers the court criticism and compliment (Orgel 1975; Marcus 1986b; 1987; Dutton 1990) or from a postmodern Marxist perspective, in which his texts are read "symptomatically" as an unintended critique of the absolutist state, driven by the transition from feudalism to capitalism (Knapp 1979; Cohen 1985; Wayne 1984; Womack 1986 and 1989; Stallybrass and White 1986; Venuti 1989).

My alternative reading of Jonson and my alternative definition of censorship emerge from a Foucauldian, post-Marxist manner of theorizing how a multiplicity of material or institutional determinations of censorship is registered in decentered subjectivity, textual heterogeneity, indeterminacy, polysemy, and so on. Like postmodern Marxists, I read Jonson's writings symptomatically in relation to early Stuart theatrical culture. Unlike these critics, however, who keep in place a hierarchy of historical determinations, giving capitalism, for example, chief importance as the final horizon of interpretation, I contend that no final horizon can rightly be said to operate consistently at all points as the determining constraint on the theater.[22] If we grant that there is no essential, fixed relationship between history and a text which would tell us in advance whether the politics of a given text is or is not inherently subversive—if, that is, we must turn to particular cases such as Jonson's to examine both the local constraints operating on his writings and the liberties those constraints enabled—it follows that we cannot determine the politics of his texts by giving literary production, intentions, or market forces necessary priority over literary consumption as the determining horizon of those texts' meanings and politics. To give any one of these determinations priority would be to keep in place the kind of ahistorical essentialist practice that postmodern historicist critical practices rightly eschew.

Once the notion of the absolute priority of a given determination or horizon is abandoned, it follows that textual ambiguities, equivocations, and indeterminacies are not necessarily strategies adopted to evade authority; they may be adopted to enforce authority as well. Intentions cannot simply be sidelined, but neither can they be regarded as the final horizon of interpretation of a text's meaning and valence since they cannot tell us definitively what a text meant at the time it was produced or what its politics were. Nor can production as opposed to consumption form the final horizon, however the content of production is defined. Thus, one cannot rightly argue that one form of censorship—say, the court's control over literary production—always has priority over another form, such as market censorship over consumption.[23] By the same token, one cannot rightly maintain that there was anything inherently progressive about contemporary criticism of Renaissance court censorship. As Jonson's case will make abundantly clear, criticism could easily be made on behalf of an extremely repressive censorship; conversely, Jonson's innovations in literary canonization and criticism could be progressive.

Saying this much is perhaps not altogether controversial given the present broad consensus that antiessentialism is, so to speak, essential to any historicist practice.[24] My more controversial revision of the postmodern Marxist symptomatic reading is that it produces a space for critique by adopting (implicitly or explicitly) the narrow, monolithic definition of censorship which, I have already suggested, is precisely what needs to be interrogated. To their credit, postmodern Marxists have implicitly departed from a humanist hermeneutics of censorship which involved a "fully-conscious arrangement" (Patterson 1984, 53) and so avoided re-inscribing a critical practice now known as the old historicism, a practice that depends on the following questionable assumptions: centered subjects (either censors or authors) determine meaning; language is always transparent, and double meanings can always be safely broken down by reasonably clever readers into two single meanings, one being a surface meaning asserting submission to authority and the other a deeper, secret meaning that resists authority; history (parliamentary debates, say) is a background that a literary text reflects topically.[25] Yet in adopting the same definition of censorship and the same oppositions between criticism and censorship and between the market and censorship, Marxists have paradoxically limited a critique of censorship, leaving unexamined the ways and contexts in which it operated outside the court and its patronage system.

A similar point may be made with regard to the argument that at least some early modern writers opposed censorship. The force of the apparent counterexample of Milton depends precisely on a narrow definition of censorship. Once this definition is in place, one can draw a line separating those who are for it from those who are against it. While I would not dispute that Milton's critique of state censorship was relatively progressive, even Milton did not advocate the end of all forms of censorship. Although he has often been viewed as contributing to the formation of a public sphere, Milton's view of censorship, as Henry Limoze (1980), Francis Barker (1984, 44–49), and Stanley Fish (1992) have shown, is considerably more equivocal than it has traditionally been made out to be.[26] Milton was in fact willing to burn libelous and blasphemous books. Moreover, he wanted to end the licensing of books not because he thought unlicensed reading opened new kinds of freedom but because it secured what Milton termed "the surest suppressing."[27]

For both critical practice and a critique of censorship, then, an appeal to History conceived as the overdetermination and hence decentering of authority will not provide political critics with an undifferentiated difference, so to speak, an Archimedean point for a critique of censorship, a critique, that is, in which critique escapes from censorship altogether.[28] Rather, the project of historicizing censorship undertaken here discloses a proliferation of differentially related subject-positions from which one could censor or exercise poetic liberty. This proliferation infinitely perpetuated a theatrical legitimation crisis by both reinforcing and unsettling distinctions between legitimate censors and author/critics, on the one hand, and illegitimate censurers and poetasters, on the other, producing a fierce dialectic between various forms of critique and various forms of censorship: local critiques of certain forms of censorship were made on behalf of liberties, which in turn authorized (and were authorized by) forms of censorship, and so on.[29]

As an intervention in political criticism in the postmodern present, my larger argument about censorship seeks not only to expand a critique of court censorship (or other forms of censorship) rather than neutralize it but to begin an examination of ways in which an ahistorical, moral definition of censorship has served to legitimate political criticism in the present. In the Conclusion, I examine how the legitimating work done by this definition bears on a larger paradox of criticism in the present, namely, that an avowedly oppositional political criticism has become critical orthodoxy.

Branding the Body, Burning the Book: Censorship, Criticism, and the Consumption of Jonson's Corpus

In "An Execration upon Vulcan," written sometime in 1623 after his library burned, Jonson imagines the destruction of his corpus, both his books and his body, as an act of court censorship: burning offensive books was the regular means of court censorship and burning authors of heretical books the means of controlling heresy, at least to 1612.[1] If Jonson's books can be consumed in a "feast of fire" (60) because they are deemed transgressive, so too can his body:

> Had I wrote treason there, or heresy,
> Imposture, witchcraft, charms, or blasphemy,
> I had deserved, then, thy consuming looks,
> Perhaps, to have been burned with my books.
>
> . . . . .
>
> Thou might'st have had me perish, piece by piece,
> To light my tobacco, or save roasted geese,
> Singe capons, or poor pigs, dropping their eyes:
> Condemned me to the ovens with the pies;
> And so, have kept me dying a whole age,
> Not ravished all hence in a minute's rage.
> But that's a mark, whereof rites do boast,
> To make consumption, ever, where thou go'st.
>
> (15–18, 51–58)

The possible penalty for discursive transgression is a near can-
nibalistic consumption of the book and "perhaps" its author as well.
Though Jonson entertains this possibility with mock seriousness,
his tone is deceptively carefree. Jonson in fact responds equivocally
to Vulcan's consumption of his corpus. On the one hand, he submits to censorship: "Had I wrote treason there . . . I had deserved,
then, thy consuming looks, / Perhaps, to have been burned with
my books." These lines begin a defense of Jonson's writings:

> But, on thy least malice, tell me, didst thou spy
> Any, least loose, or scurrile paper, lie
> Concealed or kept there, that was fit to be,
> By thy own vote, a sacrifice to thee?
> Did I there wound the honours of the crown?
> Or tax the glories of the church and gown?
> Itch to defame the state?
>
> (19–25)

On the other hand, Jonson's mock-serious tone unsettles the force
of his concession that he ought "perhaps" to have been burned with
his books if they were transgressive. Though Jonson may be submitting to censorship, he may also be undermining Vulcan by using
a hyperbolic suggestion that subtly reinvokes the repressive era
from which it came, turning any accusation against Jonson against
the accuser, who, with his "consuming looks," metes out to authors
appalling, excessive punishments.

The possibility that he is offering a critique of Vulcan is reinforced by the way Jonson articulates a defense of his liberty against
state censorship, distinguishing writing placed in public circulation
by an author from writing that Vulcan may illegitimately wish to
censor. Jonson enunciates an argument he believes Vulcan will
make to justify burning his works and then refutes it by appealing to
"public fame":

> but, thou'lst say,
> There were some pieces of as base allay,
> And as false stamp there; parcels of a play,
> Fitter to see the firelight, than the day;
> Adulterate monies, such as might not go:

>Thou should have stayed till public fame said so.
>She is the judge, thou executioner.

>(41–47)

Here, "stayed," a term for waiving censorship, is opposed to "public fame," while burning Jonson's unpublished manuscripts becomes an act of precensorship (the censors burned only printed books).[2] Against Vulcan as executioner, Jonson poses a disembodied, critical community of judges, displacing authority from a single, undiscriminating censor onto a public community of critical readers who can judge his works with distinction.

Yet it would be misleading to read "An Execration upon Vulcan" (or any of these other instances) as an unequivocal critique of court censorship. The crucial distinction for Jonson is between legitimate and illegitimate censorship, not between censorship and poetic liberty. Even as Jonson evades Vulcan's censorship, he simultaneously authorizes other kinds of censorship. When he says to Vulcan, "Thou should have stayed till public fame said so," Jonson shifts the authority to censor away from Vulcan and to the public; he does not deny the propriety of censorship altogether: public fame has the authority, or "say so," to censor.[3] Similarly, Jonson's assertion of his own authority over his text involves transferring authority to himself: keeping his text in manuscript form allows Jonson to decide if or when he will print it. At stake in "Execration" and elsewhere in Jonson's corpus are distinctions concerning who can legitimately censor Jonson's writings (Vulcan, the public, Jonson himself) and at what stage of literary production (prepublication or postpublication).

Far from closing down criticism of censorship, the need to make these distinctions opened it up, for the question was who was to make them. The answer, I contend, involved the emergence of literary criticism as an increasingly distinct prose discourse. The *Oxford English Dictionary* gives 1605 as the first instance of the use of *critic* to mean a reviewer, but Jonson uses it as early as 1599 in the Induction to *Cynthia's Revels* (186).[4] It is worth noting that much of what is now thought to constitute Jonson's literary criticism occupies a central place in the inventory of his books given in "Execration": a translation of Horace's *Ars poetica: Discoveries;* and the lost "Apology to *Bartholomew Fair.*"[5]

The very multiplicity of censors to which Jonson was subjected required that they be sorted out, some legitimated, others delegiti-mated. If in "An Execration upon Vulcan" Jonson bases a defense against the court censor on an appeal to public fame, that defense continually collapsed when the public exercised a similarly con-suming market censorship of Jonson's writings. As Timothy Mur-ray points out, Jonson struggled against any "ideology of com-munal consensus, which he often critiques for cultivating more promiscuous judgment than theatrical legitimation (1987, 79). Pub-lic fame revealed itself to be less an alternative to Vulcan (a more reliable and legitimate censor) than a version of Vulcan. Like Vul-can, who eats Jonson's writings "piece by piece," the spectator is an undiscriminating eater of plays:

> Tut, such crimes
> The sluggish gaping auditor devours;
> He marks not whose 'twas first: and after times
> May judge it to be his, as well as ours.
> Fool, as if half eyes will not know a fleece
> From locks of wool, or shreds from the whole piece?
> (*Epigrams* 56.9–15)

Similarly, in "To the Same," *Epigrams* 13, Jonson regards with resignation the privilege accorded all consumers by the circulation of his text in the literary marketplace:

> When we do give, *Alphonso,* to the light,
> A work of ours, we part with our own right;
> For, then, all mouths will judge, and their own way;
> The learned have no more privilege, than the lay.
> (1–4)

The poem's unrestrained, unregulated circulation enables the return of the repressed grotesque body ("all mouths"), thereby obliterating any distinction between critical, learned readers and uncritical, lay readers. Jonson's use of the same biological metaphor of festive con-sumption to describe both court and market censors registers their similar inadequacy, at least in Jonson's view, in distinguishing legiti-mate from illegitimate poets or their poetry, which symbolic prac-tices such as festive consumption—eating and burning books—are meant to affirm.

Through literary criticism (and the codification of criticism through biological metaphors establishing hierarchies of taste) Jonson attempted to regulate the circulation and consumption of his writings within a dispersed network of censorship practices. In saying that his literary criticism regulated consumption, I mean not only that criticism of censorship operated locally rather than globally but, more crucially, that as a form of regulation criticism was already paradoxically implicated in censorship. Criticism authorized censors to repress or to exercise discursive liberties. Moreover, the critic and the censor were complicit rather than opposed: censors operated as critics, and critics legitimated particular kinds of censorship, demanding that authors submit to critical censure. Criticism and censorship were at no point radically differentiated in early modern England. One of the meanings of *censor* was "critic" and one of the meanings of *critic* was "censor."⁶ In *Discoveries*, Jonson makes "the office of a true critic, or censor" (3199) equivalent, asserting that the critic's office is to "judge sincerely of the author, and his matter" (3203). Jonson refers to Plautus as a "great . . . master, and censor in the art" (3324). Similarly, John Donne occupied the roles of critic and censor in Jonson's writings. In "To John Donne," *Epigrams* 96, Jonson gives him the role of censor: "in thy censures . . . / Thou hast best authority to allow" (3, 19). Similarly, in "To Lady Digby," *Underwood* 78, Jonson's patron Weston "allows" (28) Jonson's poems. And as Herford and Simpson point out, the "leges conviviales" governing the behavior of Jonson and his sons at the Apollo Room made each participant a "censor morum" (H & S, 1:85). Criticism authorized the censor to differentiate liberty from license, to make the distinctions that legitimated or delegitimated specific forms of censorship.

Yet criticism and censorship did not consistently authorize each other. If literary criticism eased the felt pressure to distinguish legitimate from illegitimate forms of censorship, its legitimating function was always troubled by a counterpressure requiring the legitimation of the critic and of literary criticism; the critic, too, had to be legitimated, differentiated from the ordinary reader or mere censurer. The semantic instability of some of the terms for criticism (such as *censure*) register this difficulty. In *Epigrams* 17 and 18, Jonson juxtaposes the poems "To the Learned Critic" and "To My Mere English Censurer," placing them in implicit opposition. The critic confers on Jonson's poems a "legitimate fame," whereas the censurer uncritically compares Jonson's epigrams to Sir John Davies' (banned by the bishops in 1599) and to John Weever's. As in "To My Book" Jonson censures the mere censurer for failing to tell the difference between a text that ought to be censored and one that ought not to be. Yet in *Epigrams* 17, the implicit distinction between critic and censurer breaks down: Jonson leaves his poems to the critic's "sole censure" (4) just as in *Epigrams* 96 he mentions Donne's "censures" (3).[7] Furthermore, the regulation of criticism could take the form of court censorship. Jonson's earliest piece of literary criticism, the "Apologetical Dialogue" to *Poetaster,* was censored in the quarto edition. It is worth noting that Jonson owned a censored version of George Puttenham's *Art of English Poesie,* with four canceled leaves (see H & S, 1:264).

By drawing attention to the paradoxes of Jonson's literary criticism (which I take to be exemplary of early modern criticism in general), I mean to suggest that it, like censorship, needs to be historicized if its difference from modern and postmodern criticism is to be understood. Just as revisionists and Marxists have not contested the meaning of censorship when debating the theater's politics in general or Jonson's in particular, so too they have not contested the meaning of literary criticism. Indeed, though their accounts of theater and of Jonson are in many respects opposed, these critics have adopted a modern definition of literary criticism, implicitly or expliciting taking it to be the antithesis of court censorship.[8] In discussing the court's willingness to tolerate reformist criticism, revisionists, for example, legitimate the court and the writers it patronized by arguing that the court's tastes were sophisticated and diverse. As Kevin Sharpe puts it, "far from being sycophants, [Caroline court poets and dramatists] deployed the license of play to offer counsel through compliment and criticism" (1987, 295). Like the Whigs they often attack (Harbage 1936), revisionists project back on to the Renaissance a modern, ahistorical notion of literary criticism. The question of reception is reduced to determining what someone in the audience actually thought (did James I or Charles I actually understand the licensed criticism of the masques they patronized? for example). In answering this kind of question, revisionists mistake structures of authority and the structural distinctions that inform early modern literary criticism for supposedly empirical evidence ("taste" is unselfconsciously adopted as a critical category); similarly, a history of these structures gives way to an "evolutionary" development based on audience preferences.[9]

While Marxists have usefully criticized revisionist accounts of the Renaissance court culture, their account of literary criticism as a post-Renaissance development assumes the same definition of criticism. Along with Terry Eagleton (1984), Marxists such as Peter Burger (1984) and Peter Hohendahl (1982) have followed Jürgen Habermas (1962) in yoking the emergence of literary criticism to a specifically bourgeois social formation. It is likely that Marxist histories of criticism (Eagleton 1984) have remained beyond the purview of recent debates on the Renaissance theater precisely because those histories begin after the Renaissance.[10]

In historicizing literary criticism, I want to retain the conception of the public sphere and complicate it. Usually linked to the end of state censorship, the public sphere has also been defined by criteria such as universal participation in discourse (all can speak as equals; thus, a rational consensus can be reached); the emergence of mercantile capitalism (the commodification of discourses makes them available to a mass market); and the emergence of new technologies of cultural reproduction. The public sphere is defined against aristocratic culture in part because a different notion of publicity is said to have obtained in the Renaissance. Habermas argues, for example, that the "court aristocracy of the seventeenth century was not really a reading public. To be sure, it kept men of letters as its servants, but literary production based on patronage was more a matter of conspicuous consumption than of serious reading by an interested public" (1962, 38).

In this chapter I want to challenge this account in two respects, one historical and the other philosophical. In the next section, I argue that the paradoxes of Jonson's literary criticism and the reversibility of his model of theatrical legitimation arise in part because the agencies regulating the circulation and exchange of discourses were dispersed across several institutions that formed competing public spheres: the Revels office, the theater, the tavern, and of central importance, the library. (Modern and postmodern critics have often noted that Jonson legitimated the theater by taking his plays out of it and putting them into print. I would add that Jonson was equally interested in legitimating the theater by making a connection between the library and the critic who collects and reads books. The library keeper acted as an unofficial censor, and the library owner legitimated himself as a critic through his acquisition of legitimate books.) Criticism was never formally institutionalized through, say, the formation of a royal academy of letters or the founding of a national library. Different public spheres competed to establish criteria for the inclusion or exclusion of differing voices. As we will see in detail, these criteria were contested and were often made the basis for the delegitimation of would-be censor/critics. "Play clubs" might presume to dominate theater audiences, for example, but Jonson considered their dominance illegitimate insofar as they deprived him of the right to exercise his freedom to censure. The emergence of multiple public spheres did not necessarily imply political and social instability, but it did build a potential reversibility into Jonson's model. The dispersal of subject positions and of competing criteria allowed others to turn Jonson's own criteria of legitimation (or those of others) against him and his writings.

Attention to the specific public spheres in which Jonson circulated will enable us to read in his writings a set of neurotic symptoms that register the conflicting demands competing censors made on Jonson's model of theatrical legitimation. These conflicts resulted in the construction and deconstruction of interlocking distinctions between criticism and censorship, literary production and consumption, authors and critics, bodies and books. In addition to being paradoxically related to censorship, early modern literary criticism was an emergent discourse without a clear identity, a feature that helps to account for its elusiveness as an object of study by modern and postmodern critics.[11]

Jonson's criticism was not clearly separated from the rest of his literary corpus. Unlike Pierre Corneille, for example, who prefaced his criticism titled *Three Discourses* to an edition of his plays in 1660 (partly in response to an earlier controversy over his play *Le Cid*), Jonson's criticism took a variety of forms, sometimes spilling over into literature: prologues, epistles, the marginalia to his entertainments and masques, the catalog to his *Works,* as well as plays, epigrams, and poems such as "A Fit of Rhyme against Rhyme."[12] In his published corpus, whether in quarto or folio form, Jonson did not clearly distinguish his criticism from his literature. (The posthumously published *Discoveries* will prove to be exemplary of this lack of distinction rather than the exception it might at first appear to be.) Jonson's literary criticism is marked as early modern, in short, by its difference from modern literary criticism, which is understood to be a separate prose discourse subordinated to literature as its handmaiden and servant. Similarly, Jonson's model of theatrical legitimation required both the conflation and the differentiation of an author or reader's body and his books.

In making this historical argument, I also want to advance a philosophical critique of the Marxist account of the public sphere. In my view, the emergence of literary criticism in the Renaissance does not simply mean that the public sphere can be moved back, conceptually intact, to an earlier historical moment; it means, rather, that the usual criteria for defining the public sphere need to be revised. The standard account rests philosophically on idealist, ahistorical notions of "undistorted communication" (Habermas 1972); it assumes that uncensored discourse is a norm. Marxist histories of literary criticism have remained idealist insofar as they have placed criticism above or beyond censorship. These histories are structured by two utopian moments: a lost moment in the eighteenth century when criticism had a "real" social function (a golden age that Terry Eagleton concedes never existed) and a revolutionary moment yet to arrive when that function will be recovered and criticism will again have a transformative social effect.[13] Moreover, they have assumed a centered subjectivity (whether conceptualized in humanist terms as a fully conscious subject who intends meaning or in Marxist terms as History) and with it a repression model of discourse which governs both a humanist hermeneutics of censorship and the Marxist symptomatic reading that my historical argument about Jonson's neurotic practices calls into question.

Apart from the obvious problems an idealist, ahistorical model of discourse presents Marxist critics, this model has prevented them from attending to the paradoxes of early modern criticism as well as to specific limitations of the public sphere as they define it. Historically, that sphere has always legitimated the exclusion of certain groups, and as Peter Stallybrass and Allon White argue, "that 'idealist' realm of judgment, refinement, wit and rationalism was dependent on disavowal, denial, and projection" (1986, 108). In short, the public sphere has always involved forms of censorship, however different from those one would have found in the Renaissance.[14]

If we grant that the public sphere is itself an idealization, the criteria by which it is defined must include not only who gains access to discourse, who is denied access, and how access is blocked but on what basis. The criteria for a public sphere, that is to say, specify how discourses and speakers are legitimated and delegitimated. Revising the criteria in this way allows us to redefine the public sphere in two crucial respects. First, it is not tied to any historical moment: discourses can be exchanged between institutions without necessarily being commodified. Second, multiple public spheres may be present at the same historical moment, each operating with its own relative autonomy from the others.

In the last section of this chapter, I buttress my philosophical critique by addressing both Jonson's criticism in relation to that of his contemporaries and his centrality to a later neoclassical model of criticism. Jonson's relation to his contemporaries and his later reception call into question any attempt to differentiate strictly between a consensual notion of literary criticism practiced in the eighteenth century and an authoritarian censorship practiced in the Renaissance. The contradictions of Jonson's model cannot be resolved from a critical position that opposes censorship to criticism; the contradictions cannot rightly be recuperated by regarding them as prefiguring in an emergent form a later, noncontradictory modern model of criticism.

I

To grasp the paradoxes of early modern literary criticism and Jonson's contribution to them we need to examine the symbolic economy of Jonson's reformist, antitheatrical mode of cultural legitimation, what Stanley Fish (1984) has termed Jonson's community of the same, in relation to the various censoring agencies that helped produce the theater as a public space. According to Fish, Jonson's style serves to legitimate and delegitimate, include and exclude readers who always already were or were not members of Jonson's club: Jonson's texts are immediately readable, but only by members of his critical community. The meaning of his writings would "declare themselves" (*Masque of Beauty,* 9) to the learned, aristocratic spectator, and "only the unlucky scene need an interpreter" (*The Magnetic Lady,* Induction, 125–26). Fish and, more recently, Katharine Maus (1989) have drawn attention to Jonson's use of economic metaphors in his writings. Maus suggests that Jonson's community is founded on opposition between two symbolic economies, ideal and satiric, in which exchange occurs without change.

I would add that Jonson's community and the exchanges between authors and readers it both enables and constrains entail a reciprocal alignment between the court censor and the critic, an alignment that allows both authorities to recuperate the otherwise potentially disruptive effects of the dispersal of authority across a relatively autonomous aesthetic domain. This domain is related but not confined to what is now generally known as a literary marketplace.[15] It involved not only an economy of cash exchange but a symbolic economy in which discourses and the power to regulate them were exchanged between licensing authorities and licensed author/critics who in turn exercised their own autonomy in a self-regulating manner. Each Master of the Revels was a well-educated man of letters, not an officious or corrupt time-serving bureaucrat.[16] How the Master of the Revels acted as a critic in licensing plays can perhaps best be seen by turning to a specific example from Sir Henry Herbert's record book.[17] Consider his comments on one of James Shirley's plays: "The comedy called *The Yonge Admirall,* being free from oaths, prophaness, or obsceanes, hath given mee much delight and satisfaction in the readinge, and may serve for a patterne to other poetts, not only for the bettering of maners and language, but for the improvement of the quality, which hath received some brushings of late" (Adams 1917, 19). Herbert did not merely differentiate between censored and licensed plays on political grounds but evaluated licensed plays on moral and aesthetic grounds.

Herbert's implicit alignment of the court censors with literary critics implies a converse alignment of the critic with the censor, an alignment, as we have seen, that Jonson usefully illustrates. The exchange of power between censor and critic worked to secure a semiotic system with the king as the supreme judge, his patronage being a form of prestige attached to the company.

This exchange of power depended on a symbolic economy in which a certain model of mimetic discursive production secured cultural hierarchies. Herbert suggests in his account of *The Young Admiral* that dramatists should imitate other allowed dramatists:

> When Mr. Sherley hath read this approbation, I know it will encourage him to pursue this beneficial and cleanly way of poetry, and when other poetts heare and see his good success, I am confident they will imitate the original for their own credit, and make such copies in this harmless way, as shall speak them masters in their art, at the first sight, to all judicious spectators. . . . I have entered this allowance, for direction to my successor, and for example to all poetts, that shall write after the date hereof. July 3, 1633. (Adams 1917, 19–20)

Here the court censor differentiates the authority of judicious from injudicious spectators or critics, and expects dramatists to follow suit. Similarly, he expects future Masters of the Revels to maintain his critical model.

Jonson adopted a similar account of imitation, aligning "good" imitation with the classical body and "bad" imitation with the grotesque body.[18] Imitation and emulation become the basis for subjection and hierarchies of legitimacy in judgment. In *Discoveries,* Jonson likens poetic imitation, or *copia,* to digestion and its copy:

> The third requisite in our poet, or maker, is imitation, to convert the substance or riches of another poet, to his own use. To make choice of one excellent man above the rest, and to follow him, 'til he grow very he, or so like him, as the copy may be mistaken for the principal. Not as a creature, that swallows, what it takes in, crude, raw, or indigested; but, that feeds with an appetite and hath a stomach to concoct, divide, and turn all into nourishment. Not to imitate servilely, as Horace Smith, . . . but, to draw forth out of the best, and choicest flowers with the bee, and turn all into honey, work into one relish, and savour. (3055–63, 3065–69)

Jonson's poetics of imitation, like the court censor's view of imitation, authorizes, legitimates, and regulates the circulation of power between censors and author/critics. Jonson's metaphor for imitation—converting "another's riches" to one's "use," like the metaphor of "stamping" or making current in "Execration upon

Vulcan"—legitimates the circulation of good imitations and delegitimates the circulation of bad imitations by instituting a set of interlocking oppositions between poets and poet apes, between plagiarists and authors who truly incorporate their sources, between counterfeit and true copies, between counterfeiting rogues and counterfeiting actors, between spectators who censure a play by imitating another spectator's censure and spectators who exercise their own opinions, between critics who engage in theatrical self-display and critics who give studied, thoughtful responses. The second child in the induction to *Cynthia's Revels,* for example, attacks the self-preoccupied critic, "one civet-wit among you, that knows no other learning, than the price of satin and velvets; nor other perfection than the wearing of a neat suit; and yet will censure as desperately as the most professed critic in the house: presuming, his clothes should bear him out in't" (Induction, 184–87). Jonson served the state by formulating a way in which the court censor and the critic define and determine which discourses and which writers and readers are to be put on one side or the other of these oppositions.

The autonomy copia required for the regulation of these legitimating and delegitimating distinctions was problematic, however. As Richard Halpern notes in a discussion of humanist pedagogy, copia represented "a decisive innovation in ideological control" (1991, 47). Halpern writes: "Humanist pedagogy and writing theory both extended the realm of pleasure and granted it a certain autonomy, in the belief that it could be recuperated or 'trained' in the end. This was in a sense humanism's great wager and the source of its distinctive optimism, which was by no means naive. . . . By imposing a simulated ideological coherence on the text *ex post facto,* style also becomes the signature of a *subject,* in all senses of the word: one that has achieved a certain continuity and regularity, has learned to obey certain *decora,* is identifiable and individualized" (1991, 56). Whether the ideological strategy of licensing liberty could be fully recuperative was an open question, however. As Halpern points out, "imitation theory seems to encourage not ideological subjection but the 'self-fashioning' of autonomous subjects. . . . it seems to threaten the very mechanisms that make imitation a method of ideological control" (1991, 43). The felt pressure of this threat is registered in the censorship and expurgation of school texts. Juan Luis Vives wrote that "obscene passages should be wholly cut out of the text" (1991, 47). Moreover, at least some schools made use of beatings and whippings.[19]

Jonson formulated similar recuperative strategies in his literary criticism, but the extreme volatility of his paradoxical position as a critic/censor can be seen in the contrast between the way copia and a poetics of imitation were used in Renaissance humanist schools and the way Jonson used them in his literary criticism. Jonson disparages "servile" submission to one's model in *Discoveries,* and he adds that "nothing is more ridiculous than to make an author a *Dictator*" (2095–96). Moreover, he maintains that he is "not of that opinion to conclude a poet's liberty within the narrow limits of laws, which either the grammarians, or philosophers prescribe" (2555–57). Jonson's generic innovations in comical satire depended on a principle of legitimate poetic liberty to depart from the original the author imitated. In *Every Man out of His Humour* Asper asks why he should not be able to augment his speech "with a liberty according to elegancy and disposition of those times wherein they wrote? I see not then but we should enjoy the same license or free power, to illustrate and heighten our invention as [classical satirists] did; and not be tied to those strict and regular forms, which the niceness of a few (who are nothing but form) would thrust upon us" (Second Sounding, 256–61). Similarly, in the prologue to *Volpone,* Jonson both observes laws and departs from them. The author

> presents quick comedy, refined
> As best critics have designed,
> The laws of time, place, persons he observeth,
> From no needful rule he swerveth.
>
> (29–32)

Though Jonson follows the "best critics," he observes only their "needful rules." Similarly, in the epistle when discussing the conclusion to *Volpone,* Jonson concedes, "My catastrophe may in the strict rigor of comic law meet with censure, as turning back to my promise" (103–5). He appeals, however, to the "learned and charitable critic" (107) to justify his ending, and responds to the stricture that "we do never punish in our interludes, &c" by saying that he "took the *more* liberty, though not without example" (111, my emphasis) in choosing to end the play as he did.

Yet Jonson's literary criticism and criticism in general functioned more paradoxically as a form of discursive regulation than did schools, not only because theater censorship was never centralized in a disciplinary apparatus but because criticism regulated a wider range and circulation of discourses within diverse public spheres and permitted a greater degree of autonomy to readers and writers than did the schools. The effectiveness of Jonson's use of imitation as a mode of critical/censorial regulation was radically limited by the fact that criticism, unlike the Revels Office, was never formally institutionalized. The office of Master of Revels was centralized in 1606, putting an end to the more dispersed arrangement that had allowed Samuel Daniel to function as the licenser for the Children of the Queen's Revels from 1604. This centralization helped to crystallize a division between censor and author/critic under the early Stuarts.[20] Though poets contended for the Revels Office (John Lyly was unsuccessful in 1588), no poet ever functioned as the court censor.

Literary criticism could not easily regulate literary production and consumption, however, because any discursive model of theatrical legitimation depended on clearly institutionalized authorities that could organize distinctions between and within discourses as well as the hierarchies that followed from them. The dispersal of power among censors and critics involved a multiplicity of public spheres, and therefore, critics were authorized or would authorize themselves to determine which texts did or did not meet the criteria for legitimate discourse.

The extent to which Jonson (or anyone else) functioned outside a formally institutionalized model of literary criticism can be gauged by comparing the English institution to the Académie Française, founded by Richelieu in 1634, which had its own library and produced a dictionary (see Murray 1989). The academy, moreover, was well integrated into the state, and even genre was regulated. In 1680 the king gave Molière's troupe a monopoly on comedy (Guicharnaud 1989, 354–58). By contrast, England had no such academy. A proposal for a royal academy of letters was formulated and Jonson was on a list of members, but the proposal never materialized (Hunter 1847). It was, in any case, to be a society of antiquarians, who would not have regulated theatrical production or acted as theater critics as the French academicians did. The only English social institution approaching the French academy was the play club or faction, which met in theaters and, more important, the tavern. The Apollo Room provided some authority and prestige for Jonson and his "sons," who could admit or exclude members. In "Leges Conviviales," Jonson distinguishes the critical community that met at the Apollo Room by its civility, modesty, and intellectual ability:

> Let none but guests or clubbers hither come;
> Let dunces, fools, sad, sordid men keep home;
> Let learned, civil, merry men be invited,
> And modest, too; nor the choice ladies slighted.
>
> (1–4)

Learning, command of languages and cant, mastery of the classical canon, observance of stylistic decorum, generic hierarchies are, among others, the criteria by which Jonson's community includes author/critics, excludes dunces. Jonson similarly legitimates his "tribe" in "An Epistle to One Who Would be Sealed" by excluding those who do not restrain themselves. Linking their bodily excesses with political sedition and poetic ineptitude, Jonson excludes those "that live in the wild anarchy of drink,"

> Subject to quarrel only
>   .   .   .   .   .
> That censure all the town, and all the affairs,
> And know their ignorance is more than theirs;
> Let these men have their ways, and take their times
> To vent their libels, and to issue rhymes.
>
> (10–11, 23–26)

Yet the limit of the authority and prestige of the play club is evident not only in the mockery Sir John Suckling applies to Jonson and his tribe in "Session of the Poets" but in Jonson's own scorn for a similar self-authorized group, including the "play-club" that put down *The New Inn*.[21] As "factions," these clubs manipulated audiences by buying up blocks of tickets (see H & S, 6:15). Jonson delegitimates the club as a heterogeneous group that "scarce allowed" him to give his "censure" of Joseph Rutter's play *The Shepherd's Holiday* (1635), in "To My Dear Son, and Right-Learned Friend, Master Joseph Rutter" (*Miscellaneous Poems,* 23). Similarly,

Jonson mocks the censorious "college of critics" (3.4.93) in *Poetaster* and the collegiate ladies in *Epicoene*.[22]

We can deepen our understanding of the problem Jonson faced in legitimating literary criticism by turning to the library, a site directly linked to Jonson's critical model of imitation and copia. Some of the central metaphors for copia are also used for the library. As Terence Cave points out, "One of the particular senses of copia is 'treasure chest,' 'hoard,' or 'store'" (1979, 6). Jonson uses the metaphor of the store for his work in progress in "An Execration upon Vulcan," describing a version of *Discoveries* as "twice twelve years stored up humanity, / With humble gleanings in divinity" (101–2). Jonson refers to his library in the same way in his poem "An Epistle to a Friend," thanking him for the gift of a book: "You have added unto my store a book" (*Underwood,* 37.4).[23]

The library was of increasing importance to Jonson because it compensated for the failure of his memory. According to George Chapman, the burning of his library should not have made any difference to Jonson since he ought to be able to rewrite any burned works from memory. Chapman made this point in his caustic response to "Execration upon Vulcan," titled "An Invective of Mr George Chapman against Mr Ben: Johnson" (H & S, 11:406–11). Chapman maintained that Jonson had actually lost no manuscripts to the flames, that he was naming unwritten manuscripts, not destroyed ones (criing fire out In a dreame to kinge / Burne thinge vnborne, and that way generatt thine" [ll. 118–19]). If manuscripts had indeed perished, Jonson should surely be able to replace them:

> Canst thou lese theise by fire, and liue yet able
> To wright past Ioues wrath, fier and Ayre, things stable,
> Yet Curse as thou wert lost for euerye bable?
> Some pore thinge wright new; a Riche Caskett Ben
> All of rich Iems, t'adorne most learned men.
>
> (108–12)

Chapman's criticism had some force, for when he was younger, Jonson himself boasted that he could copy his writings from memory. In the dedication to Prince Henry in the quarto edition of his *Masques of Queens* Jonson says he has managed to annotate it "though it hath prou'd a worke of some difficulty for mee, to

retriue the particular *authorities* (according to yor gracious command . . .) to those things, wch I writt ovt of fullnesse, and memory of my former readings" (H & S, 7:281). Similarly, he says in
Discoveries: "I myself could, in my youth, have repeated all, that I
ever made; and so continued, till I was past forty: since, it is much
decayed in me. Yet I can repeat whole books that I have read, and
poems, of some selected friends, which I have liked to charge my
memory with" (598–604). But Jonson was fifty-one in 1623 when
his library burned. One can see why he might compose a poem
about its destruction, for the library served to literalize the principle
of copia on which his criticism depended: copies of books substituted for copia.

Jonson's difficulty in legitimating literary criticism was not simply a factor of his age and consequent lapses in memory, however.
More crucially, the library was not a stable alternative site of consumption and production to the unstable public theaters, for the
library was itself a public institution, another site of discursive
circulation, exchange, and consumption, which reproduced the
features of the public theaters Jonson was most concerned to avoid,
all of which concerned bad imitation.[24] Historicist critics have often
declared that Jonson legitimated his writings by moving from theatrical performance into the stabler medium of print without examining the connection between the place where books are read,
namely, the library, and the critic who reads them. Stephen Orgel
(1982) points out that the theater is legitimated in the Renaissance
largely by the high status that publication conferred on plays. He
comments further on the importance of the library:

> We see in the pattern of dramatic publication an emphasis on the
> increasing authority of the playwright. . . . The spectacle of theatre
> in this way becomes drama, a form of poetry; and as it moved
> upward on the generic scale, so it did on the social scale as well. . . .
> when plays are published in folio and sell for 1£ . . . the drama has
> new patrons: the rich, the aristocratic collectors, men with libraries;
> and the publishers assume that their clientele will be people of se-
> riousness, learning, and taste. Thus, Jonson's plays are presented as
> *Works.* . . . How new all this is may be understood if we recall that
> Sir Thomas Bodley's library at Oxford, in the terms of its foundation
> in 1611, explicitly excluded books of plays. Jonson's, Shakespeare's,
> and Beaumont and Fletcher's folios, like the volumes they imitate—

the great humanist editions of the ancient dramatists—are not playbooks. They present themselves as classics. (1982, 151)

In describing patrons, Orgel implicitly characterizes them as modern literary critics: "people of seriousness, learning, and taste." His
view of theatrical legitimation may be counterposed against another that contrasts the heterogeneity of the theater to the unity of
the book and the "defensive patriarchal academy" (Murray 1987,
192) that unity serves. "Any reader who chooses to be only a *Son* of
Ben," Murray writes, "who opts for the intellectual *possession* of the
manuscript stands forth as an unquestionable *critic* of the theater"
(1987, 104).

I would add here that as a central agent of theatrical legitimation,
the library constituted another public sphere from which the critic
could exercise his authority as a censor. The library retrospectively
conferred legitimation not only on published books but on specific
kinds of published books. Sir Thomas Bodley wished to exclude
from Oxford "pamphlets, not worthy of the custody of such a
Librarie." In a letter to the keeper, Thomas James, Bodley argued
that "the benefit [of including "idle books and riff raffe"] will
never countervaile the harme that the scandal will bring unto the
librarie, when it shal be given out, that wel stuff it full of baggage
books. . . . The more I thinke vpon it, the more it doth disgust me,
that such a kinde of bookes, should be vouchsafed a rowme, in so
noble a Librarie" (Wheeler 1926, 222). As Alexandra Halasz (1990)
points out, Bodley uses "baggage" as a term of abuse; he means
"trashy" or "filthy." Bodley effectively wanted the library keeper
to act as a censor, to take in legitimate books and keep out baggage books. The connection between libraries and censorship can
be seen even more directly in Edmund Bolton's proposal in 1617 for
a royal academy. According to Bolton, the scholars of the institution would, among other things, have given "the vulgar people
indexes expurgatory and epunctory (i.e., censored and purified) of
all books of secular learning printed in English never to be public
again" (Hunter 1847, 141; see also Irwin 1964, 236).

This distinction required stable definitions of both baggage and
legitimate books. Yet this ideal notion of copia and imitation for the
accumulation of self-identical books was complicated by the lack of
a centralized national library and the consequent importance as-

sumed by gentlemen's libraries as public institutions. Antiquarians were concerned to found a central library after the dissolution of the monasteries; others wanted to save books for the nationalistic and propagandistic purposes of the Reformation (see Sharpe 1979; Irwin 1964; Wright 1958). Proposals for a national library were submitted to Thomas Cromwell, to Queen Mary, and to Elizabeth. In the most elaborate version, Archbishop Parker, Sir Humphrey Gilbert, and Sir Robert Cotton, among others, asked Elizabeth for a charter of incorporation of the Library of Queen Elizabeth for public use "to encourage learning by public lectures, Libraries and Academies" (Edwards 1864, 160). The books would come from divers gentlemen, and they asked the queen to contribute "so many books out of History and Antiquity, as it shall please her to grant, for the better furnishing of the library" (Edwards 1864, 161). Yet like Cromwell and Mary, Elizabeth I showed no interest, and the project was abandoned (see Sharpe 1979, 51). The early Stuarts followed suit.

The lack of a national library meant that a gentleman's collection such as Cotton's could assume political significance as a public institution. Libraries were an important mode of aristocratic status display. Books bound with velvet of various colors and some adorned with gems were part of Elizabeth's collection (Edwards 1864, 161). Queen Anne gave Charles a gift of books bound in crimson velvet (Edwards 1864, 109). It was in their libraries that gentlemen such as Cotton kept their wonder cabinets (Sharpe 1979, 65–68). Royal libraries were similarly on display. Among the wonders Paul Hentzler noted during his tour of England was Elizabeth's library in Westminister (Edwards 1864, 165).

Yet there was a significant shift away from libraries as status indicators toward libraries as research institutions in the seventeenth century.[25] James I ordered that the state papers be organized in a "set form of Lybrary" (Edwards 1864, 181), and gentlemen's libraries were becoming research centers. Cotton, for example, lent books among a wide circle of friends, including courtly ones, giving his borrowers "free access" to his books (Sharpe 1979, 74). According to Sharpe, Cotton's library was a public institution (1979, 64). Sir George Buc, one of the Masters of the Revels, followed Cotton's lead and lent books from his own library as well (Sharpe 1979, 74).

The shift toward a public use of a collection could also be defined against certain kinds of censorship. Thomas James advised the curators of the Bodleian in 1627 to look to the Catholic church's *Index Librorum Prohibitorum* as a guide to titles most worth preserving and collecting (Eisenstein 1979, 416). He advised them to make sure to get the earlier and therefore unexpurgated copies (Putnam 1906, 13). According to Edmund Bolton, James I liked his proposal for a royal academy, "because it was purely for the public" (Hunter 1847, 140).

This new research or public use of gentlemen's libraries also proved troublesome to the crown. Buckingham advised Charles I to close Cotton's library in 1626. After the intervening stormy Parliaments of 1628 and 1629, Charles ordered it closed in 1629, the trumped-up charge (Sharpe 1979, 80) being that Cotton had circulated a seditious paper. Sharpe notes that the library's users cut across Whiggish divisions between court and country, but he adds that "during the debates leading to the Petition of Right, it was not the king and his councillors of Whitehall, but Sir John Eliot and the leaders of Parliament who walked a few yards to consult their neighbour Cotton's library" (80).

Cotton's library was unusual in this regard, particularly problematic for its collection of manuscripts and state papers. Yet state censorship can also be seen behind the impulse to catalog. Cotton's library was ordered to be cataloged, as was Sir Edward Coke's when he was dismissed by James in 1616. Sir Walter Ralegh's collection was cataloged by the royal library keeper "in 1619 at James' commandment" (Edwards 1864, 184) while Ralegh was in the Tower. (James had called in Ralegh's *History of the World;* according to John Chamberlain, James felt Ralegh was "too sawcie in censuring Princes" [Clare 1990, 154]. An incomplete shelf list of 494 books includes some of the commonplace books Ralegh used in writing *The History of the World* and the books he consulted as well ([Jayne 1956, 148].)

Before clarifying the impact of these dispersed public spheres on the institution of criticism and Jonson's contradictory interest in both distinguishing and refusing to distinguish between authors and critics, bodies and books, and criticism and literature, we need first to understand how the dispersal of competing public spheres complicates the repression model of discourse that continues to inform accounts of Jonson's critical practices in printing and editing his own texts. Jonson's neurotic compromises between the different forces of discursive production and consumption among which he circulated call into question the stable oppositions between public and private, author and critic, through which this repression model is structured.

In order to "fit in" with one audience, Jonson willingly censored himself; yet the censored criticism emerged in another context. He couldn't say everything he wanted to say in any one place or in any one medium. Jonson was both limited and licensed in a given sphere—the theater, the tavern, the court, the country house, the study. The same may be said for the media he used—speech, manuscript, print, or marginalia—in the vernacular or in Latin. In displacing the problems he saw in one practice, such as theatrical performance, onto another, such as print, Jonson needed to construct a new set of distinctions (the reader ordinary versus the reader extraordinary, as in the prefaces to *Cataline*) to solve the new problems this displacement opened up. In moving from one site to another, Jonson produced finer and finer distinctions between censure and vulgar censure, or between "good" and "bad" libel, as when he delegitimated in "Ode to Himself" the "vulgar censure" of *The New Inn* or, to take another example, when the boy asserts in *The Magnetic Lady* that the author is "careless of all vulgar censure, as not depending on common approbation" (Induction, 104–5). Even when discussing poems in his house, as in "Inviting a Friend to Supper," Jonson can exercise his "liberty" freely without the presence of spies because he and his friend have already internalized censorship (spies are unnecessary because they are superfluous).

These paradoxical displacements, I suggest, constitute a neurotic subjectivity not reducible to an opposition between freedom and repression. To adopt a repression model of the public sphere or of the hermeneutics of censorship would effectively dissolve the paradoxes and contradictions that mark Jonson's literary criticism as early modern. Present accounts of the public sphere tend indirectly to confirm humanist accounts of censorship in which readers are thought to decode authorial disavowals of criticism as invitations to apply the text, to read in them a double meaning. These accounts, albeit in different ways, assume the existence of a single authority that determines a single threshold between transgressive and legitimate discourses (whether or not that authority was inconsistent or capricious about when and where it drew the line or how it responded when the line was crossed). These unexamined assumptions continue to determine accounts of Jonson's exclusions and inclusions in the first folio.[26] According to recent critics, Jonson printed the first folio and called it *Works* in order to fashion an identity for himself as a legitimate court poet (see Dutton 1983; Marcus 1986b; Riggs 1988, 215–39). His choice of what to include was governed by this aim. He left half of his plays out of print (H & S, 1:143, ll. 392–93), for example, because he wanted to suppress parts of his past that did not conform to his image as a court poet. A similar model of repression governs a related issue, namely, Jonson's textual revisions. Consider, for example, the discrepancies between the quarto and folio versions of censored plays such as *Cynthia's Revels* or *Poetaster*. In both cases, critics have assumed Jonson restored passages he cut for an earlier court performance in 1601 (H & S, 4:17; Barton 1984, 80), that by 1616 Jonson had the authority to add the previously censored material or that it was now safe to do so because the censor approved it (see Riggs 1988; Clare 1990, 83–90).

Any account that appeals to Jonson's conscious intentions or to unconscious, unintended market forces takes for granted a hermeneutics of censorship that fails to explain either the contradictions of Jonson's model of imitiative poetics or his revisions of his texts (excluding material from print, restoring previously deleted material, or expanding earlier editions). Why, for example, did Jonson censor some of his poems rather than identify his victims (as in *Underwood* 20, where he writes, "Here something is wanting," and indicates that two lines are missing)? This account of Jonson's legitimation as court poet leaves out questions about his neurotic practices as a literary critic and about his literary criticism. From a perspective that adopts the assumptions informing present accounts of the hermeneutics of censorship, one can only wonder why Jonson compared the burning of his library to censorship in "Execration upon Vulcan." His library did not contain state papers of the sort that attracted many people to Cotton's library. According to David McPherson, about half the contents of Jonson's library were composed of what we would now call literature and literary criticism (1974, 9). Why, then, does Jonson give his literary criticism such centrality in the poem? For that matter, why didn't Jonson ever publish his most significant literary criticism, including a "discourse of Poesy against Campion and Daniel, especially this latter" (H & S, 1:132), a preface to Horace's *Ars poetica* and a translation of it, and the "Apology to *Bartholomew Fair*"? Why, moreover, did Jonson frequently announce in print his intention to publish texts we now consider to be literary criticism and then fail to do so? In the preface to the quarto edition of *Sejanus,* "To the Readers," for example, Jonson announced that he would "take more seasonable cause to speak, in my observations upon Horace his *Art of Poetry* which, with the text translated, I intend shortly to publish" (13–15). Jonson apparently obliquely referred to the same text in the epistle to *Volpone,* saying in reference to a work of criticism he would "have occasion to speak more hereafter" (H & S, 9:685–86 n. 124). His unwillingness to publish his literary criticism is still more puzzling given that he cites the *Ars poetica* in the prologue to *Volpone* (H & S, 9:686 n. 8). And why did Jonson often publish his literary criticism, restoring in the first folio the "Apologetical Dialogue" struck from the quarto edition of *Poetaster?*

These questions suggest that if literary criticism was a potentially transgressive discourse, its transgressive potential cannot rightly be read in terms of a distinction between one discursive space in which discourse was repressed and another in which it was free. I am concerned here not with empirical answers to the above questions (which assume an unproblematic notion of Jonson as a writing subject) but with how those questions register the neurotic instability of Jonson's model of theatrical legitimation, an instability that arises from its location in multiple public spheres. Elucidating this instability means rethinking the way political criticism has assimilated a psychoanalytic model of repression, whether in the service of "undistorted communication," in Habermas's terms (1972), the symptomatic reading elaborated by Louis Althusser (1971) and Fredric Jameson (1981), or the Foucauldian reading of a bourgeois, neurotically self-censoring subjectivity advanced by Francis Barker (1984).

While these critical accounts and practices have the merit of explicitly engaging psychoanalysis and introducing a conception of decentered subjectivity freed of pejorative moralizing connotations, they have nevertheless largely included psychoanalysis in order to exclude it. In practice, they rely on a repression model of discourse fundamentally congruent with the humanist one, thereby leaving intact humanist oppositions between freedom and repression, private and public spheres. I use *neurosis* to suggest that Jonson's decentered subjectivity marks a compromise formation between different censoring spaces and agencies. As Pierre Bourdieu argues,

> The specialized languages that schools of specialists produce and reproduce through the systematic alteration of the common language are, as with all discourses, the product of a *compromise* between an *expressive interest* and a *censorship* constituted by the very structure of the field in which the discourse is produced and circulates. This "compromise-formation" in the Freudian sense, is more or less "successful" depending on the *specific competence* of the producer, and is the product of *strategies of euphemization* that consist in imposing form as well as observing formalities. These strategies tend to guarantee the satisfaction of an expressive interest, biological drive or political interest (in the broad sense of the term), within the limits of the *structure of opportunities for material or symbolic profit* which the different forms of discourse can procure for different producers according to their position in the field, that is, in the structure of the distribution of the specific capital that is at stake in the field. (1991, 138–138)

I would add that in using neurosis as a metaphor for an inescapable censorship, the meaning of censorship begins to be destablized. Rather than simply meaning an all-encompassing, ahistorically constitutive force (which would trivialize it), censorship may include or exclude a variety of textual practices. Revision, for example, may be thought either to distort a text's meaning (by functioning as censorship) or to clarify it. In a passage in *Moses and Monotheism* which indirectly illuminates this point, Freud discusses the kinds of distortion textual revision may involve:

> The text as we have it today will tell us enough about its vicissitudes. Two mutually opposed treatments have left their traces on it. On the one hand, it has been subjected to revisions which have falsified it in the sense of their secret aims, have mutilated and amplified it and have even changed it into its reverse; on the other hand, a solicitous piety has presided over it and has sought to preserve everything as it was, no matter whether it was consistent or contradicted itself. Thus almost everywhere noticeable gaps, disturbing repetitions and obvious contradictions have come about—indications which reveal

things to us which it was not intended to communicate. In its implications the distortion of a text resembles a murder: the difficulty is not in perpetrating the deed but in getting rid of its traces. We might well lend the word *Enstellung* [distortion] the double meaning to which it has a claim but of which today it makes no use. It should mean not only to "change the appearance of something" but also "to put something in another place, to displace." Accordingly, in many instances of textual distortion, we may nevertheless count upon finding what has been suppressed and disavowed hidden away somewhere else, though changed and torn from its context. Only it will not always be easy to recognize it. (1964, 43)

By terming Jonson's practice of literary criticism neurotic, I want to suggest that there is a permanent difficulty in recognizing the difference between the "real" text and its later distortions precisely because there is no original, precensored text to be (dis)-covered. Freud's assumed distinction between a pure, genuine text and its subsequent bad, distorted revisions is mythical (even the first version, that is, is inscribed in censorship). The question of whether a revised text has been criticized or censored will often remain difficult to decide precisely because textual revision can so easily slide from rewriting as clarification (uncovering an earlier, truer "uncensored" version) into rewriting as repression (a textual cover-up). Depending on one's interpretation of a given text, revision may be registered as a negative function (of distortion and censorship) or a positive function (of clarification, itself defined as a critical activity).

Though I have reintroduced neurosis to complicate the binary oppositions that empower repression models of discourse, I do not mean to void the validity of these models altogether. Jonson's literary criticism can be partly assimilated to a notion of criticism as a secret resistance to censorship. Consider his conversations with Drummond. Jonson tells Drummond of his personal satire of Inigo Jones and fills in his censored account of the occasion of his masque for Essex. The only reason we know many of his particular codings and censures of English poets is that Drummond wrote them down. Drummond's conversations are significantly titled "Certain Informations and maners of Ben Johnsons to W. Drummond" (H & S, 1:132).

Transgressive criticism can also be seen in Jonson's marginalia in books written by other authors. Jonson restored *Chorus poetarum*'s expurgations and warned Farnaby not to acquire the expurgated edition of Martial, calling it "castrated" (H & S, 1:216). Jonson methodically supplied "all of the missing lines, using the book's upper, lower, and even side margins when necessary," including expurgated passages "in Plautus, Terence, Catullus, Horace, Tibullus, Ovid, Seneca, Persius, Juvenal, and Martial" (McPherson 1974, 12, 36). He wrote "Inigo" in the margins, and as McPherson notes, "beside Martial's IX.xxxvii, 'In Gallum,' Jonson has written what appears to be 'Vel Lu. Co: B.' [Lucy, Countess of Bedford]" (1974, 10; see also 68–70). Moreover, he made a "half dozen annotations in which [he] discusses an epigram that deals with oral sexual intercourse" (McPherson 1974, 11). His marginalia in his copy of Chapman's translation of Homer were similarly transgressive. Though Jonson spoke favorably of this translation in a prefatory poem praising Chapman's translation of Hesiod's *Works and Days,* his annotations to his copy of Homer "criticize[d] Chapman's scholarship severely" (H & S, 11:593). As Herford and Simpson ask, "Considering how sensitive Chapman was to criticism, what would have happened if he had read these annotations?" (H & S, 11:94).

If Jonson's literary criticism was potentially transgressive, it was because its legitimacy could not be taken for granted, not because it constituted a secret, coded political critique. Consider his marginalia to his own writings. Jonson authorized and legitimated editions of his entertainments and masques and delegitimated criticism offered by those who in "their tyrannous ignorance, will offer to slight me . . . and give themselves a perremptorie license to judge" (H & S, 8:249) both by printing them and by extensively annotating them.

Yet Jonson's use of scholarly authorities to buttress his text could produce negative critical responses. In his *Entertainment* for James I, Thomas Dekker glances critically at Jonson's annotated edition of Jonson's own part of the entertainments, likening the common scholar to a literary tyrant whose borrowings make him resemble a theatrical counterfeiter:

> To make a false flourish herewith he borrowed weapons of all the old Maisters of the noble Science of Poesie, and to keepe a tyrannical coile, in Anatomizing Genius, from head to foote, (onely to shew how nimbly we can carve up the whole mess of poets) were to play

the Executioner, and to lay our Cities household God on the rack, to make him confesse how many paire of Latin sheetes, we have shaken and cut into shreds to make him a garment. Such feates of activite are stale, and common among scholars. (Nichols 1828, 1:337)

Jonson used his learning in ways that amounted, at least in Dekker's view, to literary tyranny. He is perhaps responding to this kind of criticism when he defensively justifies the quarto edition of *Sejanus* (in "To the Readers"), complete with marginal notes and footnotes in Latin, as being "non-affected" to the nostrils of his readers.

The extent to which the legitimacy of criticism was open to negotiation can be seen even more clearly if we note that Jonson did not publish the criticism modern critics would take for granted as legitimate—his "censures" of other poets, including Drummond himself, among them. Many of Jonson's censures in "Conversations" are, in early modern terms, hard to distinguish from libel: "That Sharpham, Day, Dekker, were all rogues and that Minshew was one. That Abram Francis in his English hexameters was a fool. That Markham (who added his English Arcadia) was not of the number of the faithful, i.e. poets, and but a base fellow. That such were Day and Middleton" (H & S, 1:51–56). The indeterminacy of what counted as criticism is further registered by the fact that not all the decodings Jonson provided Drummond were satirical or transgressive (Jonson identified Criticus as Donne, for example). It is significant that Jonson expressed his criticism in different media, sometimes giving his censures in conversations or reading his criticism aloud from a manuscript. As Drummond notes: "To me he read the Preface of his arte of Poesie, upon Horace Arte of Poesie, wher he heth ane apologie of a Play of his St Bartholomee faire, by Criticus is understood Donne" (H & S, 1:82–85).

If the legitimacy of literary criticism was at issue in early modern England, its difference from libel or treason sometimes unclear because Jonson negotiated different public spheres, so too it was not a clearly defined self-identical discourse separate from literature. Lacking a single standard of probity, a single threshold of modesty, court censorship could not establish a systematic division between transgression and legitimacy across the board. Thus, it was impossible for authors to know in advance what one could or could not say, how to evade regulations, how to decode, and so on. The circulation of discourses among different public spheres meant that the identity and legitimacy of criticism were always subject to negotiation. If the multiplicity of public spheres and the dispersal of regulating power motivated the discourse of literary criticism, those same factors made its emergence as a fully separate and legitimate discourse difficult.

How the multiplicity of public spheres complicated the definition and legitimation of Jonson's literary criticism may be better grasped if we turn to his most fully realized literary criticism, in which he negotiated the legitimation of his corpus. *Discoveries,* a separate, prose discourse of literary criticism which nevertheless collapses the distinctions between authors and readers on which that discourse's distinctiveness depends, registers in exemplary fashion the contradictions of this difficult negotiation. It legitimates criticism through a symbolic economy of primitive accumulation which assumes stable identities and differences between authors and their works. As Timothy Murray comments:

> "Sorting," "cutting out," "woods" and in this case *Timber: or, Discoveries* are metaphors used in the Renaissance to suggest the dual process of selection and grouping together passages for contemplation. Similar to the printing of plays, the common placing of variant texts unites them in one spatially apprehensible image through which its compiler becomes trained in visually maintaining identities and differences—what is done manually in transcribing the commonplace book. In turn, so D. C. Allen claims, the compilation of these texts enhanced the gatherer's learning and literary stature: "One cannot bring together a collection of pertinent quotations without wide reading and a certain exercise of the powers of criticism." (1987, 48)

Jonson condemns writers who merely copy others: "Some, that turn over all books, and are equally searching in all papers, that write out of what they presently find or meet without choice; by which means it happens, that what they have discredited, and impugned in one work, they have before, or after extolled the same in another. . . . These, in all they write, confess still what books they have read last; and they in their own folly, so much, that they bring it to the stake raw and undigested" (719–24, 726–27). Such writers are thieves so rank that "a man may find whole pages together usurp'd from one author" (739–40).

Yet Jonson's critical practice in *Discoveries* complicates his ability to differentiate his writings from others'. In a discussion of the passage from *Discoveries* on imitation cited earlier (3055–69), Thomas Greene (1982, 275–76) notes that the emphasis on achieving an identity between the copy and the principal is Jonson's own. In practice, however, this emphasis on identity calls into question the legitimating function of his criticism, for Jonson does not clearly identify the authors and sources he cites, nor does he provide an index that enables its users "to be well ware how thei reade Common places" (cited by Murray 1987, 48).[27] The distinction between Jonson as good imitator and the authors he calls bad imitators here breaks down. It is not surprising that modern editors continue to defend Jonson against the charge, first leveled by Dryden, that *Discoveries* is plagiarized.[28]

Discoveries is paradigmatic of the contradictions built into Jonson's model of legitimate criticism: across his canon, there is no clear division between Jonson's literature and his criticism; indeed, his criticism spills over into literature (itself an engine of criticism) and takes varied and dispersed forms. The forces that made it difficult to define literary criticism also made it difficult for Jonson to give his writings definitive canonical form. The emergence of Jonson's literary criticism entailed the emergence of a set of related distinctions involving authors and books and modes of consumption (reading books whole or in pieces).

As we have seen, Jonson legitimated his writings by distinguishing between authors and their works; he also defined his works as his literary property. Thus, he signed his name and put his motto in books he acquired (H & S, 1:180), but he inscribed only his name in copies of his own books given to others as gifts (H & S, 8:661–66), thereby distinguishing the books he bought or sold from those he wrote and circulated as gifts. Yet Jonson also called this distinction into question, foreclosing the possibility of printing a definitive canon. His contradictory insistence on maintaining and dissolving distinctions between works by him and by other author/critics can be seen concretely if we return to "Execration upon Vulcan." He defends himself and his writings against state censorship by contrasting his own writings to a catalog of books that might have been in his library: "Had I compiled from *Amadis de Gaul*, / The *Esplandians, Arthurs, Palmerins*, and all / The learned library of Don

Quixote . . . Thou then hadst had some colour for thy flames" (29–31, 40).[29] In his defense, Jonson gives an inventory of some of the books he's written and offers to send Vulcan a whole set of books to "redeem" his own (63):

> The *Talmud,* and the *Alcoran* had come,
> With pieces of the *Legend;* the whole sum
> Of errant knighthood, with dames and dwarfs;
> The charmed boats, and the enchanted wharfs;
> The Tristrams, Lancelots, Turpins, and the Peers,
> All the mad Rolands, and sweet Oliveers,
> To Merlin's marvels, and his cabal's loss
>
> .   .   .   .   .
>
> With Nicholas Pasquil's *Meddle with your Match,*
> And the strong lines, that so the time do catch,
> Or Captain Pamphlet's horse, and foot, that sally
> Upon the Exchange, still out of Pope's Head Alley.
> The weekly corrants, with Paul's seal; and all
> The admired discourses of the prophet Ball
>   (65–71; 77–82)

Jonson moves from this list of books to an inventory of the writings "in his desk," giving a catalog of his works in progress.

Rather than clearly differentiate, however, books he has written from books he has acquired, Jonson undermines a strict distinction. The verb "compile" admits an ambiguity: it could mean either the accumulation of books or the composition of a volume out of other works. Jonson's use of words such as "store" and "compile" mixes books he owned or borrowed with his own writings. Moreover, the meaning of "my books" is ambiguous when Jonson objects in "Execration upon Vulcan" that he ought not to be burned with them (18): though the phrase probably means "the books I have written" it may instead mean "the books I own." This ambiguity arises in part because Jonson alternates references to papers he had written and books he had acquired:

> Had I wrote treason there, or heresy,
> Imposture, witchraft, charms, or blasphemy,
> I had deserved, then, thy consuming looks,
> Perhaps, to have been burned with my books.

> But, on thy least malice, tell me, didst thou spy
> Any, least loose, or scurrile paper, lie
> Concealed or kept there, that was fit to be,
> By thy own vote, a sacrifice to thee?
> Did I there wound the honours of the crown?
> Or tax the glories of the church and gown?
> Itch to defame the state?
>
>   (15–25)

Jonson's adoption of a similar syntactic structure in describing his writings ("Had I wrote treason . . . I had deserved") and in describing the books in his library ("Had I compiled . . . then thou") further undermines a strict distinction between books Jonson wrote and books he owned.[30]

The ambiguity of the referent of "my books" is further registered in the belated offer to exchange for Jonson's own writings books containing "proper stuff" for Vulcan. The principle of exchange through which Jonson can redeem his writings by trading others, using them as stand-ins, implies, without clarifying, the proximity between them. That is, it is not clear from where Jonson will send the writings that will redeem his own, and hence it is not clear whether he owns these books or not (since they are the sort he associates with the market). This uncertainty makes it all the more difficult to distinguish clearly between legitimate and illegitimate books based on ownership. It is worth noting that the same word, *explorata,* appears in the motto Jonson inscribed in books he compiled in his library ("Tamquam Explorata," as an explorer) and in the title of his major work of criticism (*Explorata; or, Discoveries*). The referent of "me" and "I" shifts subtly from Jonson's body to his books and back again: from "I had deserved to have burned with my books" (17) to "me perish piece by piece" (51) and "me dying" (55) back to "my desk" (85). Just as the self-identity of the books in his library is compromised in "Execration upon Vulcan," so too is the self-identity of the author/critic and his body.

We might note in passing that print complicated Jonson's literary criticism by calling into question the identity of books. That books were printed in copies or manuscripts were copied by hand had paradoxical consequences for the notion that Jonson's library contained a store of self-identical books (the identity of the work was problematic by definition, since even if the copies were identical, one would still have to ask which copy of Jonson's works was *the* works). The technology of book production created a tension between the ideal of copia and the material nonidentity of copies of books. As Stephen Orgel has shown, the unsystematic practices of printing houses ensured that no two copies of a given text were identical (Orgel 1988, 20). In that case, a metaphorics of copia could not secure the library's legitimating function as a store. The library stored not a constant, self-identical accumulation of books but copies.

We can better understand the ambiguity of Jonson's interest in legitimating his works by defining them as *his* works if we examine some of the biological metaphors central to Jonson's imitative poetics: "pieces" and "parts." If critics and books lack self-identity, so does the critical activity itself. Jonson's contradictory identification with and separation from his text registers the extent to which biological metaphors could be literalized, criticism collapsed into censorship of Jonson or at least the call for him to censor himself. Jonson thus not only unified his writings as a whole but separated them into pieces and parts as a defense against distorted, mistaken readings. In "Execration upon Vulcan," for example, representing the decontextualization of his writings as the fragmentation of his body, Jonson can sacrifice part in order to preserve the rest, can preserve the body of work, that is, by disowning objectionable "parts." After suggesting that he would gladly have substituted heretical texts and romances for his own writings, Jonson concludes:

> These, had'st thou pleased either to dine or sup,
> Had made a meal for Vulcan to lick up.
> But in my desk, what was there to excite
> So ravenous, and vast an appetite?
> I dare not say a body, but some parts
> There were of search, and mastery of the arts.
>
> (83–88)

By characterizing his writings as parts, Jonson, as his own censor, can at least make the distinctions between the good and bad parts of his corpus. Along related lines, Jonson adopts the metaphor of pieces in the first prologue to *Epicoene* to encourage his theater audiences to consume his writings on what we might term a piece-meal basis: "If those with cunning palates hither come . . . / And though all relish not, sure there will be some, / That when they leave their seats, shall make 'em say, / Who wrote that piece could so have wrote the play" (8, 10–12). Similarly, in "To My Book," Jonson willingly advises the bookseller to destroy unsold copies in order to assure that Jonson's books circulate only among fit readers.

Yet even these defenses against the possible destruction of his writings and his body were of limited effectiveness, for two reasons, one external, the other internal to Jonson's poetics. First, the codes of biological metaphors which regulated and legitimated criticism by distinguishing good from bad imitation, censure from libel, were themselves imitable and hence in need of regulation. Jonson could be criticized on his own terms. Since criticism legitimated censorship, he himself was potentially subject to censorship not only by the court but by other critics who could turn Jonson's own model of theatrical legitimation against him, giving rise precisely to Jonson's anxieties about the consumption of his writings and the potential consumption of his body. Jonson's image for Vulcan's destruction of his writings as a match "to light my tobacco" along with the image of using paper to wrap fish in Bucklersbury in "To My Bookseller" were turned against him by Alexander Gill in his attack on *The Magnetic Lady*. Gill says that the play, if it has to be printed, ought to be printed on poor-quality paper:

> As not to dare to venture on A stall
> Exceppt ytt bee of Druggers, Grocers, Cookes,
> Victuallers, Tobackoe Men, and such like men and such like Rookes;
> From Bucklers Burye let it not be barde
>
> (H & S, 11:347–48)

Jonson's relation to literary criticism and to censorship was paradoxical because he and his censor/critics saw the legitimation of criticism in precisely the same way: the point of legitimating criticism was to legitimate certain kinds of censorship and certain kinds of censors.

Moreover, if in fragmenting his corpus, Jonson defended at least parts of it from court censorship, fragmentation exposed his writings to precisely the kinds of misreadings that, he believed, unfairly subjected them to court censorship in the first place. His image of *Epicoene* as a series of pieces registers as less a bromide for his anxiety about its reception than a source of dyspepsia. After stating his willingness to please the palates of his guests rather than his own (the cook's), Jonson concludes:

> Nor is it only while you keep your seat
> Here that the feast will last, but you shall eat
> A week at ord'naries, on his broken meat.
>
> (25–27)

Jonson's insistence that his audience dine on "*his* broken meat" (they will live off his leftovers by quoting his good lines in taverns) indicates less an easy, generous invitation to the consumption of his play than an anxious need to coerce acknowledgment of the debt the audience owes him, and hence his authority over them. In breaking Jonson's meat, the consumers implicitly turn into scavengers who cannibalize his play, but Jonson takes his revenge in calling their tavern meal "broken meat," inferior to the whole.

Jonson's willingness to let a piece substitute for an imagined whole did not necessarily secure a uniformly positive response to his play. Presumably others would enjoy only particular pieces and fault Jonson for indulging the tastes of other segments of the audience. Indeed, the initial reception of *Epicoene* was not positive. According to Drummond, "When his play of a *Silent Woman* was first acted, there was found verses on the stage against him, concluding that the play was well named *The Silent Woman*, there was never one man to say 'plaudite' to it" (696–700). A more serious problem, however, was that some members of the audience might mistake a piece for the whole and attempt to censor it, as Arabella Stuart did. Indeed, the metaphor of his play as "pieces" here and in Jonson's reference to Vulcan's eating his books "piece by piece" along with Vulcan's condemnation of Jonson's writings as "pieces of . . . base allay . . . some parcels of a play" (42, 43) recall an oft-cited passage in *Discoveries* wherein Jonson asserts that his enemies "would urge mine own writings against me; but by pieces (which was an excellent way of malice) as if any man's context, might not seem dangerous, and offensive, if that which was knit, to what went before, were defrauded of his beginning; or that things, by themselves uttered, might not seem subject to calumny, which read entire would appear most free" (1674–81).

The difficulty Jonson had in legitimating a defined and definitive corpus that circulated among competing public spheres was due less to these external imitative threats than to contradictions internal to his poetics of imitation. Literary criticism could not be fully legitimated as a separate discourse and biological metaphors could not embody a unified literary corpus because production and consumption were not always clearly separable in Jonson's poetics of imitation, much less arranged hierarchically. Proper ingestion took two contradictory forms in *Discoveries*. On the one hand, it involved not only achieving identity with the ingested object but ingesting the work whole. As we saw earlier, Jonson says in *Discoveries* that he can repeat "whole books" and poems "of some selected friends" (602). Similarly Jonson maintains that the "perfecter writer . . . must have civil prudence, and eloquence, and that whole; not taken up by snatches, or pieces, in sentences, or remnants" (H & S, 8:2522–24). On the other hand, Jonson also reversed this hierarchy, giving pieces priority over the whole, as in the examples cited previously. When he was characterizing the reception of his writings, Jonson's use of bodily metaphors was sometimes explicitly paradoxical: rather than distinguish between judging a piece and judging the whole, Jonson tended to distinguish between judging a piece and judging "the whole piece" (*Epigrams* 56.14).[31]

This paradoxical formulation—"the whole piece"—indicates the instability of the hierarchy of literary production and consumption on which Jonson's model of theatrical legitimation rested, made even more wobbly by the equation in his model of criticism of copy and principal.[32] Jonson's criticism was, in principle (not, however, in practice), indistinguishable from the modes of textual appropriation and consumption he consistently censured. He insists in the epistle to *Volpone*, for example, that his "books have been allowed" by the Master of the Revels and, as we have seen, he regularly delegitimated spectators who did not distinguish licensed from unlicensed writings. Similarly, he mocks poetasters such as the fop Sir John Daw, who too easily identify an author's body with his books:

Dau. Whom do you account for authors, Sir John Daw?
Daw. *Syntagma juris civilis, Corpus juris civilis, Corpus juris canonici,*
      the King of Spain's Bible.
Dau. Is the King of Spain's Bible an author?
Cler. Yes, and *Syntagma.*
Dau. What was that *Syntagma,* sir?
Daw. A civil lawyer, a Spaniard.
Dau. Sure, Corpus was a dutchman.
Cler. Ay, both the Corpuses, I knew 'em: they were very corpulent
      authors. (*Epicoene* 2.3.72–81)

The wits dismiss Daw as "a fellow that pretends to learning, buys
titles, and nothing else of books in him" (1.3.74–76). Jonson satirizes poetasters who do not digest fully enough: Crispinus, for
example (who at the end of *Poetaster* can nevertheless be forced to
vomit up words whole precisely because he has not properly di-
gested them). Yet Jonson's censure of both spectators and poetasters
on the same grounds registers a problem with his own model of
legitimate criticism, namely, that it demands a conflation of consumption and production which effectively dissolves any distinction between author and reader, between an author's body and his
books. Jonson threatens to become indistinguishable from the figures he delegitimates: he is always haunted by the specter of the
figures he parodies, against whom he defended his legitimacy.

Jonson could achieve a degree of equilibrium only by exaggerating a distinction between an offensive crime and its legitimate
punishment, heightening a sense of crisis in order to authorize
himself as the agent of the criminal's punishment and the reformer
of the theaters. In the epistle to *Volpone,* Jonson concedes much of
the antitheatrical critique of the public theaters: "Now, especially in
dramatic, or, as they term it, stage poetry, nothing but ribaldry,
profanation, blasphemy, all license of offense to God and man is
practised" (34–36). This hyperbolic fantasy licenses an equally hyperbolic, even hysterical, fantasy of repression in the concluding
passage, in which Jonson says he will brand licentious poetasters.
Poetry "shall in just rage incite her servants (who are *genus irritabile*)
to spout ink in their faces that shall eat, farther than their marrow,
into their fames, and not Cinnamus the barber with his art shall be
able to take out the brands, but they shall live, be read, till the

wretches die, as things worth deserving of themselves in chief, and then of all mankind" (132–36). Precisely because a censurer, critic, or play club of critics might attempt to censor him, Jonson, as critic, could only respond in kind, exercising his critical faculty by reproducing court censorship: he assumed the authority to determine which texts ought to be censored and which should be licensed. As Thomas Carew put it in "To Ben Johnson vppon Occasion of His Ode to Himself":

> 'Tis true (deere Ben:) thy iust chastizing hand
> Hath fix'd vppon the sotted age, a brand
> To theyr swolne Pride, & empty scribling due,
> It can nor judge, nor write.
> (H & S, 11:335)

Jonson criticizes his critics by arrogating to himself the machinery of court censorship. He relies on a version of the spy system, which he held in contempt, to defend himself against his enemies and to gain allies.[33] Thus, he launched a preemptive strike against his dramatic rivals in *Poetaster,* responding to Dekker's *Satiromastix* before it was even performed. Similarly, Jonson invites his bookseller to be his "intelligencer" and spy out good consumers, as in "Epigram to My Bookseller": "Thou, friend, wilt hear all censures" (*Underwood* 58.10,1).

Jonson could not construct a closed community of the same without authorizing himself to imitate the court censor, excluding others who thought of themselves as critics with the authority to censure or censor him. Jonson legitimated not only his use of the brand or of fire but the adoption of the libelous tactics he often disavowed. Like the wits in *Epicoene,* Jonson lived in a "dangerous" age for poets; such coteries as his were often accused of slanderous attacks by (often justifiably) paranoid readers who "think I and my company are authors of all the ridiculous acts and moniments told of him" (1.2.8–10). Though Jonson disavowed personal satire, like the wits, he took hostile "misreadings" of his writings as a warrant to strike the first blow. In the folio edition of *Poetaster,* Jonson added a scene that is almost a literal transcription of Horace's strongest defense of his role as satirical reformer in the fifth satire. In it Virgil argues that Horace's "sharpness"

is most excusable,
As being forced out of a suffering virtue,
Oppressed with the license of the time.
(5.3.378–80)

And in *Discoveries,* Jonson makes a similar defense of his own transgressive critique:

> I have been accused to the lords, to the king, great ones, . . . nor were they content to feign things against me, but to urge things, feigned by the ignorant against my profession; which though from their hired and mercenary impudence I might have passed by, as granted to a nation of barkers, that let out their tongues to lick others' sores; yet I durst not leave myself undefended, having a pair of ears unskilful to hear lies; or have those things said of me, which I could prove of them. (149–51, 1660–69)

Jonson extends this same logic to plagiarists of his work. He ends his epigram "To Prowl the Plagiary," *Epigrams* 81, by threatening the plagiarist, "if thou leave not soon, I must a libel make" (8). Jonson contentiously censured his censurers, libeled his libelers, in order to exclude them from his critical community. He thereby voided, however, his principled claim to occupy a transcendent position above personal satire. As a self-appointed censor/critic, Jonson intermittently deconstructed the distinctions on which his identity as a critic and censor depended. He transgressed the boundaries between legitimate and illegitimate censorship, between licensed critique and transgressive libel, which grounded his authority: legitimate censorship sometimes collapsed into illegitimate censureship; liberty collapsed into libel. Unable to resolve the contradictions and paradoxes of censorship and criticism either by identifying with one authority or by submitting to another, Jonson oscillated in neurotic fashion between them, setting one against the other, sometimes unwittingly setting himself up to be censored or censured by both.

II

In calling into question any stable distinction between criticism and censorship, my account of the paradoxes and elusiveness of Jonson's literary criticism has revised Marxist accounts of the public sphere and its relation to literary criticism. Yet I have also kept in play a distinction between brutally repressive court censorship and more moderate forms of censure in order to avoid simply collapsing all forms of regulation into "power" (as Foucault has often—mistakenly, in my view—been said to have done). Marxists and other avowedly political critics might want to use this difference of degree to reinstate a difference in kind between censuring and censoring by distinguishing Jonson from his contemporaries. His difference would suggest a range of responses to the contradictions and paradoxes he registers and would, consequently, in the view of some political critics, make it possible to rank the threats of censorship and censureship hierarchically as more or less severe and then to position writers along an axis from the more progressive and radical at one pole to the more reactionary at the other. The farther censure is from censorship in the traditional sense, it might be argued, the more progressive the critic; conversely, the more eager to censor, the more reactionary the critic might be said to be.

Typically, Marxist critics have tried to salvage a progressive political potential in Jonson's neoconservative use of market forces in advancing his reactionary political and aesthetic agenda. In their account, Jonson, in spite of himself, anticipated a more enlightened moment that succeeded him. An emergent consensual criticism could be taken to be an early modern version of a later, more fully developed neoclassical model of criticism, which, even in its emergent form, stood as an alternative to Jonson's illiberal model. This account could be buttressed by contrasting the Renaissance to a later, more enlightened historical moment that put in place seemingly self-evident distinctions between authors and books, between books one writes and sells and books one reads and buys, between censorship and criticism, and so on.

I readily concede that there were multiple, plural institutions of criticism in the Renaissance arising from multiple public spheres, not a single institution of criticism. Moreover, the forms of censure or censorship that existed differed greatly in their degree of repressiveness. Jonson often savagely identified with a repressive censor in a way that put him to the right of many of his censurers. Other critics advocated burning only books. Alexander Gill, for example, called on Jonson to burn *The Magnetic Lady,* whereas Jonson wanted to brand and whip Gill as well as crop his ears. Moreover, other critics adopted a consensus model of critical authority. Gill criticized Jonson's unwillingness to accept as authoritative his audience's censure of *The Magnetic Lady:*

> But wheneas silkes and plush and all the witt
> Are Calde to see, and Censure as Befitt,
> And yff your Follye take not, thay perchance
> Must heare them selues stilde Gentle Ignorance
>
> . . . . .
>
> Calling [them] Fooles and Rogues, vnlettered men,
> Poore Narrow soules that Cannot Iudge of *Ben.*
>
> (H & S, 11:347)

The author of "The Cuntrys Censure on Ben Johnsons New Inn" makes a similar point: "sure that censure must impartial bee / whear readers and spectators both agree" (H & S, 11:51–52). Both Gill and this anonymous critic articulate a notion of communal consensus that places the audience's authority above the dramatist's.

Moreover, the subject-position of the critic could be used for different political aims depending on whether the interests of the subject who occupied it were, say, republican or absolutist. In absolutist fashion, Jonson clearly identified with the monarch in reinforcing the hierarchies of this system, as when he takes Charles as his audience at the end of "Ode to Himself," appended to *The New Inn.* Similarly, in his "Charm for a Libeller," Philip Massinger attacks Carew for criticizing the play, on the grounds that Carew is usurping the court's authority to censor:

> Why is hee
> The Poets tribune, and authority,
> Conferr'd on him to free or condemne
> All what is writ or spoken by other men?
>
> (Beal 1980, ll. 18–21)

Moreover, Massinger scoffs at Carew for acting as if he were a licensed critic: "I ne'er saw his patent" (24).

Jonson and his Caroline contemporaries registered the legitimation crisis of criticism differently, as I will show at greater length in the third chapter. In my discussion thus far, I have been concerned to identify within a general problematic of criticism a specifically Jonsonian subjectivity effect. On the one hand, Jonson and his contemporaries felt the same contradictions, used the word *critic* positively and negatively, used *censure, criticism,* and *censor* interchangeably. Richard Brome's prologue to *The Antipodes,* for instance, is titled "To Censuring Criticks." On the other hand, acute differences emerged between Jonson and his contemporaries. By the 1630s, the censorious aspect of Jonsonian satire had fallen out of fashion. As Thomas Nabbes says in the prologue to *The Weeding of Covent Garden* (1633):

> Our *Author* doth not meane
> With such vile stuffe to clothe his modest Scoene.
> Nor doth he brande it with a Satyres marke.
>
> (3–5)

Caroline playwrights departed from Jonson not only in adopting other genres but in their more submissive relation to the increasingly hegemonic status of the critic.

The difference between Jonson and his Caroline contemporaries can be seen in two prologues that bear on *The New Inn.* Whereas Jonson faulted his audience when his play failed, others criticized Jonson (and authors like him) for not submitting to the judgment of the audience. Shakerley Marmion, for example, presents a "Critick" and an "Authour" in a prologue to *A Fine Companion.* The Critick refers to some earlier London theatrical failures, possibly of Jonson's *New Inn:*

> Remember, if you please, what entertainment
> Some of your tribe haue had, that haue tooke pains
> To bee condemn'd, and laughed at by the Vulgar,
> And then ascrib'd it to their ignorance.
>
> (1979, 8–11)

The "Authour" elevates the authority of the "Critick" above his own:

> In all ages
> It hath been ever free for Comick Writers,

> If there be any that were infamous,
> For lust, ambition, or avarice,
> To brand them with great liberty, though I
> Disclaime the privilege
>
>   .   .   .   .   .
>
>   and leave all
> To be determined as you censure.
>   (1979, 54–59, 66–67)

Similarly, Massinger's relation to his audiences became less combative. He initially followed Jonson in criticizing critics in his audience, complaining in the court prologue to *The Emperor of the East* (1632), for example, that his "poor work had suffered . . . the rage, / And envie of some Catos of the stage" (15–16). Yet after another of his plays failed too in the private theaters, Massinger submitted to the critics' authority (see Massinger 1976, 1:xli, 4:107). In the prologue to *The Guardian* (which may refer to Jonson's adverse reaction to the failure of *The New Inn*) Massinger

>   submits
> To the grave censures of those Abler Wits
> His weakness; nor dares he profess that when
> The Critiques laugh, he'l laugh at them agen.
> (Strange self-love in a writer!)
>   (13–17)

Jonson's comparatively defiant relation to the critics in his audience throws into relief his characteristic subjectivity effect.

In addition to specifying his neurotic subjectivity effect by attending to significant differences between Jonson and other author/critics and between institutions of criticism, I also want to make the more general claim that the paradoxes in his literary criticism were not resolved elsewhere in the Renaissance. Thus, it would be a mistake to use the differences I have noted to salvage a history that defines literary criticism in opposition to censorship. To think that these differences involve stable oppositions between terms with stable identities is to run the risk of simplifying Jonson's politics, of reinscribing a Whiggish view of Jonson as a reactionary—in a simple, noncontradictory sense—who is always on the wrong side of free-speech issues. It risks, as well, reinscribing a similarly simplistic view of Jonson as a critic who, in Herford and Simpson's words, was a "dictator of letters" (H & S, 1:95). And it risks assimilating Jonson to a humanist, normative model of literary production, replacing Edmund Wilson's (1938) view of him as contentious, arrogant, and anal retentive with a contrary view of him as essentially healthy and well adjusted, more like (a humanist version of) Shakespeare than unlike him (see Barish 1972; Barton 1984; Fish 1984; Riggs 1988).

More broadly, what some critics might take to be a saving difference between consensus and censorship reinscribes an ahistorical view of the body. Modern critics understandably tend to register moral horror at certain forms of torture. However horrible, the meaning of bodily mutilation was nevertheless itself always open to interpretation. Michel Foucault (1977a) has shown how the symbolic economies of the Renaissance were highly unstable, open to sudden reversals. William Prynne's interpretation of the letters *SL* carved on his cheeks to mean "stigma of Laud" rather than "seditious libeler" (as William Laud intended) bears Foucault out. Even if an author were mutilated or had, in Jonson's phrase, "some parts" of his body cut off, discursive production would not necessarily be ended. Prynne continued to write and publish prolifically after he had his ears clipped and his cheeks carved, and John Stubbes, to take another example, wrote with his left hand after his right hand had been severed as the penalty for writing *The Gaping Gulf*.

My most crucial objection to Marxist accounts of the public sphere lies not in their insistence on distinguishing between forms of censorship but in the way the moral force of these distinctions depends on a hierarchy of discursive production over consumption, a hierarchy that implicitly idealizes production and its regulation. Recuperating Jonson's contradictory criticism on the basis of a distinction between postpublication critical consensus and prepublication authoritarian censorship turns out to be problematic for Marxists (and for other political critics) insofar as they have defined that consensus in an idealist, ahistorical manner. To be sure, Marxist and revisionist accounts of the theater's politics register this problem in different ways. Marxist criticism of Jonson could potentially be connected to a critique of consensus as manufactured, providing an important critique of revisionist accounts of court censorship.[34] From a Marxist perspective, revisionist apologies for the court (in which censorship is said to have been lenient and tolerant) imply a conservative notion of consensus; they recuperate and legitimate aristocratic factional inclusion of licensed voices but ignore how factionalism excludes more radical voices. Furthermore, one could argue from a Marxist perspective that revisionists have simply projected back onto the Renaissance court an eighteenth-century model of critical consensus (entirely missing the emergent institution of literary criticism in the Renaissance).

Yet a Marxist symptomatic reading of Jonson's idealized critical community does not radically depart from revisionist notions of legitimation, for it too retains an idealist model of criticism as consensus. Indeed, Marxist accounts of literary criticism imagine a resolution to the contradictions of criticism in a way that necessarily entails assuming an end to censorship. Were they to criticize Jonson by contrasting his community to a more progressive, consensual community either of his contemporaries or of his successors in the eighteenth century, Marxists would in turn reinscribe an idealist history of criticism made by nonneurotic, disembodied, centered subjects. To contrast Jonson's critical community to a more progressive consensual critical community is, in other words, to set one idealization of criticism against another.

Broadly speaking, this reinscription at best requires Marxists to ignore the regulatory, disciplinary functions of criticism and at worst requires them to license repressive, scapegoating regulatory practices that depend for their legitimacy on the institutionalized hierarchy of producers over consumers. I can best make this general point by focusing on the transitional moment on which Marxist accounts turn, taking up Jonson's centrality to post-Renaissance, neoclassical criticism formulated in the Restoration and in the eighteenth century. William K. Wimsatt and Cleanth Brooks (1964, 174–95) carefully established the debt Dryden's criticism owed to Jonson's, and more recently, Timothy Murray (1987, 101) has charted a complex ideological line from Ben Jonson to Samuel Johnson. Stallybrass and White (1986, 93–124) have argued more broadly that Jonson was central to a later, neoclassical model of literary production and authorship, one that, they point out, involved an increasingly phobic relation to the grotesque body and an increasingly regulated bourgeois subjectivity based on the codification and standardization of taste.

As I noted earlier, Marxist accounts oppose literary criticism to Renaissance authoritarianism. I would argue, however, that Jonson's importance to neoclassical criticism calls into question any attempt to differentiate strictly between Renaissance and eighteenth-century models of criticism. We can grasp more concretely how Jonson complicates any such differentiation by turning to an anonymous account of criticism titled, "At a Session of the Poets Presided over by Apollo" (c. 1687, H & S, 11:500–501). The meeting is regarded as consensual: a group of critics assigns Renaissance poets a "peculiar province of inspecting and licensing the severall Species of Poetry" (Jonson is given comedy). Censures are passed as laws. "To these in their respective stations all Authors whatsoever were to present & submitt their works, & from them to receive their Sentence without Appeal; then, & not till then might they be accepted, & should not be refus'd by their chapmen" (500). This critical modus operandi leaves open a question, however, as to which books will be allowed in, a question addressed to Jonson, who, interestingly enough, is the library keeper:

> And for the further discouragement of ignorant pretenders, Apollo thought fit to give order to the Library Keeper Ben Jonson that no Book or paper should be admitted into the Museum till it had pass'd the Censure of the Committee aforesaid. . . . Ben reply'd he had done all this & more to little purpose, as might appear by those monstrous heapes of Volumes that lay pil'd before the Library-door, waiting for admittance; for he was resolved to leave them to the moths. . . . Wherefore I humbly move that the Entrance may be clear'd of such a nusiance, & the Papers put to some more commodious use. . . . To this the whole House consented; & it was immediately voted that they be removed from thence, & otherwise dispos'd at the discretion of the Library Keeper. (501)

This view of a critical community headed by a censurer and library keeper who disposes of "monstrous heapes" of books was obviously already a fantasy, however, by the time it was written. In Augustan neoclassical poetry and criticism, the library no longer can figure a resolution to the monstrous threat the mass market for printed books poses to the orderly hierarchies of high culture. In Pope's *Dunciad* the weight of books in Colley Cibber's "Gothic library" threatens to collapse the shelves they sit on; in Swift's *Battle of the Books,* the moderns beat the ancients and manage to get their books into the Royal Library in St. James Place, the library becoming a place of contention rather than harmony and peace. And in *The Rambler,* Samuel Johnson attacks the public library as impossibly incoherent (see Kernan, 1987, 11, 243–45).

Offering this account of neoclassical criticism may appear only to displace the ground of my argument rather than decide it, since the history of literary criticism has recently been contested within eighteenth-century studies in much the same terms. Liberal humanist critics have tried to redeem Samuel Johnson and Alexander Pope from an earlier view of them as literary dictators (Kernan 1987; Mack 1987) while Marxist critics have rewritten neoclassical aesthetics in relation to imperialism and mercantile capitalism (see Brown 1985) or the history of authorship (see Stallybrass and White 1986, 27–79). And Marxists would, of course, be willing to grant that the contradictions in libraries and taste are part of the larger contradictions of literary criticism. Eagleton, for example, acknowledges the ironies and limits of literary criticism as a progressive social institution, quoting Leslie Stephen's remark that "criticism was a new tribunal or literary star chamber" (1963, 88). Eagleton concedes that

> the critical gesture is typically conservative and corrective, revising and adjusting particular phenomena to its implacable model of discourse. Criticism is a reformative apparatus, scourging deviation and repressing the transgressive; yet this juridical technology is deployed in the name of a certain historical emancipation. The classical public sphere involves a discursive reorganization of social power, redrawing the boundaries between social classes as divisions between those who engage in rational argument, and those who do not. . . . Authoritarian, aristocratic art judgments were replaced by a discourse among educated laymen. (1984, 12–13)

While Eagleton is extremely sensitive to the contradictions of criticism, he nevertheless reads them in a quite undialectical manner. Although he acknowledges that a repressive juridical technology is employed in the name of emancipation, Eagleton's notion of emancipation depends for its force upon a utopian model of criticism which reifies the politics of both Renaissance absolutism and the eighteenth-century public sphere. In order to set a reactionary pole to which he can oppose a more democratic pole represented by the consensual institution of the coffeehouse (with a serious, interiorized, literate public), Eagleton must demonize and marginalize the Renaissance as an unenlightened moment of absolutism and critical authoritarianism, a mere surface display of learning.[35]

The idealism of his history of literary criticism may be seen by examining the utopian notion of criticism that awaits full realization. Eagleton's progressive, emancipatory function of criticism reinscribes a Kantian model that contrasts critical taste to censorship by appealing precisely to what Marxists wish to discredit, namely, a transcendental, ideal, universal standard of taste.[36] In his "General Remark upon the Exposition of Aesthetic Reflective Judgments" in *The Critique of Judgement,* Kant opposes censorship to free aesthetic judgment on just these grounds:

> If we attribute the delight in the object wholly and entirely to the gratification which it affords through charm or emotion, then we must not exact from *any one else* agreement with the aesthetic judgement passed by *us.* For in such matters each person rightly consults his own personal feelings alone. But in that case there is an end of all censorship of taste—unless the example afforded by others as the result of a contingent coincidence of their judgements is to be held over us as *commanding* our assent. But this principle we would presumably resent, and appeal to our natural right of submitting a judgement to our own sense, where it rests upon the immediate feeling of personal well-being, instead of submitting it to others. . . . For, were not taste in possession of a priori principles, it could not possibly sit in judgement upon the judgement of others, and pass sentence of commendation or condemnation upon them, with even the least semblance of authority. (1790, 131–32)[37]

We may generalize from Kant's account to say that the end of censorship in the Enlightenment depends on two assumptions, first, that there is a universal, transcendental standard of taste and, second, that there are centered subjects. Eagleton (1990, 70–71, 382, 405–8) and other political critics would of course be among the first to call these assumptions into question.[38] Moreover, they reinscribe a disembodied notion of the public sphere that Eagleton (1984, 110) himself notes as a problem in Habermas. Yet if Eagleton and others are critical of Kantian idealism, it is not clear how they can write a history of criticism which differentiates consensual criticism from censorship and yet break with Kant. If universals are abandoned, how can censorship be said to have ended? How is the avowedly political critic not a regulator? On what does the critic's authority rest?

In suggesting that censorship may be said to have ended only if one reinscribes an idealist, utopian view of criticism and its history, I do not mean to suggest that the alternative is a deidealized view of criticism as a simple interiorization of censorship. If it is fair to call Jonson a neurotic, it is clear that neurosis as such cannot be tied to a specifically bourgeois mode of subjectivity, one formed by the transition from the spectacular display of bodily subjection to its private internalization, as in Francis Barker's (1984, 8–24) fine discussion of Samuel Pepys, who read a pornographic book, subsequently burned it, and then recorded both acts (in coded form) in his diary. A specifically modern criticism in the eighteenth century would require its own local analysis of new forms of neurosis in relation to new forms of censorship, new modes of bodily discipline, and so on. That analysis would involve a different set of assumptions about censorship and criticism which would enable one not to construct a theory of criticism but to perform a historically specific local analysis of a new legitimation crisis of criticism centered increasingly on the regulation of criticism itself through a standard of taste—in other words, one that examined the contradictions idealist critics such as Pope, Johnson, Hume, and Kant sought to regulate, if not resolve.[39]

The point of this historical analysis would be to interrogate further how an idealized account of discursive production and critical consensus continues to inform the regulatory practices that govern the institution of criticism in its present form. In a fine essay on plagiarism which indirectly bears on the central concerns I have addressed in this chapter, Neil Hertz (1985) suggests that the value placed on originality in accreditation procedures and the marked interest academics have in the topic of plagiarism register a need to legitimate criticism through a scapegoating procedure in which "an interior difference—the sense of self-division implicit in all linguistic activity, sometimes more pronounced, sometimes less so, depending on the social context in which speech or writing is produced—that difference is exteriorized as the difference between the offended institution and its delinquent member" (149). This practice of scape-goating, Hertz argues, rests on a fantasy—an echo of Jonson's—in which an offending author's body is identified with his writings:

> The fantasy is constructed so as to produce the sense of satisfaction that comes with contemplating a punishment . . . aptly fitted to its crime: the "author" of *this* mark [of the corruptness of his act and the disloyalty and baseness it entails], at least, will be inseparable from it; here—for once . . . mark, paper, and author will be fused. For this is a . . . fantasy of integration, of the overcoming of difference . . . at once a dream of punishment and a dream of interpretation: what is at issue is not just who is suffering but the extent to which it can be known and by whom. . . . The delinquent member is himself made to unwillingly represent an emblem of integrity, of the binding of self and signs. . . . Anxiety about the relation of authors to their words, anxiety about the relation of flesh-and-blood reality to conventional signs—these may be exorcised if they can be laid on the head of a figure not wholly unlike the fantasist. (1985, 147, 149, 159)

If one wants to read a progression from the legitimation crisis registered by Jonson's criticism with its own anxieties about the relation between authors and their bodies, about bodies and their books, about critics and censors to a more enlightened institution of criticism in which these distinctions are sorted out through well-defined, stable, regulatory procedures, then the politics of that progression can hardly be assumed to be progressive. For the progression rests on a fantasy of clear, discursive distinctions and identities, and that fantasy can be unwittingly lived in repressive ways because the hierarchy of production over consumption so important to Marxists and many other political critics is congruent with other hierarchies in the institution of criticism: teachers over students; tenured faculty with academic freedom over untenured faculty without it. These two hierarchies will not be dissolved by defining students and untenured faculty as producers. Depending on who produces it and in what context, criticism may seem like censorship. One man's critique is another's repression. The potential interchangeability of the terms *criticism* and *censorship* is a salient register of the present postmodern legitimation crisis of criticism.

I address this crisis in the Conclusion, where I argue that the present discourse of diversity (of critical practices) cannot constitute an antidote to the discourse of legitimation, since diversity is itself always being regulated (divided into legitimate and illegitimate practices). In the following chapters I continue to interrogate the related kinds of production-centered historicist readings of Jonson which have implicitly opposed criticism to censorship. I further elaborate my discursive account of censorship and attempt to neutralize in a local fashion two dominant revisionist and Marxist (more broadly, "oppositional") ways of criticizing early Stuart court culture and turning that critique to political account in the present. On the one hand, revisionists criticize Whigs and Marxists for seeing the court as a monolith and attempt to salvage court culture by seeing it as diverse. On the other, Marxist and other oppositional critics consider it no wonder that revisionist-oriented New Historicists have been so pessimistic about the emancipatory potential of the Renaissance, inasmuch as they have taken into account only canonical texts produced by an aristocratic culture (Holstun 1989). Two versions of this critique of a "New Historicist" reading of the Renaissance have followed: in one, the canonization of court culture—say, the Jonsonian masque—is regarded as a reactionary stripping of the text's sociocritical dimension (see Venuti 1989, 165–77); in another, the data base of Renaissance culture is extended beyond aristocratic canonical culture to include noncanonical texts (Hill 1986; Holstun 1989; Norbrook 1991). In the writings censored in the Renaissance or marginalized or excluded from the canon, so this latter argument goes, or in the writings of subordinate groups such as the Ranters and Diggers, one can discover a much more radical critique of court culture than any found in the canonical, elite culture. In my view, both accounts of court culture tend to reify the court, either legitimating it by attributing to it a unified diversity without even theorizing cultural differentiation between elite and popular, canonical and noncanonical texts, or criticizing the court by attributing to it a demonic unity from which a more popular text or a more fully political critical practice can be differentiated.

By contrast, I argue that cultural differentiation between elite and popular practices is itself a response to the contradictions of the court's licensing practices. In Jonson's view, the court as much as the audiences of public theaters was insufficiently critical, overly censorious, and hence in need of reform. Jonson was consequently in a paradoxical position: although he was increasingly inclined to identify with the court as the agent of reform, he was increasingly critical of it for its failure to reform the theater and for its innovations in the court and popular theaters. We will see just how paradoxical his position was by comparatively situating him and Shakespeare in relation to the court's broad licensing of social forces such as enclosure and vagabondage, on the one hand, and to the narrower licensing practices of the Master of the Revels, on the other.

Licensing Authorities: Jonson, Shakespeare, and the Politics of Theatrical Professionalism

Jonson's place in literary history and the shape of his career have been structured by differences between, for example, Jonson and Shakespeare or between Jonson's Jacobean successes and his Caroline failures. These differences have in turn been secured by assumptions about court censorship and about the theater as a site of cultural differentiation between elite and popular cultures. Some have maintained that theatrical politics are radical insofar as the theater is part of a popular tradition that takes liberties with the license granted it by the state. Anthropological and Marxist critics (Bristol 1985; O'Connell 1985; Cohen 1985) have often taken the Renaissance London authorities and Protestant antitheatricalists at their word. The theater, according to these critics, was a subversive social institution, an idolatrous counterchurch that appropriated holiday festivity and plebeian culture to interrogate the authority of the ruling elite. The theater is inherently subversive because it makes use of a native, nonaristocratic, egalitarian popular tradition. As Walter Cohen says, "The public theaters constituted part of both the base and the superstructure, their function in one in conflict with their role in the other. However aristocratic the message of the play, the conditions of its production introduced alternate effects. . . . The medium and the message were in contradiction, a contradiction that resulted above all from the popular contribution" (1985, 234). And in a similar vein, Margot Heinemann argues that plays produced in the popular theaters were the most radical and, hence, the ones subject to censorship: "The most forthright plays, those which involve not merely glancing topical allusions but a whole alternative way of seeing the situation, seem . . . to have been those of the popular theatres like the Red Bull and the Fortune, a great part of whose repertory has been lost. The existence of many of the opposition and radical plays is known to us only through the records of censorship and prosecution" (1980, 201). Many of the playwrights in the period are less radical than they otherwise might have been, she suggests (1980, 203), precisely because they attempted to forge a consensus between crown and Parliament which excluded popular forces.

The argument that the theater's politics were radical because its audience or mode of representation was popular is often accompanied by a call to rewrite the literary history of Renaissance drama. Yet that history has changed little. Despite recent critiques of his canonization and assertions of the marginality of his theater, Shakespeare continues to occupy a central place in New Historicist and Marxist accounts of the theater as a social institution, while Jonson has often been relegated to the margins. Shakespeare has been regarded as the central poet of the nation, a representative of the progressive, popular voice, while Jonson has been regarded as a conservative, antitheatrical reformer, interested in sorting out and stabilizing the heteroglot practices of the popular playhouse (Bristol 1985; Womack 1986).

This view of Jonson's place in literary history does not really challenge the Whig distinction between two cultures drawn by Alfred Harbage (1967) so much as reinscribe it. Just as Harbage favored a drama of the nation over a drama of the coterie, so Robert Weimann (1978) and Walter Cohen (1985) favor a drama of a nation, a scene indivisible (Weimann 1968). In other cases, either the cultural division is deferred to the 1630s or it is redrawn, narrowing the court as much as possible, enlarging the popular as much as possible. Moreover, Shakespeare's cultural centrality is reaffirmed. He represents the supposed unity of Elizabethan culture. Weimann writes, for example, "Shakespeare's universal vision of experience was so secure and remained essentially unshaken because he had access to the fully developed techniques and values of a popular theater turned into a national institution. The two modes [of natu-

ralism and convention], far from being mutually exclusive, helped
to constitute the universalizing pattern in Shakespeare" (1978).
Similarly, Harbage's Whig views are repeated in only slightly different ways in the work of Walter Cohen (1985), Steven Mullaney
(1987), and Annabel Patterson (1989). Although they abandon Harbage's neat division between public and private theaters, these critics nevertheless retain Harbage's division between the popular theater of a nation and the theater of a coterie, valuing the former and
devaluing the latter. Cohen maintains, for example, that the cen-
tralizing tendencies of absolutism ultimately destroyed the public
theater precisely because its popular component was subversive. He
writes off the Caroline drama as largely produced for the private
theaters of a courtly aristocracy, concluding that "Shakespeare,
Marlowe, and Jonson had no successors" (1985, 275).

Taking *The Winter's Tale* and *Bartholomew Fair* as my focus for
comparing Shakespeare and Jonson, I wish to challenge this account
of the theater's popular, radical politics and of Jonson's and Shakespeare's place in literary history, not merely on the grounds that it
reinscribes the Whig historiography revisionists have discredited.
(As we shall see, revisionists themselves remain prisoners of this
traditional historiography insofar as they merely invert Whig judgments, saving the court by showing that it licensed serious criticism
rather than merely cultivated decadent sycophants.) I want to challenge it primarily by contesting its central assumption, namely, that
a popular voice was both radical and autonomous from a court that
sought to contain, absorb, and if necessary, censor (in the negative
sense) its potentially unruly energies. An examination of the court's
contradictory licensing practices will show that the relation between popular and courtly practices was more complex than present accounts allow.

The heterogeneity of the court's practices precludes any attempt
to oppose Jonson to Shakespeare by regarding the latter as radical
and the former as conservative: from the perspective of licensing,
the two can be seen to be much more similar than has generally been
thought. In *Bartholomew Fair* and in *The Winter's Tale,* Jonson and
Shakespeare legitimate the court's licensing practices by differentiating professional from criminal entertainers.[1] In *The Winter's
Tale,* Shakespeare attempts to recuperate problems attendant on the
court's own innovations in theatrical representation by thematizing

theatrical representation in terms of an economy of loss specific to the genre of pastoral: the natural is always already lost, available only in the compensatory form of fiction, which paradoxically recovers nature by acknowledging it as always already lost. Calling attention to the limitations of "play" enables the elevation of an autotelic aesthetic symbolic economy above cruder criminal and commercialized deceptions. In *Bartholomew Fair,* Jonson invokes the multiple authorities of the contract, the Master of the Revels, and the king to distinguish licensed from licentious entertainments. Both Jonson and Shakespeare are "antitheatrical" not in any ahistorical, essentialist sense of "theater" but in their desire to exclude and delegitimate particular theatrical and paratheatrical practices.

Yet Jonson's critique of Shakespearean romance indicates a central problem with this strategy. In Jonson's view, far from legitimating the theater, Shakespeare contributed to its delegitimation. For Jonson, the legitimacy of any form of theatrical representation is dependent on a specific institutional site of theatrical production and consumption. Thus Jonson wanted to enforce distinctions between elite and popular culture, between, say, the court masque and puppet shows. Shakespearean romance, however, undermines precisely these distinctions. Thus, in the induction to *Bartholomew Fair,* Jonson warns his audience that they will not see the kinds of entertainments included in Shakespeare's romances: "If there be never a servant monster i'the Fair; who can help it? he says; nor a nest of antics? He is loth to make nature afraid in his plays, like those that beget Tales, Tempests, and such like drolleries, to mix his head with other men's heels, let the concupiscence of jigs and dances reign as strong as it will amongst you" (112–17). Jonson's "nest of antics" is generally assumed to allude to a moment in the sheepshearing scene of *The Winter's Tale,* which itself apparently alludes to Jonson's own *Masque of Oberon:*

> Master, there is three carters, three shepherds, three neat-herds, three swine-herds, that call themselves Saltiers, and they have a dance which the wenches say is a gaullimaufry of gambols, because they are not in't; but they themselves are o' the mind (if it be not too rough for some that know little but bowling) it will please plentifully. . . . One three of them, by their own report, sir, hath danced before the king. (4.4.325–31, 337–38)

Jonson extends the critique of Shakespearean romance in *Bartholomew Fair* itself. As Muriel Bradbrook (1976, 241) and Richard Dutton (1983, 168–69) have pointed out, Jonson includes in the play a critique of *The Two Noble Kinsmen*. Quarlous and Winwife imagine themselves as Palamon and Arcite as they compete for Grace's hand. Moreover, *The Two Noble Kinsmen* appears to endorse unequivocally the kinds of pastimes Jonson represents from a more jaundiced perspective in *Bartholomew Fair:* Theseus interrupts his own "country sport" (hunting) to watch and approve the morris dancing of country folk (3.5) performed by "a merry rout" (3.5.105) complete with a "Lord of May, and Lady" (3.5.124), a Bavian (the fool of the morris dance) and taborer, and "a maypole" (3.5.143).

Yet Jonson's critique of Shakespearean romance and popular audiences implies a potential critique of the court's willingness to license professional playwrights such as Shakespeare to represent courtly forms like the masque on the common stage. Consider the morris dance in *Two Noble Kinsmen*. Far from being genuinely rustic, it was borrowed directly from Beaumont's masque for the wedding of Princess Elizabeth and the Elector Palatine. Moreover, the court received these plays favorably. *The Winter's Tale* and *The Tempest* were performed at court in 1611; both were also performed, along with twelve other plays, as part of the wedding festivities for Princess Elizabeth and the Elector Palatine in 1612. Jonson's critique is most deeply directed at the court, I am suggesting, and it focuses on Shakespeare largely because of Shakespeare's favorable reception there. In allowing Shakespeare and others to adapt the masque to the public stage and in receiving these plays favorably in its own theater, the court undermined the very distinctions between legitimate and illegitimate theater which Jonson wished to uphold.

Jonson's antagonism toward Shakespeare and his critique of the court register, I suggest, a broad ideological conflict that took shape in early seventeenth-century England over the authority to license not only the theater but other traditional forms of popular culture as well.[2] The monarchy and its delegated officials licensed and authorized players, promulgated dramatic entertainments, and passed proclamations on behalf of other forms of popular culture. In 1618 the king issued the *Book of Sports,* to be read in all parish churches, which defended the "lawful sports to be used" on

Sundays (Tait 1917; Govett 1890). These sports included dancing, archery, leaping, vaulting, May games, Whitsun ales, and morris dances. Charles I followed suit. In 1633 after Thomas Richardson, the Lord Chief Justice in Somersetshire, ordered that revels be suppressed on the sabbath, Charles reissued the *Book of Sports,* making additions that more expressly linked the subject's support for rural sports with obedience to royal and ecclesiastical authority (Barnes 1959). These rural festivals depended on aristocratic patronage; in order to maintain them, James issued a proclamation in 1615 and gave a speech to the Star Chamber in 1616 urging the aristocracy to live in the country rather than in London and to "keepe hospitalitie" by conspicuously displaying generosity toward their tenants (Tanner 1960, 343, 344). As Peter Stallybrass (1986) and Leah Marcus (1986b) have shown, feasting was a pastime that tied aristocratic to peasant interests. Far from undermining Stuart hegemony, the forms of culture the elite licensed—traditional rural pastimes as well as the masque and the drama—in fact helped to underwrite the reign. Without public festivals, James argued in the *Book of Sports,* men would set up "filthy tipplings and drunkenness," breeding "a number of idle and discontented speeches in their ale-houses" (McIlwain 1965, 27).

During the sixteenth century, state institutions had been established in order to limit the effects of burgeoning capitalism on the aristocracy. Nonetheless, these same institutions depended both on the economic power of capital and on the dislocation of traditional social customs and distinctions brought about by capital. Enclosure undermined traditional pastimes in several respects: urbanization lessened the ties of feudal hospitality because the lord was no longer present at his estate; furthermore, the peasantry was fractured, giving rise to vagabonds and "masterless men."[3]

Cultural differentiation between the elite and the popular may be viewed as a response to this social contradiction. By professionalizing the theater, Jonson and Shakespeare in different ways affirmed the monarchy's interest in gaining a monopoly on the acting profession: the court licensed certain theatrical practices in order to ensure that its power would be celebrated while competing forms—potentially subversive of state and church authority—were suppressed. Rather than a radical alternative to the disciplining of masterless men and the repression of holidays advocated and undertaken by many of the "middling sort," the theater was itself a site of discipline: dramatists such as Jonson and Shakespeare reformed their audiences by legitimating certain theatrical practices and delegitimating others.[4] The increasing reliance of aristocratic culture on a proto-bourgeois rather than strictly artisanal mode of production, its reliance, that is, on a specifically "common" player, sought symbolic resolution in the drama through an early modern construction of a domain of poetic liberty separate from mercenary deceptions. Acting companies accrued symbolic capital as they effaced the economic capital on which they depended. Shakespeare and Jonson helped authorize the professional theater by disciplining it through local antitheatricalism, dividing culture into high and low, elite and plebeian, creating a division that secured aristocratic culture from its potential subversion by the market, by identifying the market with licentiousness, rebelliousness, and criminality (Burke 1978; Stallybrass and White 1986).

Yet, as my readings of *The Winter's Tale* and *Bartholomew Fair* will demonstrate, this division between elite and popular, high and low, could never be fully secured because the court was in the contradictory position of having to license cultural innovations in order to conserve older cultural practices threatened by enclosure. The court relied on new kinds of theatrical representations and social practices to maintain older social divisions. Moreover, licensing was penetrated by the very market forces it sought to regulate. As I will show in detail, the licensing of plays, players, and playhouses was a profitable business. Far from settling the legitimacy of theatrical practices, licensing negotiated a set of political questions raised by the displacement of ritual and the circulation of theatrical practices within a nascent culture industry: What institutions did the theater authorize? Who was licensed to entertain? And through which symbolic forms? Who could capitalize on the exchangeability of certain discourses and practices?

It would be a mistake to try to answer these questions by appealing to a notion of popular culture as unconnected to the ruling elite or as a set of practices the ruling elite appropriated to repress the populace. Broadly speaking, the popular is itself a constructed category, and there is nothing inherently progressive about it (Hall 1981; 1986). Critics who oppose a radical popular tradition to a conservative court culture revert to the notion of popular culture as folk culture and of the folk as an idealized collectivity, one without its own set of hegemonies and divisions. More narrowly, to view stage liberty or license as part of a subversive popular tradition is to ignore, as Tony Bennett points out, that "there is no point at which it is possible to locate a game in pre-industrial society that was ever or immediately the people's, that was not in some way caught up in the patronage of local notables, the church, or the crown" (1979c, 75). For this reason, Peter Stallybrass (1991) argues, it is difficult to use a Bakhtinian model of carnival as subversion of the court by the popular: the court itself sponsors and participates in carnival (see also Stallybrass and White 1986, 104). Moreover, any appeal to a genuinely popular culture is further complicated by the difficulty, under the early Stuarts, of drawing any strict distinction between the representation of pastimes in the theater and "genuine" rustic pastimes. Though rural pastimes were often revived after James authorized the *Book of Sports,* that revival was complicated. The rituals could not simply be reproduced in their earlier form; rather, the patronage of pastimes was staged as a partisan struggle, and that staging was itself increasingly a matter of display, as in the collection *Annalia Dubrenisa,* which celebrated Robert Dover for his patronage of such pastimes (and to which Jonson contributed a poem).

This is not to say that there were no recognizable popular interests that might resist attempts from above to discipline "low" theatrical tastes. As we saw earlier, the threat staged by Beaumont in *The Knight of the Burning Pestle* was sometimes realized. My point is that we need to look at cultural differentiation as a construction generated out of the court's licensing practices rather than assume that we can recover utopian elements of Shakespearean romance and theatrical representation in the popular theater and criticize the repressive elements of Jonsonian comedy and the court masque. In essentialist fashion, that would mean ahistorically linking a political effect to a specific mode of cultural production, namely, theatrical representation. A more historically specific analysis requires that we look at the politics of theatrical representation in terms of the specific problems of enunciation produced by the court.

Though both Shakespeare and Jonson, were antitheatrical, they differed, as we have already seen, in the specific practices they criticized. Shakespeare focused on a distinction between licensed and unlicensed entertainments and Jonson concentrated on a distinction between licensed entertainments such as puppet shows and licensed entertainments such as his own plays. Moreover, though both *The Winter's Tale* and *Bartholomew Fair* inscribe a critique of the court, Jonson's is the more strident. Shakespeare's Autolycus implies a potential critique of the court, for he is not a vagabond pure and simple but a former courtier who masquerades as a vagabond. Jonson was more conservative, more critical of the court than Shakespeare, in wanting to reform the theater in a way that, as he came to recognize not long after *Bartholomew Fair,* was finally impossible because of the court's own contradictions. (And as I will show in the next chapter, those same contradictions mean that the court theater did not provide an alternative authority to the public theaters, which Jonson abandoned in 1616 after *The Devil Is an Ass*.) These differences between Shakespeare and Jonson register not a unified popular critique of the court but a theatrical legitimation crisis. Jonson, that is, could direct his antitheatricality not only at a licensed puppet master but at a leading playwright whose licensed plays were regularly performed by the King's Men in both the public and the court theaters.

Before turning to Jonson's analysis of Shakespearean romance, we first need to examine Shakespeare's own strategy of theatrical legitimation in *The Winter's Tale* in relation to the particular way he differentiates the professional theater from unlicensed cultural forms and practices, a difference figured by cozenage. *Cozenage* meant deception, fraud, and imposture. Most often associated with coney-catchers, it also served as a trope for a broad range of practices, including those of unlicensed criminal vagrant players and papists, from which professional acting companies were marked off. With the passage of the vagabond statute in 1572, licensed players were distinguished from "Roges Vacaboundes and Sturdy Beggers" (*ES,* 4:122). The Protestant attack on Catholicism as a "devil Theater" and "the Pope's playhouse" also helped to differentiate the player from the papist (Greenblatt 1988, 112, 113). In *The Discoverie of Witchcraft* (1576), Reginald Scot exposed as frauds not only witchcraft, exorcisms, and resurrections of the dead but juggling and other magic tricks, "common juggling knacke[s] of flat cousenage . . . among the simple," which entertainers attempted to pass off as "miracles" (258–60, 268–98). Samuel Harsnett, a disciple of Scot's, went on to expose cases of exorcism in similar terms. In

A Declaration of Egregious Popish Impostures (1603), Harsnett called the false miracle workings of exorcists acts of "legerdemaine: bewitching by . . . counterfyte miracles, the mindes of the ignorant" (sig. A5).

Yet the difference between players and cozeners was not always secure. The professional theaters were regularly linked with crime, rebellion, and idolatry by city aldermen and Protestant antitheatricalists. Theaters, London's mayor wrote, "are the ordinary places for vagrant persons, Maisterles men, thieves, horse stealers, whoremongers, Coozeners, Conycatchers, contrivers of treason, and other idele and daungerous persons" (*ES*, 4:322). And Protestant antitheatricalists equated players with cozeners. In *An Anatomy of Abuse,* for example, Philip Stubbes writes: "Who will call him a wiseman that plaieth the part of a foole and a vice: who can call him a Christian, who playeth the part of a devil, the sworne enemie of Christe: who can call him a juste man, that playeth the part of a dissembling hypocrite: And to be brief, who can call him a straight dealing man, who playeth a Cosener's trick" (Stubbes 1583, sig. M). The same charges were made against rogues, players, and papists: as cozeners, all were sources of disorder, riot, and tumult.

It was difficult to differentiate the professional cozener from the criminal cozener in part because the displacement of ritual into a culture industry opened up competing forms of cozenage. Players were differentiated from rogues administratively, discursively, and economically through the creation of a Master of the Revels and the expansion of the powers of his office, through the renewal and prosecution of the vagrancy and recusancy laws, through the production of a discourse about vagabonds, and through economic policy. Coney-catching literature was initially written by magistrates such as Thomas Harman, whose *Caveat for Common Cursitors, Vulgarly Called Vagabonds* appeared in 1566. Harman and others attempted to understand what we might term a "semiotics" of cozenage. The codes adopted by rogues were discovered and exposed by civic-minded writers; cant, peddler's French, over twenty orders of rogues, cozeners, as well as the names of a number of rogues are all made ready by Harman for official surveillance. Harman, who learned these codes by examining the vagrants who were presented before him, even translated a typical dialogue between two rogues. The rogue's chief crime was deception, which Harman and his readers could pierce, discovering the false rogues among the true poor by breaking their codes (Beier 1985, 135–37; Agnew 1986, 65–66). Indeed, it was precisely because all vagrants, as Harman implies, played at being vagabonds (so that even their "lowliness" was a disguise) that a semiotics of cozenage was necessary.

The distinction between player and rogue was similarly reinforced through economic policy. The emergence of a professional theater coincided with a neoconservative monopolistic strategy of restricting trade to a specific profession or company (see Ashton 1965, 12–13, 33–120). In the official Elizabethan account, the depression in the middle decades of the sixteenth century was caused by overcompetition in foreign trade. The solution was to restrict trade to a specific profession, to merchants rather than retailers and shopkeepers. The crown adopted a neoconservative policy: chartered companies with limited membership were given a monopoly of trade within a particular area. This policy aided not only merchants but the crown itself, which charged the companies increasingly large amounts for patents of monopoly.

Yet if the granting of a monopoly created a difference between licensed and unlicensed entertainment, it was a difference that could not be maintained in practice. The number of presentments of vagrancy show how ineffective this policy was: the two groups most feared, masterless men and recusants, especially when they appropriated plays, continued to perform and were often well received in the provinces. Recusant players and the gentlemen who invited them to play appear with great frequency in the quarter sessions presentments of the North Riding of Yorkshire. In a typical case, "Ralph Rookby, Esq. of Marske," was presented "for receiving . . . a traveling company of unlicensed players" made up of "Geo. White, weaver (24 years of age), John, Rich. and Cuthbert Simpson, cordiners (25, 24, and 18), all of Egton and Recusants . . . as players of enterludes, vagabonds, &c . . . in his dwelling house, giving them bread and drink, and suffering them to escape unpunished, &c" (*ES,* 1:304–5, 328). Similarly, at Topcliffe on October 2, 1610, Thomas Pant, apprentice to Christopher Simpson of Egton, shoemaker, was released from his indentures because "he hath been trayned up for three years in wandering in the country and playing of interludes . . . and for the said Simpson is an obstinate convicted popish Recusant" (Atkinson 1893, 1:204, 260). At

Helmesley on January 9, 1616, a number of gentlemen and yeomen were presented for receiving players and giving them bread and drink: "John, Richard, and Cuthbert Simpson, recusants, of Egton, Robert Simpson of Staythes," and four other players were fined 10 s. each (Atkinson 1893, 3:110, 119, 197).

By failing to prohibit unlicensed playing, the courts also failed to end subversive performances. In one case a gentleman named Sir John Yorke, and his wife and brothers were "fined and imprisoned for a scandalous play acted in favor of popery" (Bruce and Hamilton 1858–97, 9:77 n. 58). Similarly, in 1628 Christopher Malloy appeared before the Star Chamber for playing the devil in a performance at Yorke's house in Yorkshire, in which part he carried King James on his back to Hell, and alleged that all Protestants were damned. The clerk's court record makes clear an overlap among recusancy, the unlicensed playing of vagrants, and rebellion: "pluss del audience fueront recusants. . . . Le Chief Justice dit q. players de enterludes sont Rogues per le statute . . . le very bringing de religion sur le stage est libell" (*ES,* 1:328 n. 3). The enforcement of the vagrancy laws was a way of linking recusancy and vagrancy with subversion, and of distinguishing them from licensed playing.

Even the licensing of players could not always secure their conformity. Licensed players and entertainers might use their entertainments in criminal, unauthorized ways. Consider, for example, the case of William Vincent, an officially licensed itinerant magician who originated the phrase Hocus Pocus (which he used as a stage name).[5] In November 1625 Vincent was accused along with two confederates of having "cosened and deceyved of ix*li* [shillings] in money" a gentleman named Francis Lane in a tavern in Reading. Vincent apparently took his stage name from the words he said as he performed his tricks, "Hocus pocus, tontus talontus, vade celeriter." The words *hocus pocus* parodied the putative miracle of transubstantiation—"Hoc est enim corpus meum"—in the Catholic mass, implying that it is merely a magic trick. Yet Hocus Pocus did not perform his tricks only to reaffirm the Protestant view of the mass as theater, exposing priests as professional entertainers. At the tavern in Reading, he seems to have put his skills of legerdemain to less than benign uses. When searched, Vincent was found with 105 pounds on him, a suspiciously large sum at the time. There is no record of whether he was convicted. If so, his punishment had no serious effect. Vincent appeared in Coventry in 1638 with the King's Men, maintaining he was licensed to perform "feats of legerdemaine" by Charles I.

The differentiation of the player from other cozeners was complicated not only because the practice of licensing was open to unauthorized uses and proved difficult to enforce but because neither players nor masterless men occupied a fixed socioeconomic position. The emergence of the professional player depended on an expansion of socioeconomic divisions and on the creation of trades that could not be accommodated to the elite view of the social order. Many of the unlicensed rogues made a living as part-time entertainers. Ballad singers, minstrels, jugglers, and magicians were also part-time laborers and part-time criminals who lived on the verge of poverty and vagrancy (Beier 1985, 96–99, 141; Slack 1974; McMullan 1984). In 1599 a man who was "a cooper by trade, but uses the art (as he says) of a tumbler," was accused of vagrancy (Beier 1985, 99). A Wiltshire musician seized in 1605 was "sometimes a weaver, sometimes a surgeon, sometimes a dyer, and now a bullard" (a drover of bulls); he was accused of having "no trade to live by" (Beier 1985, 102). Masterless men did not fit into the hierarchy as conceived by the ruling elite.

But the professional players did not quite fit into the social order either. They were neither artisans nor aristocratic servants, though they had connections with both: the first theater was financed by John Burbage, a carpenter, and acting companies were patronized by the aristocracy and by the monarchy. That Shakespeare's theater was neither strictly artisanal nor strictly aristocratic can be grasped in a letter by Samuel Cox (1591). Cox laments the disappearance of systems of patronage which gave, he nostalgically believes, the actors a proper sense of their role, either as servants or as artisans:

> I could wish that players would use themselves nowadays, as in ancient former times they have done . . . without making profession to be players to go abroad for gain. . . . The [earlier] sort were artisans in good towns and great parishes, as shoemakers, tailors, and such else, that used to play either in town-halls, or some time in churches, to make people merry, where it was lawful for all persons to come without exacting money for their access, having only somewhat gathered of the richer sort by the churchwarden for their apparel and other necessaries. (*ES*, 1:223)

The theater has been described as an artisanal mode of production in the service of aristocratic hegemony (Cohen 1985). But that description seems closer to the patronage relationship Cox describes or to the relationship between the rude mechanicals and the Athenian aristocrats represented and mocked by Shakespeare in *A Midsummer Night's Dream* than it does to the market relationship between Shakespeare's play and its audience. The professional actor emerged from an artisan class, but he was separated from it by virtue of the way in which he made his money. Unlike the artisan or the servant, the player had no master (*ES,* 4:237).

Moreover, the player and the rogue were linked socioeconomically because neither had a profession. Both arose out of similar social forces that eroded traditional social distinctions. And as Jean-Christophe Agnew suggests, both coney-catching literature and the theater responded to the rise of an impersonal market, indeed, were symptomatic of the potential for fraud inherent in the timeless, placeless market (1986, 61–67). Instead of confining themselves to a single trade, both masterless men and players were free to play at a variety of professions. As one Jacobean satirist put it:

> The statute hath done wisely to acknowledge [the player] a rogue and errant, for his chiefe essence is, *A Daily Counterfeit;* he is but a shifty companion; for he lives effectually by putting on, and putting off. He hath been familiar so long with outsides, that he professes himself, (being unknowne) to be an apparent Gentleman. . . . If his profession were single, hee would think himself a simple fellow, as he doth all professions but his owne: His own therefore is compounded of all Natures, all humours, all professions. He is politic to perceive the commonwealth doubts of his license, and therefore in spite of Parliaments or Statutes he incorporates himself by the title of a brotherhood. (*ES,* 4:255–57)

The similarity between player and rogue can be remarked too in the description of a rogue in *The Groundwork of Cony-Catching* (1592), which is just as applicable to actors:

> This monstrous dissembler, a crank all about,
> Uncomely coveting, of each to embrace
> Money or wares, as he made his race;
> And sometimes a mariner, and a serving-man,
> Or else an artificer, as he would feign then.

> Such shifts, he used being well tried,
> Abandoning labour, until he was espied.
>
> (Kinney 1990, 220)

Like the professional player, then, the criminal cozener played at all professions.

The juridical apparatus and economic policy could not efface the embarrassing contradictions of the player's socioeconomic position. The theater after all was a radical innovation. If it confirmed social distinctions, it also put them into question. Indeed, the similarities between player and masterless man made the player vulnerable to the charge commonly made against rogues, namely, that they furthered idleness. The author of *Orders Appointed to Be Executed in the Cittie of London for the Setting of Rogues and Idle Persons to Work* (1582) argued that the "playing of Enterludes" was a "great wasting and loss of thrift of many poor people" (*ES*, 4:291). The city often echoed this complaint, arguing that the theaters "maintain ideleness in such persons as haue no vocation & draw apprentices and other seruantes from their ordinarie workes" (*ES*, 4:322). The contradictions involved in the reliance of the aristocracy and the monarchy on common players to celebrate their power could not be resolved by appealing to traditional feudal ideals of hospitality and service.

By professionalizing the theater, however, dramatists could at least symbolically resolve these contradictions. Professional players could lay claim to a monopoly on the profession of cozening since they were neither criminal vagrants nor cozening papists. Acting companies were licensed joint-stock companies, a version of the monopoly. The theater was linked to other monopolies as well. Many actors, for instance, were apprenticed to guilds, and the play text, when printed, was the property of the printers' monopoly. Dramatists such as Shakespeare and Jonson deployed the same strategies used by the juridical apparatus and displayed in coney-catching literature: they sorted out the player's profession from the laborer's, the player's cozening from the papist's.

I

With this account of cultural differentiation between legitimate player and illegitimate rogue in place, we may turn to *The*

Winter's Tale to examine a particular instance of theatrical legitimation in detail. Here Shakespeare discursively constitutes himself as a
professional dramatist by criminalizing competing forms of cozenage, separating theatrical play from the potential subversiveness of
holiday and of mercenary cozening practiced by Autolycus.

In discussing the displacement of religious ritual in the popular
theater, Michael O'Connell offers *The Winter's Tale* as an illustration of the subversiveness of the theater. In the last scene, he argues,
"Shakespeare does not counter, finally, but embraces the charge of
idolatry" (1985, 304). For O'Connell, the theater is a counterchurch
that competitively challenges the authority of church and state. He
and other anthropological critics are certainly correct in observing
that religious rites are absorbed by the theater and by Shakespeare.
The miracle Shakespeare appears to perform at the end of *The Winter's Tale*—Hermione's resurrection—echoes Christ's death and resurrection. "Bequeath to death your numbness," Paulina says to
Hermione, "for from him / Dear life redeems you" (5.3.102–3),
and the language of grace suffuses the final scene. Moreover, Paulina commands Leontes and the audience to "awake" their "faith"
(5.3.95) in what they initially take to be a miracle.

Yet Shakespeare's absorption of sacred rite is less subversive than
anthropological critics believe. One obvious problem with their
account is that sacred rite and magic trick are differentiated in
the play. The possibility of possession is raised and ruled out by
Leontes: "One worse, / And better used, would make her sainted
spirit / Again possess her corpse, and on this stage, / Where we of-
fenders now appear" (5.1.56–59). Moreover, unlike representations
of Christ's death and resurrection in the Corpus Christi mystery
plays and processionals, which were planned, produced, and promulgated to celebrate the miracle of the Eucharist, Shakespeare's
"resurrection" of Hermione is an illusion, not a miracle; that is,
Shakespeare does not stage the miracle as a miracle; Leontes' spir-
itual "recreation" (3.2.240) is made possible in the final scene
through Paulina's deceptive recreation. And just as Paulina, herself a
stage manager, deceives Leontes, so Shakespeare deceives his audience. Like Leontes, the audience is "mocked with art" (5.3.68).
("Mocked" was synonymous with "deceived," "beguiled," and
"cheated.") By first deceiving the audience about Hermione and
then calling attention to his deception, Shakespeare puts his audience's faith not in rite but in self-consciously theatrical illusion as

illusion. The final scene thus subverts religious orthodoxy less by competing with it than by legitimating the theater. Shakespeare defines his theatrical "magic" as an "art / Lawful as eating" (5.3.110–11) by staging a miracle of death and resurrection as a show.

Even more crucially, the anthropological view of the final scene as subversive fails to take Autolycus into account. Shakespeare marks off from his dramatic practice not only charismatic exorcists but criminal, "popish" entertainers as well. He brings the rogue Autolycus into the romance in order to establish a structural parallel between his own dramatic practice and that of Autolycus (Cox 1969). Shakespeare and Autolycus appropriate magic; both pass off illusions as miracles; both tell tales the credibility of which is in question; both deceive their audience. Like Shakespeare's dramatic illusion, Autolycus's songs are a form of enchantment. The Clown describes with wonder how Autolycus sings his wares: "Why, he sings 'em over as they were gods or godesses: you would think a smock were a she-angel, he so chaunts to the sleeve-hand and the work about the square on't" (4.4.207–9). In Autolycus's first song, the lark "tirra-lyra chaunts" (4.2.8). Just as Shakespeare allows his characters and his audience to believe that they are watching a miracle at the end of the play, so does Autolycus allow his audience to believe his wares have the power of relics, "as if they were a . . . source of benediction to the buyer" (4.4.603–4).

The structural comparison between Shakespeare and Autolycus serves to differentiate between forms of cozening. Shakespeare attempts to guarantee the legitimacy of his theater by contrasting professional forms of autotelic deception to criminal, mercenary forms. Autolycus is a criminal cozener who haunts "wakes, fairs, and bull-baitings" (4.1.102), a mercenary who "sings several tunes faster than you can tell money" (4.4.183). As Autolycus tells the Clown, "Since he was a servant of the prince" he has been "an ape-bearer, then a process server, a bailiff. Then he compassed a motion of the Prodigal son, and married a tinker's wife within a mile where my land and loving lies, and, having flown over many knavish professions, he settled only in rogue" (4.3.92–97). The legitimate professional playwright differs from the criminal cozener in that the playwright heightens the distinction between magic and miracle, whereas the cozener blurs the distinction between sacred and profane. The rustics become so fully absorbed by his songs that Autolycus can easily cut their purses. Describing his success at cheating them, Autolycus tells us:

> I have sold all my trompery; not a counterfeit stone, not a ribbon, glass, pomander, brooch, table-book, ballad, knife, tape, glove, shoe-tie, bracelet, horn-ring, to keep my pack from fasting. They throng who should buy first, as if my trinkets had been hallow'd and brought a benediction to the buyer; by which means I saw whose purse was best in picture, and what I saw, to my good use I rememb'red. (4.4.596–604)

Autolycus's role as a peddler of wares and his reference here to his trompery pick up a trope commonly used by Protestant polemicists against Catholics (Kaula 1976). These writers may well have used this word for tawdry finery because of its derivation from the French *tromperie,* suggesting deception and trickery. In *A Declaration of Egregious Popish Impostures,* Harsnett denounces "craftie priests, and lecherous friars" who "enrich their purses, by selling their Pope trumpery (as *Medals, agnus dei, Blessed beades, holy water, hallowed Crosses, peripats, amulets, smockes of proofe,* and such) at a good rate" (137–38). Harsnett also invites his readers to scorn "all the trinckets, toyes, & pedlars ware in the Popes holy budget" (125). Similarly, the author of *The merchandises of popish priests* (Chassinon 1604) asks, "Is it not an extraordinary aptitude, to sell well, and in selling, to be well payd, and that the buyer (finally) shall haue nothing at all, but the mere sight of his wares? . . . these men, like to Iuglers or Mummers are deeply skild in this kinde of dealing, and know very readily, to sell, & resell the whole sight of their trompery" (sig. C3v). It is precisely because the rustics naively believe that Autolycus's "popish" peddled wares have the sacramental efficacy of relics that he can cut their purses. Thus, the popular tradition as exhibited by Autolycus does not here subvert the authority of church and state; rather, that tradition is positioned by Shakespeare as criminal and popish, and is set against his own dramatic practice so as to differentiate between them.

Like Shakespeare, Autolycus knows the difference between fraud and miracle: what the rustics take to be holy is hocus pocus to him. Unlike Autolycus, however, Shakespeare, as is frequently observed, conspicuously calls attention to his art and to its deepest

limitations. In the final scenes art does not bring a statue to life, nor
does it bring Mamillius and Antigonus back to life. Sixteen years
cannot be restored; the wrinkles on Hermione's face cannot be
erased. Asking the audience knowingly to awake its faith in an
illusion is asking it to raise this play above the other kinds of
commercial shows available to the London public, and thereby to
legitimate, license, and authorize professional forms of cozenage
rather than the kind practiced by marginal and occasionally criminal
entertainers such as Autolycus. Because his professional form of
cozenage differs from religious miracle and from criminal deception, Shakespeare redeems and authorizes it, makes his "art / Lawful" (5.3.110–11). It would therefore be a mistake to conclude, as
have some modern critics, that Shakespeare's self-consciousness
about his art in *The Winter's Tale* enables it to transcend history and
ideology; rather, as Louis Montrose (1980) suggests, we should see
that the play's apparently autotelic deceptiveness, its self-confessed
pleasure in illusion for its own sake, issues from a strategy Shakespeare employs to legitimate his art.

Attending to the cultural differentiation enacted in *The Winter's
Tale* can help us to understand why Shakespeare should turn to
pastoral romance as a way of authorizing a professional form of
cozenage. The archaizing use of a native popular tradition, initiated
in *Pericles* with Gower's "old" song "sung at festivals, / On ember
eves and holy-ales" (Prologue 1, 4–5) and elaborated in *The Winter's
Tale* with the figure of Time (whose language and costume were
probably drawn from popular pageants) and with the comparison
of Perdita's return to an "old tale" (5.3.29), demonstrates how
Shakespeare attempts to efface the embeddedness of his own art in
commercial forms of exchange. Autolycus's ballads "in print" are
commodities, the more valuable because they are "but a month old"
(4.4.260, 267). Moreover, this equation is thematized in one of the
ballads (about a usurer's wife), and in Autolycus's songs:

> Lawn as white as driven snow,
> Cyprus black as e'er was crow,
> Gloves as sweet as damask roses
> Masks for faces and for noses.
>   .   .   .   .   .
> Come buy of me, come, come buy, come buy.

Buy, lads, or else your lasses cry.
Come buy.

(4.4.216–20, 226–28)

And as the ballads are sung, the shepherd decides what to buy
(4.4.267, 269, 307). By contrast, Shakespeare's "old tale" stands as if
it were outside commercial exchange. The contrast between the
commercial ballad and the noncommercial old tale enables Shakespeare to displace a balladmaker like Autolycus: "such a deal / Of
wonder is broken out within this hour," a gentleman remarks, "that
balladmakers cannot express it" (5.1.23–25).

Shakespeare thus salvages an aristocratic notion of play by mark-
ing it off from commerce, displacing the commodification of narrative onto a cozener and onto the country. Although the market has
penetrated the sheepshearing feast, the aristocracy remains immune
to it. The Clown goes off to buy a variety of spices for the feast,
many of which were only recently available in England: "Let me
see, what am I to buy for our sheep-shearing feast? Three pounds of
sugar, five pounds of currants, rice. . . . I must have saffron to
color the warden pies; mace; dates? none—that's out of my note;
nutmegs, seven, a brace or two of ginger, but that I may beg; four
pounds of prunes, and as many raisins o' the sun" (4.3.35–38, 43–
47). Significantly, however, Florizel does not buy any of Autolycus's goods: "You have let him go / And nothing marted with
him," Polixenes says, and Florizel responds, "Old sir, I know / She
prizes not such trifles as these are" (4.4.344–45, 349–50).

The political effects of this division between aristocratic art and
rustic commerce are twofold: Shakespeare authorizes not only the
theater but the court that licensed it as well, neutralizing some
forms of resistance while authorizing others. Autolycus's critical
potential is closed down—he helps Florizel and Camillo escape and
thereby "remains constant to [his] profession" (4.4.682)—and the
disobedience of a courtier such as Camillo (who disobeys both
Leontes and Polixenes) and of a lady such as Paulina (who chastises
Leontes) take the form of benign, penitential deceptions. The unruly energy of the sheepshearing (which threatens to subvert Polixenes' authority over Florizel) is displaced and absorbed by the concluding festivities at Paulina's house, where the court will celebrate
and "sup" (5.3.104). And Florizel's change of disguise with Auto-

lycus (under Camillo's direction) is similarly legitimated. As Autolycus puts it, "What a boot is here with this exchange" (4.4.679).
The social mobility of the Clown and the shepherd is potentially
subversive, but they are comically excluded from the final festivities: the rustics are not invited to Paulina's house.

Play is redeemed from the sexual promiscuity with which Leontes had earlier associated it. Leontes' imagination, "in rebellion
with" itself (1.2.353), his fantasy that Hermione has cuckolded him,
is triggered by her playful entertainment of Polixenes: "Go play,
boy, play, / Thy mother plays too, and I play too" (1.2.186–87).
Leontes' fantasy threatens to compromise play altogether as he
extends it into the audience:

> There have been, or I am much deceived, cuckolds ere now;
> And many a man there is, even at this present,
> Now while I speak this, holds his wife's arm,
> That little thinks she has been sluic'd in's absence
> And his pond fished by his next neighbor, by
> Sir Smile, his neighbor.
>
> . . . . .
>   Many thousands on's
> Have the disease and feel't not.
>
> (1.2.189–95, 205–6)

By addressing the audience directly—"many a man there is, even at
this present"—Leontes here comes close to the charge so frequently
made by antitheatricalists, namely, that the theater was a market of
bawdry, a place of whoredom. The ending of the play inverts this
vision by bringing under control Leontes' imagination, so dangerous when he confuses fantasy with reality. When Leontes is
finally able to recognize his fantasy about Hermione as fantasy, the
imagination can become an art as lawful as eating. This control is
brought about, as we have seen, through Autolycus and Paulina,
who make the characters and the audience self-consciously recognize the imagination and play for what they are (Florizel's un-
selfconscious commitment to playful Ovidian transformations does
not succeed either.) Sexual promiscuity is by the end of *The Winter's
Tale* exclusively associated with the rustics and with commerce.

Though the legitimation of play helps to legitimate Leontes and
his court, it also reproduces the contradictions it attempts to man-

age. Two facts complicate the cultural differentiation of licensed player from unlicensed rogue on which this legitimation depends. First, as I mentioned earlier, Autolycus is not a vagabond but a courtier. He was initially the servant of Prince Florizel, who in his "time wore three-pile" velvet (4.3.13–14), and he becomes a courtier again near the end of the play. Second, he is played by an actor. The character and the actor are in these respects similar to and a part of the King's Men. But we may account for these complications by examining Autolycus's role more closely.

The part was probably written with Robert Armin in mind, the sophisticated (and, in social terms, upwardly mobile) *courtly* fool, as distinct from William Kemp, who affected the country bumpkin (see Wiles 1987, 156–57). The son of a Norfolk tailor, Armin became an apprentice with the prestigious London company of goldsmiths (from which he was released by 1592) and, like Shakespeare, had bought a coat of arms before he died in 1616. Why, then, does Shakespeare inform his audience that Autolycus was Florizel's servant? I suggest Shakespeare wants to remind the audience that the actor playing the role is a celebrated player of court fools. (Autolycus's ballads may have served as a similar reminder. The year before *The Winter's Tale* was first performed, Armin published a ballad in an apparent and unsuccessful bid for court patronage.) Shakespeare's dramatic practice is thus self-legitimating: he can playfully call attention to the actor playing the rogue in the confidence that, for his Globe/Blackfriars/court audience at least, the argument that the player and rogue are distinct has already been won. In this connection, Simon Forman's eyewitness account of the play is worth bearing in mind. Forman is usually viewed as an unsophisticated playgoer, but in the context of my analysis, his account reveals him to be an informed observer of licensing practices, and thus perhaps, his observations ought to carry some weight: "Remember also the rogue that came in all tattered like Coll Pixie; how he feigned him sick and to have been robbed of all he had. How he cozened the poor man of all his money. . . . How he changed apparel with the King of Bohemia's son, and then how he turned courtier, etc. / Beware of trusting feigned beggars or fawning fellows" (Rowse 1976, 311). To Forman at least, the distinction between player and rogue was perfectly clear.

Still, some critics might want to salvage a critique of the court by suggesting that Autolycus's connection to the court enables a subtle (perhaps too subtle for Forman) critique of it; that is, Autolycus's status as a courtier and vagabond, some might conclude, serves to disenchant the court's "magic" as mere show, revealing the court to be full of vagabonds who play a confidence game on their subjects. The difference between courtier and vagabond deconstructs, enabling the audience to see that the court is selling it a bill of goods. Such a reading might be buttressed from *Gypsies Metamorphosed,* a masque wherein Jonson explicitly collapses the distinction between vagabond gypsies and courtiers by having many of the courtiers who performed in the masque dress as gypsies. Dale Randall (1975) has maintained that Jonson's equation between courtier and gypsy is intended to be unflattering.

My reservations about this way of salvaging a critique of the court are twofold. First, it assumes that the court would have disliked being compared to predatory vagabonds or gypsies. Yet one can argue forcefully that the opposite could be the case. Martin Butler (1991) has contested Dale Randall's account of *Gypsies Metamorphosed,* claiming that the masque was orthodox rather than oppositional.[6] My second reservation is perhaps already apparent. My imagined critique of *The Winter's Tale* depends, like Randall's account of *Gypsies Metamorphosed,* on assumptions about cultural politics which ignore precisely those contradictions that I have insisted both legitimate the court and produce a potential critique of it. Autolycus and Florizel's "exchange" (4.4.679) of clothes is at the same time an exchange of aristocratic and cozenage codes which both undermines and underwrites legitimating distinctions. Autolycus's heterogeneous status as courtier/vagabond registers, I would argue, a larger contradiction through which the broad receivability by both popular and courtly audiences of Shakespeare's thematic of "play" necessitates crossing boundaries between public and court theaters.

II

It is precisely an understanding of the court's contradictions that enables us to historicize early Stuart "antitheatricality" in general and to rethink in particular the relationship between Jonson and

Shakespeare in terms of comparative degrees of antitheatricality. We may elaborate this rethinking by turning now to *Bartholomew Fair*. Jonson's play extends the critique of the court by directly thematizing its licensing practices, comprehensively addressing holiday pastimes, puppet shows, and the like.[7] Jonson's critique of Shakespeare's audience is part of a reactionary critique of the Stuart court's all too permissive (in Jonson's view) licensing practices. Jonson dramatizes the Stuart appropriation of popular culture as a contest, pitting the fair's would-be reformers, who "prophesy the destruction of Maygames, wakes, and Whitsun ales, and . . . sigh and groan for the Reformation of these abuses" (4.6.80–82), against the fair's spectators and entertainers. James had asserted his authority over Bartholomew Fair in 1603, when he closed it because of the plague, declaring that "the citizens and inhabitants of London . . . shall not holde the saide faires, nor anything appertayning to them, at the times accustomed, nor any time til they shall be licensed by us" (Larkin and Hughes 1973, 1:46). Sometime thereafter, James commissioned Jonson's play. According to John Aubrey, "King James made [Jonson] write something against the Puritans, who began to be troublesome in his reign" (H & S, 10:171). In the epilogue to *Bartholomew Fair,* Jonson invites James to judge whether the players "licence break" (7), and in the play itself, he represents the dispute between Busy and Leatherhead over the puppet show as a contest over institutional authority. Against Busy's charge that it is "licentious" (5.3.14), Leatherhead defends his show by pointing out that it has been "licensed by authority" and that he has "the hand of the Master of the Revels for it" (5.5.13, 16).

Jonson's festive comedy reproduces without resolving a central problem with licensing: because it alienated authority, it was open to abuse by forgers. Jonson registers this possibility in the absent scrivener, who sells a forged warrant to Knockem and an authentic warrant to Overdo. But Jonson is more deeply interested in how licensing made it possible for an entertainer to subvert as well as support the social order. Officially licensed mercenary entertainers might stage any "get-penny" (5.5.11) thing, regardless of whether it affirmed authority. The license is subversive for Jonson insofar as it commodifies authority, conferring it upon anyone with the money to purchase it.

Jonson's concern with the commercial aspects of licensing en-

ables us to grasp two central related issues in *Bartholomew Fair*—
moral judgment and the generic definition of the play as a festive
comedy—which I would like to examine in that order. Jonson does
not make it easy for his audience to determine the moral status of
the fair and its entertainments. In the epilogue to *Bartholomew Fair,*
to be read at court, Jonson invites King James to judge whether or
not the play "be profane":

> You know the scope of writers, and what store
>   Of leave is given them, if they take not more,
> And turn it into license. You can tell
>   If we have used that leave you gave us well;
> Or whether we to rage, or licence break,
>   Or be profane, or make profane men speak?
> This is your power to judge, great Sir, and not
>   The envy of a few.
>
> (Epilogue, 3–10)

Jonson clearly presumes that James will make an affirmative judgment of the play; that the king alone has the authority to judge
affirms his power all the more. In this respect, poetics and politics
are mutually authorizing: under the rubric of dramatic art, the king
licenses the subversion of authority within the fair, and that subversion in turn issues in an invitation to James to reassert his political
authority. Yet Jonson's appeal to James's authority is itself problematic. For the very invitation to judge the play evinces a tension
between the king and the actors, who may, in fact, have exceeded
the king's leave by admitting licentiousness and profanity into the
play. That there is no record of a subsequent performance at court
suggests that James, who made no secret of his aesthetic likes and
dislikes, did not especially enjoy the privilege of judging Jonson's
play (H & S, 9:245).[8]

Many of the fair's entertainments are indeed difficult to judge, as
the history of divided critical responses to them testifies.[9] It is hard
to tell whether they constitute forms of festive release or of anarchic
rebellion. In the game of vapors, for example, unbounded liberty to
dispute takes the form of nonsensical, contentious contradiction,
finally erupting into violence. Jonson himself clearly views the
game equivocally. Quarlous maintains that he is free to engage in
vapors: "Sir, you'll allow me my Christian liberty. I may laugh, I

hope" (4.4.114–15). Yet Quarlous's liberty is not taken for granted. Cutting replies: "On some sort you may, and in some sort you may not, sir" (4.4.116–17). And Mistress Overdo's view of the vapors is the opposite of Quarlous's. For her, vapors constitute a form of anarchy: "Why gentlemen, why gentlemen, I charge you upon my authority, conserve the peace. In the King's name, and my husband's, put up your weapons" (4.4.108–10). When the men fail to heed her, Mistress Overdo accuses them of rebellion: "What mean you? are you rebels, gentlemen? Shall I send out a sargeant at arms for a writ o'rebellion against you? I'll commit you, upon my womanhood, for a riot, upon my justice-hood if you persist" (4.4.138–41). Mistress Overdo's objections are of course comically overstated, but her fears of riot and rebellion cannot simply be dismissed, for the men proceed to fight, and as a result, Captain Whit manages to steal the cloaks and hats they drop. The game of vapors thereby asks a question Jonson does not resolve: Are vapors a form of Christian liberty or of anarchic riot?

The status of the puppet show is even more equivocal, equally open to the antithetical views that it is licensed and that it is licentious. Like the fair, the puppet show licenses the subversion of gender, aesthetic, and class distinctions on which the social order is based. Instead of ultimately affirming these distinctions, however, the show undermines them, and the result is social disorder. Prostitution, drunkenness, insults, and violence abound. Drunk on sack in a London alehouse, Hero is a whore; the men "whoremasters" (5.4.220) all. Rivals for Hero's favor, Damon and Pythias proceed to fall to blows over her. The disorder within the puppet show is infectious. Although Leatherhead maintains that his actors are a "well-governed" (5.3.95) company, the puppets Damon and Pythias hit him when he tells Cokes that they are both whoremasters.

Moreover, the mercenary motives of upstarts such as Littlewit and Leatherhead predominate over didactic or moral ends. Whereas puppet shows were performed at fairs for didactic purposes, as religious drama, before the Reformation,[10] Leatherhead's shows exploit religious themes, dramatizing them as forms of rebellion in "modern" (5.3.12) terms for commercial purposes: "O the motions that I, Lantern Leatherhead, have light to i' my time, since my Master Pod died! *Jerusalem* was a stately thing; and so was . . . *Sodom and Gommorrah,* with the rising of the 'prentices and pulling down the bawdy houses there, upon Shrove Tuesday; but *The Gunpowder Plot,* there was a get-penny. I have presented that to an eighteen or twenty-pence audience nine times in an afternoon" (5.1.6–12). Moreover, the money Leatherhead charges for *The Gunpowder Plot,* about the abortive Catholic conspiracy to blow up Parliament, implicitly links political rebellion to commercial success.[11] Leatherhead's puppet show not only subverts political authority but calls into question the poetic authority of text over performance as well: "But do you play it according to the printed book?" Cokes asks Leatherhead. "By no means sir," Leatherhead replies, adding that Marlowe's poem must be "reduced to a more familiar strain for our people; made . . . a little easy and modern for the times" (5.3.98–99, 108, 111–12) in order to attract and hold an audience that could not otherwise understand it.

Despite its potential subversiveness, however, Leatherhead's show is not judged to be licentious; indeed, it is not judged at all. Instead, Jonson presents a dispute over its legitimacy between puppet master and Puritan without resolving it:

> *Lea.*   Sir, I present nothing but what is licensed by authority.
> *Busy.*   Thou art all licence, even licentiousness itself, Shimei!
> *Lea.*   I have the Master of the Revels' hand for it, sir.
> *Busy.*   The master of the rebels' hand thou hast—Satan!
>
> (5.5.13–17)

Busy and the Puppet Dionysus, who takes over for Leatherhead, extend the dispute, each in turn comically asserting antithetical positions about the show:

> *Busy.*   Yet I say his calling, his profession is profane, it is profane, idol.
> *Pup. Dio.*   It is not profane!
> *Lea.*   It is not profane, he says.
> *Busy.*   It is profane.
> *Pup. Dio.*   It is not profane.
> *Busy.*   It is profane.
> *Pup. Dio.*   It is not profane.
>
> (5.5.59–65)

This dispute is comic precisely because Jonson cannot be said to align himself with either the puppet master or the iconoclast: although Busy will not endure the puppets' "profanations" (5.5.2), he is equally profane in his own protestations; Winwife says of him, "What a desperate, profane wretch is this!" (5.5.40). Neither puppet nor iconoclast has more learning or eloquence than the other. The puppet Dionysus declares, "I'll prove, against e'er a rabbin of 'em all, that my standing is as lawful as his; that I speak by inspiration as well as he; that I have as little to do with learning as he; and do scorn her as much as he" (5.6.97–100). Busy is of course confuted and converted by the puppet, but the force of his conversion is deeply qualified, first, because the puppets have no legitimacy of their own which might justify his conversion and, second, because Busy's conversion is based on the absence of gender difference rather than a reassertion of it. The dispute over the puppet show ends (and Busy converts) when the puppet holds up his garment to reveal that puppets have "neither male nor female amongst" (5.5.91–93) them. Rather than a return to clear social order based on clear gender distinctions, Busy's conversion marks the continuation of the fair's social disorder. The status of the show is left unresolved and judgment is suspended.

The problem of judging the puppet show is a synecdoche for judging the play as a whole. In neither case does anyone successfully pass judgment on the fair or on the spectators who have used (or abused) the liberty of it. All authority is suspended. The court of pie-powders was traditionally a court of appeal for crimes committed within the fair, but it is never held in Jonson's play (4.6.61). Similarly, the puppet show is interrupted, first by Busy and then by Overdo, both of whom unsuccessfully attempt to assert their authority over it. No figure of authority judges Leatherhead's puppet show. To be sure, Jonson appeals to James I in the epilogue, but that appeal would, of course, be made only at the court, not during performances in the public theater. By the end of the play—at least when performed in the public theater—the "date of . . . authority is out" (5.4.97–98).

The questions remain, How are we to interpret this suspension of judgment and authority at the end of *Bartholomew Fair*? What are its political implications? And what is its impact on the generic definition of Jonson's play? The suspension of authority should not be taken, I believe, as subversive of social order. Indeed, it is regularly interpreted as Jonson's humanist reconciliation of characters and audience alike, all of whom learn the virtue of tolerance and the liabilities of judgment (Barish 1972; Donaldson 1970, 77). [12] In this humanist account, the play ends as a clearly defined festive comedy: Busy will become a beholder with the rest of the audience and Overdo accepts Quarlous's advice that he remember he is "but Adam, flesh and blood! You have your frailty; forget your other name of Overdo and invite us all to supper. There you and I will compare our discoveries, and drown the memory of all enormity in your bigg'st bowl at home" (5.6.95–98). Judgment is suspended, in this reading, to be displaced by an inclusive festivity in which even the actors will be brought along.

Yet the political effects of this festivity seem to me more complex than this account allows. Far from being politically progressive, the festivity has both conservative and radical political implications. On the one hand, the absence of judgment may not be so undesirable from an official point of view. Social harmony depends on preventing the Overdos, Busys and Trouble-alls, and Wasps from asserting their own judgment, and the status quo is thereby preserved intact. On the other hand, this conservative effect is achievable only through a radical means: order is formed not by putting an end to festive license but by indulging that license indefinitely. Thus, the distinctions on which social order is founded are suspended.

Without the presence of a central authority to pass final judgment, Jonson is unable to define his play as a festive comedy. The potentially corrosive effects of this absence of authority are present in the kind of festivity with which he closes his play. Quarlous's suggestion that Overdo and he "drown" enormity in Overdo's biggest bowl of wine suggests a somewhat licentious form of feasting. But even more clearly corrosive effects are present in the marriages that conventionally define the genre of comedy. Here a comparison with Shakespeare is again instructive. In contrast to Shakespeare's festive comedies and his romances, which typically end by sanctifying marriage, however tentatively, Jonson's play ends with the discovery that two wives, Win Littlewit and Alice Overdo, have used the liberty of the fair to become prostitutes. Nor does the ending unambiguously affirm the prospective marriages between Winwife and Grace and between Quarlous and Dame Purecraft.

Jonson's refusal to do so, I suggest, is directly linked to the fact that the marriages are authorized by a warrant and a license, respectively. Just as Leatherhead is licensed by the Master of the Revels, so too the prospective marriages announced at the end of the play (and thus the play's status as a festive comedy) depend on Cokes's license and Overdo's warrant. Yet Jonson's puns on "warrant" and "licence" underline the problematic status of the prospective marriages. Quarlous justifies Grace's marriage by saying to Overdo, "Here's warrant for it" (5.6.83–84); similarly, in reference to his own marriage, Quarlous wishes to thank Cokes "for my license" (5.6.87). The force of these puns—generating the sense of "text" and of "justification" as well—is to question whether or not his uses of the texts are indeed licensed and warranted, for Quarlous uses neither in an unequivocally justifiable way. Not only has the license that permits him to marry Dame Purecraft been stolen and the warrant that enables Grace to marry Winwife been misappropriated by him, but Quarlous takes mercenary liberties with the license and warrant, thereby indirectly linking marriage with its negation, prostitution.[13] The sanctity of marriage is undercut by the fact that Quarlous's primary interest is Dame Purecraft's money: "It is the money I want; why should I not marry the money, when 'tis offered me? I have the license and all" (5.2.74–76).

Perhaps because Quarlous is so clearly mercenary, many critics have regarded Grace and Winwife as the normative center of the play. In my view, the problematic status of warrants and license calls into question any notion of a normative center. To be sure, the warrant does save Grace from marrying Cokes. More specifically, it saves her from being Overdo's ward. As Grace explains, she came to be engaged to Cokes "through a common calamity; [Overdo] bought me . . . and now he will marry me to his wife's brother, this wise gentleman that you see, or else I must pay value o' my land" (3.5.25–53).[14] According to Jackson Cope, the play ends as a comedy because the marriage between Winwife and Grace transcends mercenary considerations: "Winwife has Grace, not bought but won, albeit with the concord of a mad destiny, and their concord alone has transcended the chaos of the Fair" (1967, 151). The ending of the play seems to me to be more equivocal than Cope believes, however, precisely because Grace is bought. Quarlous uses the warrant to force Grace to pay him what she would have had to pay Overdo: "Master Winwife, give you joy, you are Palamon; you are possessed of the gentlewoman, but she must pay me value, here's warrant for it" (5.6.82–84). Although Grace is freed from Overdo, she is not freed from wardship; rather, she becomes Quarlous's ward, and Quarlous thus stands to profit from her marriage to Winwife. Mercenary considerations have not been decisively transcended, and for that very reason it is difficult to establish the difference (here between Overdo as a blocking agent and Quarlous as romantic hero) that would enable the play to affirm marriage and thus achieve closure as a festive comedy. The generic indefinition of the play is symptomatic of the alienation of authority in licenses and warrants noted earlier: without the presence of an overriding authority figure, Jonson cannot institute a final and unequivocal distinction between marriage as a form of sacred, sexual exchange and commercial, unrestrained, profane forms of exchange such as prostitution.

If the alienation of authority within *Bartholomew Fair* helps to explain the play's generic indefinition, it also helps to explain its double frame—the induction for the performance at the Hope Theater and the prologue and epilogue for the court performance.[15] Both the Articles of Agreement (set forth in the induction) and the epilogue attempt to resolve the problems of authority dramatized within the play. In the induction, the scrivener and the bookholder allow the audience freedom to censure as they wish. Yet at the same time, Jonson forces them to make the judgment he wants them to make: "In witness whereof, as you have preposterously put to your seals already (which is your money) you will now add the other part of your suffrage, your hands" (135–37). Jonson's neurotic relation to the audience—at once cajoling and coercive—registers the extent to which the commercial form of exchange between author and audience threatens the author's ability to control the reception of his play (Kaplan 1970; Wayne 1982; Agnew 1986). Jonson grants his audience liberty to judge because he has "departed with his right" (78) over his play, which he explicitly defines as a commodity or "ware" (143). Yet Jonson can compensate for this loss of control only by forcing his audience to clap before the play has begun. The induction does not constitute, then, an easy resolution to the problem of license dramatized within the play itself. Like the license and warrants in the play, the contract and Jonson's play are themselves alienable commodities, hence open to misjudgment.

The alienation of authority in licences not only impinges on the play's generic definition; it also puts into question the capacity of licensed commercial entertainment in general to affirm the established social order. For just as Cokes's license and Overdo's warrant are put to subversive uses, so, too, the license to perform puppet shows indirectly subverts poetic and political authority.

Yet why do these tensions arise? Why should Jonson at once submit to the king's authority and resist it? Jonson's ambivalence toward James registers the extent to which the court was implicated in the kinds of commercial and acquisitive activities Jonson wanted it to restrain. If no authority is present in *Bartholomew Fair* to pass judgment and if, consequently, Leatherhead and Jonson cannot be decisively distinguished, it is because both entertainers are licensed by the same absent authority, namely, the Master of the Revels. By licensing poets as well as mercenary poetasters, to put my point more generally, the Stuarts called into question the moral distinction between dramatic poet and mercenary poetaster that Jonson wanted them to authorize.

How licensing enabled Jonsonian and Shakespearean forms of antitheatricalism in *The Winter's Tale* and *Bartholomew Fair* can be understood if we situate them more precisely in relation to the licensing practices I have noted. A closer analysis of the Masters of the Revels and the Stuart monarchs shows the degree to which they were implicated in the kinds of licentious social and poetic disorder Jonson opposed. Shakespeare's and Jonson's antitheatricality were symptomatic of a wide cultural and economic crisis in early Stuart England.

III

As the debate over the puppet show in *Bartholomew Fair* makes clear, Jonson was especially sensitive to the way the cultural contradictions of early Stuart court culture were registered in the Revels Office itself (and perhaps Jonson sought the office so that he would be better positioned to resolve them). Those contradictions expressed the penetration of the office by market forces. Indeed, the office itself was alienable property. Taking Sir John Astley's sale of it to Henry Herbert on July 20, 1623, for 150 pounds as an example, Janet Clare points out: "The episode is a singular illustration of the fact that the Revels Office, once acquired, was a proprietary right capable of being assigned to a purchaser. There is no evidence that the transfer of privileges required, or received, the Crown's specific approval" (Clare 1990, 14). Indeed, the alienability of the office kept Jonson from getting it. He had obtained a second reversion (Astley himself had obtained the first reversion from Sir George Buc) on October 5, 1621, but obviously, the reversion was not enforceable.

What concerned Jonson, at least as early as *Bartholomew Fair,* was a narrower but perhaps even more significant effect of the market on the Office of the Revels: the Master alienated authority in licenses, often for commercial gain. According to Andrew Gurr, "The main point of licensing companies and playhouses seems to have been not so much the control it established as the revenue it gave the Master" (1970, 52). I would add that in the seventeenth century, the Master's desire to gain money often outstripped his concern to regulate the drama.[16] Sir Henry Herbert obtained a small annuity of thirty pounds from his rather stingy elder brother, Edward (who controlled the inheritance), and was thus greatly in need of financial supplement (see Charles 1977, 48, 58). This is not to say that Herbert was necessarily or wholly corrupt; certainly he was no match for certain stationers who pirated books or reprinted censored books with new titles in order to sell them legally. Yet the Master's desire to gain as many fees as the market would bear often came at the expense of what the monarch would bear. Consider, for example, the relationship between Christopher Beeston, the manager of the Phoenix Theater, and Herbert. Beeston regularly paid gratuities to Herbert—what G. E. Bentley politely terms "good investments"—and even gave Herbert's wife a pair of gloves that, Herbert speculates, "must have cost at least twenty shillings" (*JCS,* 6:63). As Bentley points out, these gratuities helped Beeston keep the Phoenix open when he later ran into trouble because of Shirley's play *The Ball* (*JCS,* 6:59–65). Herbert said that he "would have forbidden the play, but that Biston [Christopher Beeston] promiste many things which I found withal should be left out." The Queen's Players later went so far as to grant Herbert a share in the company, presumably in order to ensure that both actors and Master had a mutual interest in the fortunes of the company (*JCS* 6:65). Herbert owned shares valued at a hundred pounds each in all the companies except the King's Men (*ES,* 1:353 n. 2). And one of his deputies,

William Blagrave, was part owner of the Salisbury Court Theater
(*JCS,* 7:238).

A notorious example of how the Master's pecuniary interest outstripped his concern for regulation is the licensing of Thomas Middleton's immensely popular play *A Game at Chess.* After an unprecedented run of performances for nine days, King James stopped the
play because the Spanish ambassador complained. Secretary Sir Edward Conway sent a letter to the Privy Council complaining about
the "boldness of the company that permitted it to be so acted" and
asking the council to "restrain such insolent and licentious presump-
tion for the future" (Middleton 1964, 1:lxxix). When the Privy
Council ordered the players and Middleton to appear and "demanded by what licence and authority" (Middleton 1964, 1:lxxix)
they had presumed to act the play, the players produced a copy of the
play which had in fact been licensed by the Master of the Revels.
Two weeks later, after the Lord Chamberlain intervened on behalf
of the Master of the Revels and the players, James allowed the
company to perform "any common play lycensed by authority,"
except *A Game at Chess* (Middleton 1964, 1:lxxix). Although a local
case was decided, the larger institutional problem of licensing remained unresolved. Nor was *A Game at Chess* in any way exceptional. Virtually all the plays that were the subject of political controversy in the Renaissance had been previously licensed by the
Master of the Revels.

I do not mean to revert to a kind of economic determinism here in
explaining the contradictions in Herbert's practices as a censor. My
point is that both economic and symbolic forms of capital shaped
the censor's interests. Although Herbert usually charged a fee for
reading plays he refused to license (Adams 1917, 19, 23), in 1623 he
returned *The Winter's Tale* to the King's Men "without a fee" because he found it needed no corrections (Adams, 25). On another
occasion Herbert set aside his fee in order to advance his interests at
court. He refused to take ten pounds from a French troupe in 1635
"and did them many other curtys, *gratis,* to render the queene
my mistres an acceptable service. . . . The Frenchmen were commended to me by the queene, and have passed through my hands
gratis" (Adams 1917, 61, 62). Through the office, Herbert gained
power and prestige at court and helped consolidate the Pembroke
faction.

This kind of prestige could in turn be literally cashed in, as we can see by examining a specific attempt by the Lord Chamberlain, William Pembroke, a cousin of Sir Henry Herbert, to get the reversion of the office for his secretary, John Thoroughgood. Pembroke had nearly bankrupted himself in maintaining his political influence, and Thoroughgood was one of his principal creditors. Pembroke would presumably have been better able to arrange for debt relief because of the symbolic debt Thoroughgood would have owed him (see Brennan 1988). Thoroughgood was an attractive candidate, in other words, for reasons having to do with various forms of capital rather than for reasons having to do with his qualifications as a censor who might effectively smell out sedition.[17]

Just as the Master of the Revels contributed to political instability, however indirectly, by licensing controversial plays, so he undermined the very aesthetic distinctions that Jonson wished to affirm. As I have already indicated, in the later Renaissance the Master of the Revels (and even the early Stuart monarchs) licensed an increasingly varied range of popular entertainers. In 1610 Sir George Buc licensed three men "to shew a strange lion brought to do strange things, as turning an ox to be roastyed" (*JCS*, 6:298). Similarly, Sir Henry Herbert gave a "warrant to Grimes for shewing ye Camell for a yeare from 20 June" at the Hope Theater in 1632 (*JSC*, 6:212). Among the other entertainments Herbert licensed were dancing horses, including "a bay nagge wch can shewe strange feats"; dancers on the ropes; fencers; a woman with no hands; a child with no arms; the story of the World's Creation; a "portraiture of Jerusalem"; portraits of the queen and king of Bohemia and their children; and waterworks (Murray 1963, 2:251, 248, 252, 351, 354, 357). Even King James and King Charles licensed marginal entertainers. In 1605 Roger Lawrence "brought the Kyng's warrant . . . to shewe two beasts called Babonnes" in Coventry; a man produced "the Kings Ma^ts warrant to shewe tricks with poppits" on his way through Coventry in 1616; and in 1639 one Larzeus Colletto presented a license to Norwich authorities permitting him to display "a monnster"; the license was "signed," the clerk writes, "with his Maties own hand" (Murray 1963, 2:338, 246–47, 251, 359; Bawcutt 1984a, 326–27).[18]

According to G. E. Bentley, "All London theatres appear to have accommodated more miscellaneous spectacle than we are accus-

tomed to associate with theatres" (*JCS* 6:212 n. 1). This accom-
modation turned to uneasy competition, however, in the later Renaissance as more and more entertainers were licensed. Theaters
were not strictly used for plays; instead actors competed with other
kinds of entertainers. By the 1620s paratheatrical shows, entertainments, and exhibitions such as prizefighting, fencing, acrobatics,
displays of halberds and pikes, among others, increasingly displaced plays at the Swan, the Rose, the Hope, and other theaters
(Ashton 1983, 7).

These newly licensed forms of popular culture directly impinged
on the professional company that performed *Bartholomew Fair,*
namely, the Lady Elizabeth's Men. This company performed in the
Hope Theater, newly reopened in 1614 as a combination theater and
bull- and bearbaiting arena. As Jonson complains in the induction to
Bartholomew Fair, the Hope is "dirty as Smithfield, and as stinking
every whit" (Induction, 141). Bearbaiting and dramatic entertainment did not comfortably coexist at the Hope (*JSC, 6:200–214*).
The bear masters had a controlling interest in the theater and staged
more baitings than the Lady Elizabeth's Men thought tolerable,
possibly as many as three a week. The players complained to Philip
Henslowe, the entrepreneur who had arranged the contract, but
found no relief. After disbanding in 1615, the Lady Elizabeth's Men
were replaced by Prince Charles's company, which faced the same
difficulty. After 1617 no standard acting company resided at the
Hope.

If the contradictions between the court's interest in licensing
entertainments that competed economically and symbolically with
the attempts of Shakespeare and Jonson to professionalize the theater were not fully resolvable, the shapes of Shakespeare's and
Jonson's careers suggest that there were significantly different ways
to manage these contradictions. I would not want to concede,
however, that the difference between the two strategies is as sharp
as it might seem at first sight. By elevating his own professional
cozenage above its lowly kin, Shakespeare was able to retire comfortably from the theater. Yet that elevation retrospectively confirmed Robert Greene's estimate of him as an "upstart crow"; that
is, in professionalizing the theater, Shakespeare helped not simply
to reinforce hierarchical social distinctions but to initiate a transgressive social mobility as well.[19] Like the shepherd in *The Winter's*

Tale, Shakespeare became "a gentleman born," buying a coat of arms for his father. Moreover, even if, as I have suggested, Shakespeare wished to help his acting company secure a monopoly, he himself invested in a free market, speculating in Midlands textiles even as clothworkers unsuccessfully attempted to maintain a monopoly on textile production.[20]

The degree to which the court's contradictions structured Jonson's career can be seen by turning now to a crucial moment when the model of theatrical legitimation which had worked successfully for Jonson in the Jacobean court broke down at the Caroline court. Just as the court's contradictions drove Jonson out of the public theaters in 1616, so its contradictions later drove him out of the court theater.

Th'Only Catos of This Critick Age:
Late Jonson and the
Reformation of Caroline Tastes

In 1631, relatively soon after James died, Charles I sided with Inigo Jones in the bitter dispute between him and Jonson over the place of poetry and spectacle in court masques. Jonson was displaced from his self-appointed position as the leading public or courtly poet by entertainers he considered marginal and mercenary. Inigo Jones became for Jonson the image of the kind of entertainer from whom he wished to differentiate himself. When Jones, not he, had been put in charge of festivities welcoming the Spanish Infanta to England in 1623, Jonson had disparaged him as but a man "who guides the motions and directs the bears" ("An Epistle to One Who Would Be Sealed," 50). In "An Expostulation with Inigo Jones," written sometime after he left the court, Jonson returned to the terms of *Bartholomew Fair* to condemn Jones as a mere puppet master like Leatherhead: "What would he do now, giving his mind that way, / In presentation of some puppet play?" (75–76). Jonson was dismayed that once-trivial puppet shows, formerly relegated to fairs, were now performed as masques at court. Licentious commercial entertainment had triumphed:

> O shows! Shows! Mighty shows!
> The eloquence of masques! What need of prose,
> Or verse, or sense, to express immortal you?

You are the spectacles of state! 'Tis true
Court hieroglyphics, and all arts afford
In the mere perspective of an inch board.
You ask no more than certain politic eyes,
Eyes that can pierce into the mysteries
Of many colours, read them, and reveal
Mythology there painted on slit deal.
Oh, to make boards to speak! There is a task!
Painting and carpentry are the soul of masque.
Pack with your pedling poetry to the stage,
This is the money-get, mechanic age!

                                        (39–52)

The "Expostulation" registers the near-complete collapse of Jonson's career as court poet and public dramatist. Neither of his two Caroline masques was a success. His project "to make the spectators understanders" in *Love's Triumph through Callipolis* (1631) had failed. Similarly, *The New Inn* had failed miserably in its first performance in 1629; the title page says that the play was "squeamishly beheld and censured"—a complaint Jonson reiterates in "Ode to Himself":

              pride and impudence in faction knit,
        Usurp the chair of wit:

                .   .   .   .   .

        Let their fastidious, vain
        Commission of the brain
        Run on and rage, sweat, censure, and condemn.
                                        (3–4, 7–9)

In the audience of *The Magnetic Lady*, Jonson's next play, Inigo Jones sneered along with another of Jonson's victims, Nathaniel Butter, satirized in *The Staple of News*. As Alexander Gill writes:

        O how ye friend Natt: Butter gan to melt
        When at the poorness of your plate he smelt
        And Inigo with laughter then grew fat
        That there was nothing there worth laughing at.
                                        (H & S, 11:347)

By 1633 Gill's advice that Jonson burn his play was almost beside the point. And in 1634 the court performance of *A Tale of a Tub,* already censored at Jones's insistence, was "not liked" presumably because the satire of Jones was still in the play. This failure may have seemed to seal Jonson's fate; it was one of a long list of misfortunes he suffered during Charles's reign, including a stroke in 1628 and the loss of his post as city chronologer.

Recently, Anne Barton (1984, 321–24), David Norbrook (1984a), Leah Marcus (1986b, 132–38), David Riggs (1988, 295–350), Peter Womack (1989), and Martin Butler (1989) have attempted to re-cuperate the late works by defending them from Dryden's charge that they were Jonson's dotages, regarding them instead as symp-toms of his general disaffection with the values of Caroline court culture. In their view, Jonson opposed both the ascendancy at court of spectacle over poetry and the rise of a Neoplatonic cult associated with Henrietta Maria.[1] More recently, Martin Butler (1990; 1992) has reversed himself, arguing that even late in his career Jonson was orthodox rather than oppositional. Butler points, for example, to the end of the "Ode to Himself," appended to *The New Inn,* in which Jonson identifies Charles and Henrietta Maria as his au-dience.

These accounts of late Jonson have been central to an understand-ing of his career and to antithetical views of Caroline theatrical culture in general. His career is said to be shaped as follows: after an initial period of difficulty, Jonson enjoyed decades of stability at the Jacobean court and then faced new difficulties at the Caroline court. His relation to other playwrights has been used to buttress both opposition and revisionist accounts of the court either as out of touch with its subjects or as an enlightened and competent admin-istration. Martin Butler contrasts Jonson's fate to that of his con-temporaries in the Caroline popular theaters in order to underline and celebrate the popular theater's anticourt sentiments: "It is naive and frankly starry eyed to suppose that the professional dramatists were tumbling over each other in a pell-mell race for court favours; they had only to look at Jonson—paralysed, penniless, and forgot-ten—to see where that led" (1984, 102). Conversely, revisionists such as Malcolm Smuts (1987; 1991) and Kevin Sharpe (1987) have sought to redeem the Caroline court. Sharpe sees Sir William Davenant as the chief successor to Jonson as a writer of didactic comedy and masques. In Sharpe's view, the high moral seriousness of Davenant's writings puts him within reach of the benchmark left by Jonson. Butler's account of Jonson as opposed to the court assumes a sharp division between middle and late Jonson and between Caroline drama in general and Jonson in particular, while Sharpe's revisionist account assumes fundamental continuities between them.

Though opposition and revisionist critics differ in their literary histories of late Jonson and of Caroline masque and drama, they both assume the same model of politics: Jonson was either oppositional or orthodox. I wish to challenge this assumption and rewrite the literary history that follows from it not by advancing new readings of Jonson's late plays and masques but by attending to problems of reception faced by Jonson and other Caroline playwrights. I want to resituate Jonson's career and his position vis-à-vis his contemporaries in relation to the Caroline court's licensing and censorship practices. In so doing, I do not want to deny that Jonson's career is broadly marked by shifts from an early period of difficulty to consolidation in 1604, and then to a renewed crisis in the late 1620s and into the 1630s. Jonson's epistles mendicant to the king's exchequer, Arthur Squib (*Underwood* 45, 54), to King Charles (*Underwood* 62, 71, 76), to the Household (*Underwood* 77), and to his patron the earl of Newcastle (H & S, 1:213) asking for financial relief make that crisis evident enough.

I do think, however, that it is a mistake to overstate the differences implied in this account of his career. Jonson was by no means consistently a failure during Charles's reign. There are no records of court performances in the late 1620s, and it is thus far from clear whether Jonson chose to withdraw from the court and cease writing masques or was not preferred. Moreover, the failure of *The New Inn* has overshadowed the success of *A Tale of a Tub,* at least on the professional stage. Nor did Jonson entirely lose favor at court. In 1634 his entertainment *Love's Welcome at Bolsover* was performed for Charles and Henrietta Maria at the earl of Newcastle's estate. In it, Jonson satirized Inigo Jones as Colonel Iniquo Vitruvius (the very name the Master of the Revels had censored in *A Tale of a Tub*). Surprisingly, Charles seems not to have been disturbed by the satire; he subsequently intervened with the city authorities on September 18, 1634, forcing them to pay the pension of one hundred nobles they were refusing Jonson on the grounds that he had done nothing for the city. (The city subsequently paid it until Jonson died.) And *Epicoene* was revived and performed at court in 1635, and *Volpone* in 1638. Moreover, just as Jonson's position was never entirely destabilized at the Caroline court, so his position was never entirely stabilized at the Jacobean court. "An Execration upon Vulcan" (a poem, as we have seen, concerned with the censorship of Jonson's writings) was written in 1623, soon after *Time Vindicated* (1621), a masque concerned with censorship of political satire, which was "not liked" by the court. In "An Expostulation with Inigo Jones" Jonson explains his failure at the Caroline court in terms of a fundamental continuity in the licensing practices of the early Stuarts which reaches back from 1631 to *Bartholomew Fair*. Jonson denigrates Inigo Jones through a double allusion to that play, recalling his satire of Jones as the puppet master Leatherhead and equating him with the incompetent Justice Overdo: "How would [Jones] firk, like Adam Overdo, / Up and about, dive into cellars, too, / Disguised, and thence drag forth enormity" (79–81).

Just as the internal divisions in Jonson's career are not as sharp as has been commonly assumed, so too the external contrast between his failures and the successes of other Caroline playwrights has been overstated. Jonson's troubles are often regarded as peculiar to him, but in fact, they were widely shared. Indeed, one can find the equivalent of any problem Jonson faced during Charles's reign in the careers of a number of his Caroline contemporaries. Massinger, Shirley, Nabbes, and John Ford all faced similar difficulties.[2] If *The Magnetic Lady* and *A Tale of a Tub* were censored, so too were plays by Massinger, Davenant, and Shirley, among others. And if Jonson's plays failed on the public stage, so too did the plays of other dramatists. The dedicatory poem for Nabbes's *Unfortunate Mother* by C.G. alludes to *The New Inn* as compensation for the failure of Nabbes's play:

> I doe not wonder that great *Johnson* Play
> Was scorn'd so by the ignorant, that day
> It did appeare in its most glorious shine.
> (1882–89, 10–12)

(Nabbes's fourth play was rejected by the actors of the Salisbury Court Theater.) Similarly, Thomas Carew comforts Davenant for the failure of *The Just Italian* by suggesting that Davenant is in good company:

> For they'll still slight
> All that exceeds Red Bull, and Cockpit flight
> Behold the benchers bare, though they rehearse
> The tearser Beaumonts or great Jonson's verse.
>
> (Davenant 1872, ll. 20–23)

As we saw in Chapter 1, Caroline dramatists voiced complaints similar to Jonson's about their censorious audiences. In the epilogue to *Covent Garden Weeded* (1632), for example, Thomas Nabbes preemptively attacks censorious Catos:

> 'Tis arraigned [the play];
> And doubtful stands before your *judgements barre,*
> Expecting what your severall *censures* are.
> Some that pretend *commission* to the *Stage.*
> As th'only *Catos* of this *Critick Age.*
>
> (Nabbes 1882–89, ll. 9–13)

Jonson generally registered the analogy between censor and theater audience in relation to his failures, but he was by no means exceptional in this regard. Though Carew criticized him for showing "immodest rage" at the production and reception of *The New Inn,* antagonisms between other playwrights and their audiences revealed similar problems. Massinger's "Charm for a Libeller" alludes to Jonson's "Ode to Himself," attacking the "velvet and plush" members of the audience. Moreover, in the same poem Massinger is as aggressive as Jonson. He employs the trope of the brand Jonson had used in the epistle to *Volpone* and elsewhere:

> Nor shall the brand
> of infamie stamp't on thee by my hand
> bee washt of by thy barbers subtillist arte
> but still growe fresher.
>
> (Beal 1980, 124–27)

In his dedication to Davenant's play *The Wits,* Carew employs tropes Jonson regularly used to the same end, namely, to criticize the audience's judgment in relation to its "liberty" and "privilege":

> It hath been said of old, that plays are feasts,
> Poets the cooks, and the spectators guests,
> The actors waiters: from this simile
> Some have deriv'd an unsafe liberty,
> To use their judgments as their tastes; which choose,
> Without control this dish, and that refuse.
> But wit allows not this large privilege.
>
> (Davenant 1872, ll. 7–13)

Similarly, the epilogue of *The Unfortunate Lovers* satirizes the privilege the audience exerts over Davenant's play. Moreover, Jonson was no more antagonistic to other playwrights than they were to each other, as the second war of the theaters (among Massinger, Davenant, Carew, and Shirley) makes clear (Bas 1963; Grivelet 1954).

To account for the divisions and the continuities in Jonson's career as it traverses the Jacobean and Caroline courts, and to account as well for how those divisions and continuities structure the relationship between Jonson and his Caroline contemporaries, we need to theorize reception in relation to the heterogeneous tastes of Jacobean and Caroline audiences rather than assume that the reforms of the Caroline court involved a decisive break with the Jacobean court which made some genres of drama receivable and others unreceivable.[3] That assumption fails to account for the uneven reception of the works of major and minor Caroline dramatists. As Martin Butler points out, Caroline theatrical repertoires denied firm distinctions between audiences (1984, 129–32). And Kevin Sharpe has rightly argued that the court did not attempt to impose an official agenda on the theaters:

> The court appears to have staged a broad spectrum of plays from the professional theater. It would seem that most of the court plays subsequently enjoyed a life on the public stage. . . . Contrary to traditional generalizations about "cavalier" drama, the evidence suggests that the king's tastes ranged widely and did not occlude political

debate and discussion. A list of performances at court dispels any myth of a uniform courtly mode characterized by effete style, trivial subjects, and fawning flattery. (Sharpe 1987, 35, 39)

While I agree with Butler and Sharpe that court tastes were heterogeneous, I differ in my account of the politics of the court's cultural heterogeneity. Butler's and Sharpe's accounts of Jonson and Caroline drama follow from their reading of this differential system, particularly the relationship between the court and popular theaters. They wish to resolve the court's contradictions. Butler attempts to recuperate a unified oppositional politics in most of the Caroline drama by differentiating popular theaters (private and public) from the court theater, locating this difference in two audiences, one composed of a parliamentary urban gentry, the other of courtiers who lived in the "hothouse atmosphere of Whitehall" (1984, 129). Butler's account has been rightly criticized by Malcolm Smuts (1987) and Kevin Sharpe (1987, 31–35) on two counts: first, the audiences included both Whitehall and the town; there was no radical split between them. Second, as Butler himself points out, dramatists circulated in both court and popular theaters. There was no enclave of unified opposition outside the court itself.

Yet the revisionist account of the court has its own problems. If Butler is wrong to overstate the difference between popular and court theaters and their audiences, Smuts and Sharpe are equally wrong to dissolve it. They recuperate Caroline theatrical culture by ignoring the diversity of the court or by turning its heterogeneity into a unified principle, arguing that it licensed criticism across the board(s), as it were. Smuts, reverting to Alfred Harbage's (1936) Whig notion of a "uniform" court taste, ignores the fact that members of the court circulated among different theaters. Sharpe ignores the problems of reception faced both by Jonson late in his career and by other playwrights. Furthermore, he recuperates Caroline theater by canonizing the masques and drama in strikingly ahistorical terms. In their plays and in their court masques, he says, Caroline playwrights and court poets "addressed ethical and political questions which entitle them to a central place 'of an age' and to some recognition as 'for all time'" (Sharpe 1987, 53).

Ironically, both opposition and revisionist accounts of the court face the problem I noted in Chapter 1. In seeking to rehabilitate

Jonson, these critics reinscribe the kind of unity in Jonson's writings assumed by critics such as Dryden or Edmund Wilson who thought Jonson senile late in his career or immoderately angry throughout it. Just as Dryden and Edmund Wilson (1938) read Jonson's criticisms of his audiences through a unified notion of his personality (all his criticisms were regarded as symptoms of the same mental failings or pathology), so Butler and Sharpe, among others, regard Jonson's plays and masques as forms of criticism the court either licensed or censored.

In my view, it is precisely Jonson's late career that calls into question these strategies for recuperating the drama (or the court). Both opposition and revisionist accounts reinscribe and recuperate a unified opposition outside the court or a unified orthodoxy within it. By contrast, I want to continue to stress the court's contradictions and the incoherence of its model of cultural legitimation. The contradictions of that model shape Jonson's career, moving him toward the court, yet driving him from it at the same time. The court-centered trajectory of Jonson's career may be seen less as a radical decline than as a complex response to the Caroline court's increasingly incoherent model of poetic legitimation and to the way it increasingly undoes the distinctions Jonson wishes to inscribe. With this understanding, we will be able to see that Jonson and his "sons" were equally unable to resolve the contradictions common to Jacobean and Caroline theater.

I

Given the contradictions opened up by the court's own licensing practices, it would be a mistake to view Jonson as simply abandoning a problematic public theater for an unproblematic court theater in 1616. John Sweeney contends that James's authority in the court theater enabled Jonson to resolve the problems that had plagued him in the commercial public theaters: "The royal presence imparted order and meaning that the playhouse could never offer, and, able to assume this kind of authority, in the sense of both relying on it and taking it upon himself, Jonson easily dramatized the problems of response and judgment which were the crux of his misgivings about his spectators. The great masques enact such problems in their antimasques, then resolve or banish them in the display of majesty" (1985, 204). Yet the uneven reception of these Jacobean masques suggests that even James's authority did not enable Jonson to generate easy resolutions in his court masques. We are prevented, therefore, from drawing a strong distinction either between the public theater (in which authority is alienated) and the court theater (with royal authority embodied in the monarch) or between Jacobean and Caroline theater.

The extent to which the critique of court tastes in "An Expostulation with Inigo Jones" is confirmed by both the Jacobean and Caroline court and public theaters can be made clearer by comparing the reception of a late play such as *The Magnetic Lady* (1632) with the reception of Jonson's Jacobean and Caroline masques. *The Magnetic Lady* is Jonson's last in a series of attempts to control the gentry audience which extends back to the satire of the audience in the intermeans of *The Staple of News* and to the satire of Fitzdotterol's attendance at Blackfriars in *The Devil Is an Ass*. In the chorus of *The Magnetic Lady,* what appear to be members of the private theater audience evaluate the play between acts and argue on stage with a character who represents the author's point of view. By including hostile audience criticism within his play, Jonson is able to satirize it, apparently in the hope that similar responses in the play's real audience might thereby be forestalled and corrected. More specifically, Jonson draws a distinction between popular entertainments such as juggling, which he views as the province of artisans, and his own didactic comedy, which he reserves for the gentry: "Do they think this pen can juggle?" Jonson's representative asks the onstage audience. "I would we had Hocus Pocus for 'em then, your people; or Travitanto Tedesko" (Chorus before act 2, 26–27). (Tedesko was an Italian rope dancer.) The boy later upbraids Master Damplay and Master Probee in similar terms: "You are fitter spectators for the bears than us, or puppets. This is a popular ignorance indeed, somewhat better apparelled in you than the people: but a hard-handed and stiff ignorance, worthy a trowel or a hammer-man" (Chorus before act 3, 62–66).

Yet Jonson reveals within the play itself the futility of these attempts to satirize and correct the gentry's taste. Neither Probee nor Damplay accepts the playwright's authority. "This were a strange empire," Damplay exclaims, "or rather a tyranny, you would entitle your poet to, over gentlemen, that they should come to hear and see plays, and say nothing for their money" (Chorus before act 3, 48–50). Somewhat later, Damplay refuses to accept any judgment but his own: "I will not have gentlemen lose their privilege, nor I myself my prerogative, for ne'er an overgrown or superannuated poem of 'em all. He shall not give me the law; I will censure, and be witty, and take my tobacco, and enjoy my Magna Charta of reprehension, as my predecessors have done before me." The boy weakly responds, "Even to license, and absurdity" (Chorus before act 4, 19–24). The gentry insist on their freedom, significantly figured by Damplay as deriving from the Magna Charta, as their freedom from royal authority, to censure as they please, "even to license." As we have seen, *The Magnetic Lady*'s elite audience censured Jonson's play.

The court theater hardly provided an alternative, however, for the judgment of his royal audience often proved no better than that of his public theater audiences as far as Jonson was concerned, even when he was most in favor with the Jacobean court. His reading of the loss of legitimating distinctions in the Caroline theater in "An Expostulation with Inigo Jones" is borne out by attending to the innovations in the performance of masques. The early Stuart court masque was always culturally heterogeneous insofar as it included professionals and courtiers. But that heterogeneity had been sorted out in the Jacobean masque by restricting speaking parts to actors and by opposing them to the court through the antimasque and masque structure. With the growing influence of the duke of Buckingham and Henrietta Maria, however, that distinction ceased to operate, producing what I would call a crisis of difference. Buckingham, along with Henrietta Maria, had lords participate in a masque of November 1626 (since lost) based on Rabelais's *Gargantua and Pantagruel*. It "featured the tall porter (a court notable) as Gargantua, being instructed by the Duke of Buckingham as a fencing master, the Earl of Holland as a school master, and George Goring as a dancing master." The response was not uniformly positive, as the anonymous letter to the Reverend Joseph Mead makes clear: "His grace [Buckingham] took a shape . . . which many thought too histrionical to be come him. . . . never before then did any privy counsellor appear in a masque" (Orgel and Strong 1973, 1:230). As Suzanne Gossett (1988) maintains, early

Stuart masques became increasingly incoherent as the identification between the player and his or her part ceased to obtain. In the Caroline masque, only the king and queen coincided with their roles.

Though the negative reception of his two Caroline masques suggests Jonson had particular difficulty accommodating specifically Caroline practices, the crisis of difference generated by the Caroline court's licensing and censorship practices exacerbates one already present in the Jacobean court. Buckingham had already begun to erode the distinction between courtier and professional under James. The anonymous correspondent of the Reverend Mr. Mead was apparently unaware of *The Gypsies Metamorphosed,* in which Buckingham and other courtiers played parts in the antimasque. Similarly, according to one report, "at Salisbury, August 5, 1620, Buckingham spoke the lines of an Irish footman in an entertainment in which the Marquis Hamilton was a pirate and Sir William Fielding a Puritan" (Gossett 1988, 104).

This continuity between Caroline and Jacobean court theatrical practices can be further established by attending to a contradiction in Jonson's *Masque of Augurs* (1622), possibly a satire of Buckingham's "taste for riotous and farcical anti-masques" (Norbrook 1984b, 84). In this masque, Jonson does not simply mention bears; he actually brings them into the court. A Dutch artist named Vangoose offers to present three dancing bears from the Paris Garden as a masque, but he is forced by the Groom of the Revels to present them instead as an antimasque. Jonson had used bears earlier, in *Oberon* (where they drew Prince Henry's chariot), but by presenting them here as an antimasque and by counterpointing the "rare artist" Vangoose to himself and satirizing him, Jonson attempts to distinguish his own elevated poetry from a popular entertainment such as dancing bears. Yet Jonson's use of bears also registers the court's desire to see the kinds of popular entertainment Jonson regards as uncourtly. Indeed, the very sports and forms of feasting Jonson satirizes and contains through the antimasques were enjoyed not only by favored courtiers such as Buckingham but by James as well. James created an office of "Master of the Kings Bears, Bulls and Dogs" with the power to license commercial entertainments at the Paris Garden, a bearbaiting arena, and James himself watched lion baitings in the Tower of London.[4] Thus an uncomfortable contradiction begins to emerge between Jonson's desire to restrain riotous entertainments such as bearbaitings and the Jacobean court's desire to license them. Jonson is left in the difficult position of having simultaneously to capitulate to court taste and to coerce the court into changing its taste.

The reception of masques such as *Pleasure Reconciled to Virtue* (1618) and *Time Vindicated* (1623) show even more clearly that the problems of license which drove Jonson out of Caroline court theater were continuous with the Jacobean theater; indeed, they are versions of the problems that had initially driven Jonson out of the public theater and into the Jacobean court after *The Devil Is an Ass*.[5] Both masques affirm a distinction between license and liberty and thus, one might think, would have pleased James. *Pleasure Reconciled to Virtue* was occasioned in part by the *Book of Sports,* and distinguishes licentious forms of revelry from licensed and authorized forms (Marcus 1979).

Yet James and his court disliked both masques. Their disfavor may well have been linked, we may reasonably speculate, to the contradiction they reveal between the court's willingness to license forms of revelry and Jonson's desire to suppress them. In *Time Vindicated,* for example, Jonson satirizes carnivalesque forms of entertainment, presenting them as antimasques. The "spectacles" and "sports" licensed by Chronomastix are criticized by Fame:

> You do abuse the Time. These are fit freedoms
> For lawless prentices on a Shrove Tuesday,
> When they compel the Time to serve their riot,
> For drunken wakes and strutting bear baitings,
> That savour only of their own abuses.
>
> (208–12)

(It is worth noting that the second antimasque is composed of tumblers and jugglers.)

As a final instance of the continuities between Jacobean and Caroline Jonson and between popular and court theater, I would like to take up *The Staple of News,* a play that reproduces material from Jonson's masques in the 1620s, including *Neptune's Triumph* and *News from the New World;* its satire of particular figures, such as George Wither and Nathanial Butter, link it to *Time Vindicated*

(1624), and its satire of the news staple as a project links it to the satire of Merecraft in *The Devil Is an Ass*. The recycling of this earlier material, I suggest, marks the near complete collapse of cultural distinctions Jonson masques are designed to affirm.

The Staple of News and the 1620s masques it recycles were in part a topical response to a controversy between the crown and Parliament over freedom of speech (see Young, Furniss, and Marsden, 1958). James had issued a proclamation in 1620 titled "Excess of Lascivious and Licentious Speech," making it punishable for anyone to speak on matters of state (Larkin and Hughes 1973, 1:495). By 1621 he felt that members of Parliament, news writers, and political satirists were exceeding the terms of the proclamation, and so he reissued it. These proclamations coincided with the introduction of a news monopoly and the creation of a news licenser.

In *The Staple of News*, Jonson takes an extreme reactionary position on news and other discursive forms the court regarded as licentious speech. Jonson censures Middleton's *Game at Chess*, a censored play, as we have seen, by imagining its pages as toilet paper used by Gondomar, the Spanish ambassador satirized in Middleton's play:

> *Thomas Barber.* What news of Gondomar?
> (Gondomar's use of the Game at Chess, or play so called)
> *Lickfinger.*   A second fistula,
>   Or an excoriation (at the least)
>   For putting the poor English play was writ of him
>   To such a sordid use as (is said) he did,
>   Cleansing his posteriors.
>
> (3.2.207–11)

The context of this satire, namely foreign news, reveals the implication of the theater in the very kinds of illegitimate discursive practices that prompted Jonson to leave it after *The Devil Is an Ass*.

In the court theater, *Time Vindicated* was Jonson's first attempt to represent the court's position. In the antimasque, the curious believe that the "saturnalia" (28) initiated by Chronomastix, their "Lord of Misrule" (21), will afford them freedom by inverting political hierarchies so that

Ears. Men might talk and do all they list.
Eyes. Slaves of their lords.
Nose. The servants of their masters. And subjects of their sovereign. (30–32)

For these antimasquers,

Eyes. The time's now come about.
Ears. And promise of all liberty.
Nose. Nay, licence

. . . . .

[to talk of] the king.
Ears. Or state.
Nose. Or all the world. (59–60, 173–74)

In response, Fame, the court's spokesman, draws a fine distinction between liberty and license:

> A comely licence! They that censure those
> They ought to reverence, meet that old curse,
> To beg their bread and feel eternal winter.
> There's difference 'twixt liberty and license.
> (177–80)

One would think James would have appreciated the satire of Wither, inasmuch as Wither confessed himself a libeler in *Abuses Strippt and Whipped,* for which he had been briefly imprisoned:

> Yet doe not thinke I meane to blaze your shame,
> In scattered Libels, that shall want a name.
> No, I hate that: I'le tell the illes you doe,
> And put my name for witnesse thereunto.
> Then 'tis but fetching me *ad Magistratum*
> And laying to me *Scandalum Magnatum.*
> (H & S, 10:652)

Indeed, Jonson is at pains to distinguish between Wither and himself, to make clear that his masque, as Sara Pearl (1984) argues, is not a political satire but a critique of political satire. This may well have been Jonson's aim, but it is precisely this distinction between satire and a critique of it that the masque undermines: Jonson engages, as he so often does, in the sort of personal satire he condemns when others practice it. As noted, the court's response was unfavorable. According to Chamberlain: "Ben Jonson is like to hear of it on both sides of the head for personating George Withers a poet or poetaster as he terms him, hunting after fame by being a cronomastix or whipper of the time, which is become so tender an argument that it must not be touched on in jest or in earnest" (*JCS,* 4:674).

Jonson's reactionary and contradictory position emerges in relation to the court's more permissive view of free speech. His inability to make a distinction between legitimate and illegitimate forms of satire registers a larger contradiction in the court's licensing practices, not only of entertainments but of speech and news. The proclamations are not entirely against free speech. In fact, they allow it. According to the first proclamation, dated December 24, 1620: "We doe well allow of convenient freedom of speech, esteeming nay over curious or restrained hand carried in that kind rather as a weaknesse, or else over much severity of Government than otherwise" (Larkin and Hughes 1973, 1:495). But this "greater opennesse, and libertie of discourse, even concerning matters of State," was not vouchsafed to everyone: such matters "are no Theames, or subjects fit for vulgar persons, or common meetings" (Larkin and Hughes 1973, 1:495). Jonson's view is rather different. He imagines that maintaining a distinction between legitimate and illegitimate satire involves abolishing news and popular satire altogether.

The court ended up seeing things Jonson's way. In 1632 after one of the monopolists, Nicholas Bourne, had appeared twice before the Stationers' Company for printing "unfit speeches" and once before the Court of High Commission for associating with the radical printer Michael Sparke, Charles withdrew his patent. But James's earlier, more permissive view of satirists and printers registered the fact that the court's licensing and censorship practices were not consistently aligned with Jonson's interests, in part because the monopoly system was a means of both licensing and censoring specific instances of discourses such as satire instead of censoring them *tout court.* Thus, James might suppress what Jonson wanted to licence, as when he censored *Neptune's Triumph.* The Venetian ambassador comments that the "usual verses written for the masque containing some rather free remarks against the Spaniards, they were altered by his command" (Green 1872, 196). Jonson was concerned to uphold a distinction between his account of the triumph and others that were anti-Spanish. He wrote the masque a year after Charles returned from Spain, a delay he raises as a problem in the masque itself. Replying to the Cook's question about the delay, the poet replies:

> It was not time.
> To mix this music with the vulgar chime.
> Stay, till th'abortive, and exemptoral din,
> Of Balladry, were understood a sin,
> Minerva cried: that, what a tumultous verse,
> Or prose could make, or steal, they might rehearse,
> And every songster had sung out his fit
> That all the country, and the city wit,
> Of bells, and bonfires, and good cheer was spent,
> And Neptune's Guard had drunk all that they meant.
>
> (115–24)

Presumably Jonson wanted to heighten the distinctions both between his account and others' and between his medium and others'—court masque versus news, ballads, and plays such as *A Game at Chess*. Yet if these contrasts were clear to Jonson at the time the masque was to be performed, they were apparently not so clear to James, who canceled the masque when a dispute over precedence broke out between the Venetian and Spanish ambassadors.

The unfavorable reception of many of Jonson's Jacobean masques (and the uneasy mixture of capitulation to and coercion by the court in them) suggests, then, that the court theater itself and not merely the Caroline instance of it, was never a transcendent court of appeal, a clear alternative to the public or private theaters. It was not only the "multitude" at the public theaters, who, as Jonson remarked in the preface to *The Alchemist,* would "commend a writer as they do fencers or wrestlers" (14–15), or the gentry of the private theaters, who liked Hocus Pocus as much as they liked comedy, but the court itself that failed to distinguish rigorously between elevated courtly spectacle and "low" popular entertainment, between discursive practices as different as the news and the masque. Thus Jonson could no more resolve the contradictions in licensing within his masques than he could in his plays.[6]

II

The cultural contradictions within the court itself explain not only the emergence of a full-blown critique of court tastes in "Expostulation with Inigo Jones" and other such poems but a series of related critiques made by a wide range of Jonson's dramatic contemporaries, including Ford and Shirley, as well. These critiques arose from a specifically Caroline reformation of the representation of the aristocratic body. As a number of critics and historians have shown, this reformation turned back the excesses of the Jacobean court, making the genre of pastoral romance receivable in new ways that required alterations in the court masque, the royal couple rather than the monarch being the focus. As a salient example of this shift, Annabel Patterson (1984, 173) has pointed to the successful 1634 revival of *The Faithful Shepherdess* (which had failed in 1612).

Both professional playwrights and the court faced new problems of reception and a broader, disenchanted critique of the court itself (as opposed to local critiques of particular plays it did or did not license) largely because the reformation involved not the return to a more stable set of theatrical practices but the authorization and licensing of striking theatrical innovations, involving the potentially transgressive circulation of actors, plays, costumes, and props, and assignment of speaking parts (transgressive if circulation meant crossing class and gender boundaries). The most controversial of these concerned the representation of aristocratic women on the stage. While the 1634 revival of *The Faithful Shepherdess* was very successful at court, it provoked the most intense criticism (and most fiercely punished) of the early Stuart court's theatrical innovations, namely, William Prynne's.

To be sure, representations of the aristocratic body and of the monarch in the public theaters had also been a concern for James and his censors.[7] Censorship of the representation of the aristocratic body occurs as early as *The Second Maiden's Tragedy* (1611). Similarly, the court censor had been increasingly concerned to regulate the representation of the monarch's body on the stage. Jonson's representation of Elizabeth at the end of *Every Man out of His Humour* was controversial, but the representation of the monarch's body on the public stage was made illegal only under James's reign.

The king's physical presence in London had an important inhibiting effect on what the players might perform, how far they might go in satirizing the court. In his absence, however, they might take liberties in "personating" aristocrats and monarchs. The French ambassador reports, for example, that on "April 8, 1608, I caused certain players to be forbid from acting the Duke of Byron; when, however, they saw that the whole Court had left the town, they persisted in acting it; nay, they brought upon the stage the Queen of France and Mademoiselle de Vernueil" (Bentley 1971, 175). Similarly, *A Game at Chess* was performed when James was out of the city (Bentley 1971, 170). Yet precisely because the monarch was sometimes absent from Whitehall, it was necessary to regulate the representation of his body. *A Game at Chess* was censored, for example, at least partly because it violated the statute against representing a living monarch on the stage. In a letter written August 12, 1624, Secretary Conway addressed the Privy Council:

> His Majesty hath received information from the Spanish Ambassador of a very comedy acted publikly by the King's players, wherein they take boldness and dishonorable fashion, to represent on the stage persons of his Majesty, the King of Spain, the Conde of Gondomar, the Bishop of Spalato, &c. His Majesty remembers well there was a commandment and restraint given against the representing of any modern Christian kings in those stage plays; and wonders much at the boldness now taken by that company. (Middleton 1964, 1:lxxviii–lxxix)

Instead of being in a position to decide the differences between good and bad imitation by codifying good and bad taste, the monarch found it necessary to regulate potentially subversive representations of his body. The very need to regulate the monarch's theatrical representation in the public theaters and the failure to do so effectively (as in these two cases) reveal James's inability to ground legitimating differences.

By the end of his reign, James's court masques also contributed to a decline in the estimation of the court. As David Norbrook writes:

> In the words of one critic, James made "the temple of honour a common theater, into which the basest were suffered to enter for their mony." Unlike stage plays, masques were meant to be exclusive

aristocratic pursuits and not open to the public, but especially after
the inflation of honours the court seemed to have become a corrupt
theatre in which courtiers danced at the king's—or Buckingham's—
bidding. The court masque had come to be a symbol of the dissolution, rather than the defence, of the traditional hierarchical order.
(1984b, 102)

The Caroline court was regularly subjected to an even more tren-
chant critique because of its licensing innovations, even if criticism
of those innovations could be regulated or defused. A number of
cases of court censorship—*The Tamer Tamed* (the 1633 revival); *The
Ball* (1630); and *The Young Admiral* (1632)—mark a specifically
Caroline interest in the reformation of the public theaters.[8] Sir
Henry Herbert's censorship of the revival of *The Tamer Tamed*
suggests the scope of this self-critical reformation. Herbert used
this play as an occasion to rethink censorship of revivals in general:
"It concernes the Master of the Revells to bee carefull of their old
revived playes, as of their new, since they may conteyne offensive
matter, which ought not to be allowed in any time," and added,
"In former times the poetts tooke greater liberty than I allowed"
(Adams 1917, 20, 21). He further specified that copies of the plays
be left with him (so that he could show what he had allowed or
censored) and that actors refrain from learning their parts until he
had licensed the play.

In addition to Herbert's increased control over the public theaters, the court could control reception in other theaters by restricting the audience. William Cartwright's "Prologue to the University" in *The Royal Slave,* to take one example, contrasts the
uniformly positive reception his play will receive from its homoge-
neous audience to the factious response plays performed in commercial theaters will receive:

> No envy then or Faction fear we, where
> All like your selves is innocent and cleare.
> The stage being private then, as none must sit
> And, like a trap, lay wayte for sixpence wit;
> So none must cry up Booty, or cry downe;
> Such mercenary Guise fits not the Gowne.
> No Traffique then: Applause, or Hisse elswhere
> May passe as ware, 'tis only Iudgement here.
>   (1951, 31–38)

Yet Cartwright's assertion that his audience was above faction was short-lived precisely because his play circulated outside its intended university setting. After *The Royal Slave* was performed at Christ Church, Henrietta Maria asked that it be performed by her acting company at Hampton Court. The university and religious authorities tried to keep the scenery from being transferred, as the following report from Archbishop Laud makes clear: "The Chancellor desired that the King and Queen make efforts to ensure that neither the play, or Cloaths, nor Stage, might come into the hands and use of the common players abroad" (Harbage 1936, 152). Similarly, another official made a related objection: "These players had procured from the university all their apparel and the scenes, which the university did not altogether approve of; yet they lent them, but with a letter to my Lord Chamberlain, that because they had provided that entertainment only for their majesties against their coming to Oxford, they humbly besought, that what they had done for the entertainment of their majesties might not be made common upon a stage" (Cartwright 1951, 180). This request was overruled by Henrietta Maria, who nevertheless attempted to observe their wishes: "In ye Meane time you may be confident no Part of these things yt are come to our hands, shall be suffered to bee prostituted vpon any Mercenary Stage, but shall be carefully Reserv'd for our owne Occassions and particular Entertainments at Court" (Cartwright 1951, 181).

But the queen's figure for the illegitimate circulation of theatrical costumes—"prostituted"—was as likely to intensify as it was to ease anxiety on the part of the university. The problem with these new ways of circulating actors, props, poets, and audiences was that they involved transgressing gender divisions that had hitherto kept women actors off the stage. A French troupe with women actors performed in London in 1629, and the queen acted in a French pastoral in 1626 and then in the courtier Walter Montague's *Shepherd's Paradise* in 1632. The depiction of women by boy actors had always been controversial, and a woman playing a woman was perhaps even more alarming (see Orgel 1988). Thomas Brande, for example, on November 8, 1629, criticized the French troupe that played in London:

Furthermore you should know that last daye certaine vagrant French players, who had been expelled from their owne contrey, and those women did attempt, thereby giving just offense to all vertuous and well-disposed persons in this town, to act a certain lascivious and unchaste comedye in the French tonge at the Blackfryers. Glad I am to saye they were hissed, hooted, and pippen-pelted from the stage, so I do not thinke they will soone be ready to try the same againe. Whether they had a licence for so doing I know not; but I do know that, if they had licence, it were fit the Master [of the Revels] be called to account for the same" (*JCS*, 1:25)

Brande's account is of course a fiction. The troupe performed three times without interference. Yet even the fiction had force. Apparently sensitive to Brande's kind of criticism, Charles restricted the audience for the queen's first performance as an actor at court. The Tuscan dispatch reports on the marquis de Racan's *Artenice:* "The performance was conducted as privately as possible, inasmuch as it was an unusual thing in this countrey to see the Queen upon the stage; the audience was consequently limited to a few of the nobility, no others being admitted" (Orgel and Strong 1973, 1:384). Similarly, Sir Thomas Puckering comments satirically on the restrictions the court imposed on the performance of *The Shepherd's Paradise:* "My Lord Chamberlain saith no chambermaid shall enter, unless she sit cross-legged on the top of a bulk. No great lady shall be kept out, though she have but meane apparel, and a worse face, and no inferior lady or woman shall be let in, but such as have extreme brave apparel and better faces" (*JCS*, 4:918).

Yet Charles's restrictions did not prevent censure of his court's theatrical innovations, which were received negatively by courtiers, gentry, and ambassadors. In a report on *Artenice,* for example, the Venetian ambassador comments: "It did not give complete satisfaction, because the English objected to the first part (attione) being declaimed by the Queen" (Orgel and Strong 1973, 1:385). Similarly, commenting on Montague's *Shepherd's Paradise,* Chamberlain states: "A queen on a stage would once have been thought a strange sight" (*JSC,* 4:113). And Henry Manners remarks on the same performance: "I heare not much honor for the Queen's maskes, for, if they were not all, soome were in men's apparell" (Harbage 1936, 12).[9]

Of course the most vociferous attack on women actors was made in *Histriomastix* by William Prynne, who also mentioned the recent visit of French players: "as they now have female players in Italy, and other forraigne parts, and as they had such *Frenchwomen Actors,* in a Play not long since personated in Blackfriers playhouse, to which there was great resort" (1632, 214). Some "Frenchwomen, or monsters, rather," he continues, "in Michaelmas term, 1629, attempted to act a French play at the playhouse in Blackfriars, an impudent, shameful, unwomanish, graceless, if not more than whorish attempt" (214). And the authorities saw Prynne's index entry "women actors notorious whores" as a libelous attack on Henrietta Maria for having acted in *The Shepherd's Paradise.*

In response to these censures, the court did not further restrict audiences for the queen's theatricals but instead addressed, with varying degrees of directness, a broader public. At Charles's command, *The Shepherd's Paradise* was performed at court the day after Prynne was sent to prison, the point being, we may reasonably infer, that the court publicly repudiated him. Further, Ford's *Love's Sacrifice* and Shirley's *Bird in a Cage* (both performed in private theaters) took up the issue of women actors presumably to legitimate the court's practice.

Yet in doing so, these plays compounded a problem already present in Prynne's critique, namely, the paralleling of contemporary politics with those of the past. As part of his legal defense, Prynne disavowed paralleling as a critical technique in *Histriomastix,* claiming that Montague's play was performed after he had written his book. Annabel Patterson (1984, 105–7) sees Prynne's disavowal as a general model for the drama, but it is precisely the assumption that the meaning of a parallel could be readily determined that Prynne's case calls into question. There is no reason to assume that Prynne in fact intended the critique. He may well have. Certainly his argument that the book appeared in print before the queen's performance in *The Shepherd's Paradise* and thus could not have been intended as a critique is belied by its registration at the Stationers' Company after the play was performed. Nevertheless, it does not follow that Prynne necessarily had it in mind. Whatever his intentions, determining the meaning of a parallel between past and present court theatricals was difficult not only because the parallel could be a means of legitimation as well as critique but because the meaning of the parallel was hard to control either by critics or by the authorities and their dramatic supporters.

Dramatists who established a parallel ostensibly to legitimate the queen did so in ways that were at best disquieting, at worst verging on unintended vindication of the critique attributed to Prynne. Consider *Love's Sacrifice,* the first dramatic response to Prynne's attack. A rewriting of *Othello,* Ford's play includes an interlude in which ladies act. The Duke (the equivalent of Othello) advises a courtier, Ferentes: "Be it your charge to think on some device / To entertain the present with delight." Ferentes responds that he saw

> The duke of Brabant welcome the Archbishop
> Of Mentz with rare conceit, even on a sudden
> Perform'd by knights and ladies of his,
> In nature of an antick; which methought,
> (For that I ne'er before saw women-anticks)
> Was for the newness strange, and much commanded.
>
> (1:439–40)

Critics are divided over which Caroline theatrical practice Ford alludes to here. Whereas Frederick Fleay thought that the ladies mentioned were the unpopular (with certain critics) French players of 1629, Bentley (*JCS,* 4:124) has argued that Ford's play represents the queen's theatricals, approvingly. I take this critical debate to be an index of the problem faced by a dramatist such as Ford.

Fleay and Bentley make their respective choices on the shared assumption that *Love's Sacrifice* either approves or disapproves of women actors, but in fact, the play contradicts precisely this assumption. When Ferentes suggests that the ladies perform, he commends them, as Bentley notes. But Ferentes is himself a licentious character. He has propositioned all the ladies who perform in the masque, and in a fine piece of dramatic irony, they take their revenge through the masque itself. The stage direction reads:

> The women hold hands and dance about Ferentes in divers complimental offers of courtship; at length they suddenly fall upon him and stab him; he falls, and they run out at several doors. The music ceases. (1:452)

Not surprisingly, Ferentes then changes his mind about the desirability of women actors, exclaiming: "A pox upon your outlandish feminine anticks!" (1:452). The murder by the ladies is received within the play in contradictory ways. Initially, the Duke commands that the ladies be sent to prison, but Julia, one of the women actors, interrupts him: "We did it and we'll justify the deed" (1:453). Since Ferentes pledged himself to all three women and compromised them, she explains, they have taken matters into their own hands: "unable to revenge our public shames, but his public fall, / . . . thus we have contrived. For thee monster" (1:454). Just as Julia's justification appears to win the Duke over, she proceeds to stab Ferentes again. Alienated by Julia, the Duke then falls in with Ferentes, ordering Julia and the other women to cease: "Forbear you monstrous women! Do not add / Murther to your lust; your lives shall pay this forfeit" (1:454). Ferentes, still not dead, chimes in, "Vengeance on all wild whores" (1:454). The Duke then condemns "those monstrous strumpets" to prison. The language here confirms Prynne's critique: "monstrous," "whore," and "strumpet" all echo the rhetoric of *Histriomastix*. The play does not confirm this unsettling parallel, however, for the Duke does not have the last word. The scene closes with the Abbot moralizing upon the murder in a way that is partly sympathetic to the ladies: "Here's fatal sad presages; but 'tis just, / He dies by murther, that hath lived in lust" (1:453–54). Rather than simply establish the unequivocal meaning of the parallel between the play and the court, Ford's play reveals the difficulty of doing so.

This kind of difficulty is even clearer in the case of James Shirley, the court's point man in the theatrical attack on Prynne. Shirley apparently made his way into favor by defending the court, particularly Henrietta Maria, against Prynne's charge that women actors were notorious whores. (Shirley was preferred by Queen Henrietta and made a valet of her chamber.) In *The Ball,* Shirley had defended the French troupe. The character Freshwater, speaking of his travels in France, says: "But there be no such comedians as we have here; yet the women are the best actors, they play their own parts, a thing much desired in England by some ladies, inns o'court gentlemen, and others" (1833, 3:79). Shirley wrote a dedicatory poem in *Love's Sacrifice* and went on to satirize Prynne in the dedication of *The Bird in a Cage.* Shirley's play, performed by Queen Henrietta's Men, comprehends "another play or interlude, personated by Ladies" (of course played by boy actors).

The interlude of *The Bird in a Cage* parallels the queen's performances in a number of respects. Its audience is carefully regulated. Donella remarks to the other ladies: "We can receiue no disparagement, our spectators cannot jeere vs, for weele speake but to the people in the hangings" (3.3.10–12). The interlude also observes the traditional convention of suiting the part to the masquer. The casting of Eugenia is tied to her present circumstances as a prisoner at court. As Donella tells her: "You shall play *Danae,* that is shut up in the Brazen Tower" (4.2.19–20). Eugenia answers: "Well I'm contented, 'twill suit with my present fortun" (4.2.20–21). Donella notes a similar parallel, remarking on Eugenia's performance of her part: "This is excellent, she has plaid the part before" (4.2.31). Similarly, Shirley draws a parallel between the actors and himself: Donella ends her prologue by exclaiming "hang Still you learned Cricks of the Time" (4.2.19). Her terms recall Shirley's dedication, which attacks Prynne and laments that Shirley must write in "such a critical age."

The politics of these parallels are difficult to determine. Some critics might want to regard the play as a critique of Caroline culture. Lawrence Venuti (1989), for example, argues that the tension noted by Stephen Orgel and Roy Strong between the Caroline court masque's Platonism and its Machiavellianism forms the basis for a critique of its engagement in sexist oppression. Along similar lines, Martin Butler (1984) points out that in the second scene of *Love's Cruelty* Shirley alludes to Jonson's *Neptune's Triumph* in the dramatic context of an attempted seduction of an aristocratic lady. Conversely, Kim Walker (1991) has said that *The Bird in a Cage* is orthodox, containing women in the service of patriarchy.

Critics arguing either case can certainly adduce evidence in support of their readings. Opposition critics could point out that the interlude authorizes a critique of the father's restraint. As Eugenia exclaims:

> Was ever Father to his childe
> So unkind, it makes me wilde.
> When to beguile a tedious houre,
> From the very top of this high Tower,
> I see every other Creature
> Injoy a Liberty by Nature.
>
> (4.2.21–26)

The play ends with Philenzo announcing to Eugenia, "You are free" (5.1.36), as she is permitted to leave her prison and marry him, the man she has wished to marry all along.

Yet one could also maintain that this critique is in the service of orthodoxy. The interlude upholds the modesty of the court lady, saving the woman actor from Prynne's critique. Shirley's play is thus not a critique of court seduction but an authorization of the court lady who knows how to read it and not be seduced. Eugenia is always already obedient and modest. Her father is viewed as mad for attempting to restrain her. The interlude is followed by Rollardio's attempted and unsuccessful seduction of Eugenia (who doesn't recognize him), upon which Rollardio reveals himself to her as her lover, the previously banished Philenzo. Female honor turns out to be nonnegotiable: the daughter's inner restraint is stronger than her father's absurd, superfluous external restraint.

In further support of this orthodox reading, one could point to the play's disavowal of male transvestism. The courtier Morello wears a petticoat to attempt a passage to the sequestered ladies. He is caught and sentenced to wear the petticoat for a month or be perpetually exiled from the court. At the end of the play, his "petticote is discharged" (5.1.35), and he is brought back into the Duke's service. Significantly, it is Morello's strategy from which Rollardio's is distinguished: "Nor could counterfeit another sex becommingly as t'other gaudy Signior, to introduce me to the Ladies, yet with your Princely licence I may say, 'tis done" (5.1.9–12).

Rather than merely confirm the orthodox reading, however, I suggest that *The Bird in a Cage* vacillates between opposition and orthodoxy. The play is faithful and most parallel to the court in its very incoherence, an incoherence due to the way that part and actor do not coincide (as in the public theater itself). The play participates in the Caroline collapse of the distinction between court and public theaters. If, like the queen's theatricals, the interlude is restricted to a coterie audience, the audience of Shirley's play of course is unrestricted, open to jeerers. Similarly, the play confuses the question of women actors, inasmuch as the women's parts are performed by boys.

Apart from these problems of theatrical representation, the interlude raises the very problems about sexuality and women actors the Caroline court was concerned to resolve. If Shirley seeks to widen the scope of "princely license," the interlude raises disquieting questions about the "poeticall license" taken by women actors. The ladies make bawdy puns about their status as players. As Donella says, "There be some call themselves Poets, make their Rimes straddle so wide, a 12. Moneth will hardly reconcile 'em, and I hope, a lady may straddle a little by Poeticall Licence" (4.2.16–19). Similarly, Donella remarks, "Doe not distrust your own performance, I ha' knowne men ha' bin insufficient, but women can play their parts" (3.2.3–4). Further, the interlude is derived from the myth of Jupiter and Danae, a myth that calls into question the court's orthodox notions of sexual behavior. Shirley points to Jupiter's bisexuality. "I to day / Have bid *Ganimed* goe play" (4.2.9–10), Donella says as she acts the part of Jupiter (perhaps recalling gossip that Buckingham was James's Ganymede?). And Shirley interrupts the interlude (through the device of a bell) just as Donella is about to bed Danae. The possible consequence of the interlude's gender confusion—a lesbian transvestite affair—is not simply awkwardly shoved aside by the interruption but awkwardly called to our attention. Donella concludes: "Beshrew your Belman, and you had not wak'd as you did madam, I should ha' forgot myself and play'd Jupiter indeed with you, my imaginations were strong upon me; and you lay so sweetly" (4.2.32–35). The interlude confuses actor and part in a near scandalous way. The careful parallels Shirley draws between dramatic part and actor are not entirely under his control. Indeed, Shirley parallels most closely the most heterodox figure in the play, the theater manager/critic/actor Donella.

But perhaps the more serious problem with the orthodox reading is that the play's orthodoxy is itself nearly oppositional in a crucial respect, namely, its inconsistent distinction between Eugenia and the other ladies, particularly Donella, whose abilities as an actor ("I'll wanton Jove it," 4.2.34) call her modesty into question. The play within the play does not uphold a clear distinction between modest and immodest women actors. The play itself is selected by Eugenia, but the idea for the play is suggested by Donella when Eugenia is absent. Donella, not Eugenia, asks the ladies for their approval: "D'ye allow it" (3.3.9). Yet Eugenia's solidarity with the women is reaffirmed at the end of act 4, after the interlude has been performed. Thus, Eugenia is positioned contradictorily, both identified with the other ladies and differentiated from them. The play evades two uncomfortable ways of resolving the contradiction: if Eugenia is just like Donella, she is vulnerable to the antitheatrical critique; if she is redeemed from this critique through her distinction from the other women actors, however, she is also implicitly in opposition to Henrietta Maria.

Despite the contradictions I have noted, the reception of *The Bird in a Cage* appears to have been favorable, and Shirley was preferred to write the next court masque, *The Triumph of Peace,* sponsored by the Inns of Court to make up for Prynne's attack on the court. But there is no reason to believe that everyone favored *The Bird in a Cage* for the same reasons. Some may have liked it as an endorsement, others as a critique of the woman actor. Furthermore, the play opens up interpretive possibilities rather than closes them down. The ladies' interlude is interrupted, for example, and hence neither approved nor disapproved by its audience. In allowing for a range of conflicting interpretations of the woman actor, the contradictions and indeterminacies of Shirley's play are similar to those of his masque *The Triumph of Peace* and help, perhaps, to account for its mixed reception.[10] But Shirley's checkered career suggests that indeterminacy had its limits as a strategy of theatrical and cultural legitimation. *The Ball* had been censored in 1630. And though Herbert went on to praise *The Young Admiral* the same year, Shirley struck back at him in *The Lady of Pleasure* (licensed in 1635). After *The Triumph of Peace,* he fell out of favor at court and left London for Dublin in 1636.

As a final instance of how the contradictions of the court's licensing practices affected Caroline playwrights other than Jonson, we may turn to the emergence of the courtier dramatist. During the 1630s, the distinction between courtiers and professional dramatists blurred as courtiers ceased to disdain having their plays either published or performed. Unlike their Jacobean counterparts, such Caroline poets as Thomas Killigrew, Walter Montague, and Sir John Suckling were more clearly part of the court. Carew was made a personal servant in Charles's retinue, and Davenant and Edmund Waller both had secure positions in the queen's entourage. According to Malcolm Smuts (1987), their position was therefore more secure than that of their precursors. Moreover, the plays of courtiers required no license at all (Harbage 1936, 99). The blurring of the distinction between courtier and professional, however, did not mean that the court consolidated its hold over the theater; it increased rather than decreased friction.

The most prolonged and deep-seated antagonism of courtier and professional was that between Richard Brome and Sir John Suckling, and it is to Brome I now turn. Suckling's *Aglaura* was performed by the King's Men with extravagant costumes and printed in a folio edition mocked by Brome, who brought the conflict to a head in *The Court Beggar*. Brome's play was unlicensed and subsequently banned; the theater manager was briefly imprisoned and permanently stripped of his position.

Modern critics have tended to focus on the play's satire of monopolies granted by the court and to downplay its personal satire of Suckling and Davenant, treating it as a separate issue. Debate turns largely on the status of the play's conclusion, in which all projects are canceled and the projector is thrown out of doors. Martin Butler (1984, 220–28) sees the play as a radical critique of monopolies, whereas Albert Tricomi has maintained that the play is a reformist critique (and hence favorable to the court), that its reformist intentions were aligned with the court's own inclinations (1989, 182–85). Charles had already voided a number of patents, and Tricomi therefore concludes that the play was dramatizing a winning opposition issue, that it was censored only because it satirized Suckling, though Tricomi, like Butler, regards this personal satire as incidental to the main satiric target, court monopolies. While Tricomi is no doubt right to say that Butler overstates his case, Tricomi's account of *The Court Beggar* more accurately describes *A New Way to Pay Old Debts*, Massinger's satire of the monopolist Sir Giles Mompesson, which reproduces the court's own critique of monopoly.[11] As a reformist play, *A New Way* went uncensored.

I suggest that the politics of *The Court Beggar* become intelligible if we think of them as transgressive in reactionary rather than revolutionary terms. To do so it is necessary to see the personal satire as inseparable from the critique of monopolies. Unlike the earlier moment in which Massinger wrote, by the mid-1630s the court monopoly system was threatening to collapse the difference between courtier and professional dramatist. Brome, like Jonson, was a social conservative (Kaufman 1961), defined, in this case, as one who upheld a guild-centered monopoly system, especially with regard to plays. In the prologue to Thomas Goffe's *Careless Shep-*

herd (1638), probably by Brome, the court's monopolistic practices are satirized insofar as they infringe on the theater. Thrift speaks:

> Sir, was a Poet, or a Gentleman
> That writ this play? The court, the Inns of Court,
> Of late bring forth more wit, than all the Tavernes,
> Which makes me pity playwrights; they were poor
> Before, even to a proverb; Now their trade
> Must needs go down, when so many set up.
> I do not think but I shall shortly see
> One Poet sue to keep the door, another
> To be prompter, a third to snuff candles.
> Pray, Sir, has any Gentleman of late
> Beg'd the Monopoly of Comedies?
>
> (Bentley 1971, 59)

Brome wrote, as far as we know, exclusively for the professional theater, and he and others saw the theater as a guild. Jonson's dedicatory poem to *The Northern Lasse* contrasts an older, stable relation between master and servant-apprentice (Brome is Jonson's "old faithful servant") to the current crossing of professional boundaries:

> I had you for a servant, once, Dick Brome;
> And you perform'd a servant's faithful parts,
> Now, you are got in a nearer room,
> Of fellowship, professing my old arts.
> And you do them sell, with good applause
> Which you have justly gained from the Stage
> By observation of those comic lawes
> Which I, your master, first did teach the age.
> You learn'd it well, and served for your time
> A prentice-ship: which few do nowadays.
> Now each Court-hobby-horse will wince in rhyme;
> Both learned and unlearned, all write plays.
> It was not so of old: Men took up trades
> That knew the crafts they had been bred in right:
> An honest Bilbo-Smith would make the blades,
> And the physician teach men spue or shite,
> The cobbler kept him to his nail, but now
> He'll be a pilot, scarce can guide a plough.
>
> (Brome 1653, 3:ix)

Similarly, John Hall contrasts Brome to courtiers on the basis of his apprenticeship: "You do not invade; / But by great Johnson were made free o' th'trade" (Brome 1653, 3:345).

The satire of Davenant's theater project and of Suckling may be seen in this light.[12] Davenant's license, blocked, apparently by Sir Henry Herbert, had originally been granted by James in the early 1620s to three entrepreneurs, probably showmen rather than actors. They were permitted to build a huge amphitheater in Lincoln's Field with the unprecedented seating capacity of twelve thousand spectators. These entrepreneurs intended to present not only sea battles, prizefights, and sword fights, but Latin plays, masques, and tilts, the latter an exclusively royal form of entertainment hitherto performed only for the court at Whitehall (*JCS* 6:292–97). When alerted that the license included tilts, James responded by excepting them, drawing a distinction between courtly and commercial entertainments: "We are likewise pleased to . . . grant them a . . . Licence (at all lawfull Tymes) to shew to their best advantage . . . all kinde of Shewes whatsoeuer wch they can deuise, pleasant or delectable to the People Excepting Tilte, (wch no Subiect can sett vpp wth out our Licence) Tourney, Course at the Field, Barriers and such like reserued for Solemnities and Triumphs of Princes, and not to be vilified dayly in the eyes of the Vulgar for money offered" (*JSC,* 6:298). James was further concerned to distinguish the proposed commercial entertainments from aristocratic instruction. He granted the license on the condition that the showmen "practise all these thinges only for Spectacle to the people, not pretending to make yt an *Academy* to instruct, or Teach the Nobilitie or Gentrie of this *Kingdome* onely possible and fitt for Princes to Vndertake, and not to be mixed with *Mercenary* or *Mechanik* ends" (*JSC,* 6:298). The personal satire of Davenant and Suckling is inseparable from a satire of the court monopoly system. For the court's willingness to grant patents threatens the guild-based freedom on which Brome's profession depends. And though Brome's aim, as Tricomi suggests, is reformist, his reform is transgressive because it puts the authority and liberties of his guild-based profession in direct conflict with the crown's prerogative to grant theater patents, a conflict that focused not only on Davenant's license, but perhaps on the authority of the Master of the Revels to license Brome's play as well.

But Brome was on shaky ground in his critique of the court, not only because of the daring of his solution in the play—abolishing patents—or the daring of performing it unlicensed but because it defended an institution that did not really exist. Acting companies were not in fact guilds, though actors were members of guilds, and hence the theaters could not be returned to a guild system free of monopolies. Boy actors (Brome himself was one) were apprenticed to recognized London guilds, not to theater companies (see Orgel 1988). Jonson's poem in praise of Brome throws into relief this problem with Brome's reactionary critique of monopolies. Though Jonson contrasts the apprentice/master relationship to the aristocratic amateurs who invade the trade, Jonson's career contradicts the idealized norm celebrated in his dedicatory poem: Jonson was, after all, a member of the bricklayer's guild.

Far from mounting a revolutionary critique of the court which can be contrasted to Jonson's neoconservative critique, Brome's plays, like Jonson's, were occasionally transgressive because they were reactionary. Thus, if Brome and Jonson shared a common fate, namely, displacement from the Caroline theaters, it would be misleading to see their (and Shirley's) failure to resolve Caroline problems of cultural legitimation as an "opposition" to the court and to courtier dramatists such as Suckling or would-be courtiers such as Davenant. There was in fact no clear opposition between professional and courtier appropriations of Jonson. Jonson's sons came from both groups. Thomas Nabbes, another son of Ben, dedicated his *Covent Garden* to Suckling in 1638, speaking approvingly of *Aglaura:* "Your late worthy labour ha[s] prevented the intentions of many to dignifie in you which are so farr above them." This statement was accompanied by another piece of shameless flattery in which Nabbes contrasted Suckling's "piercing judgment" to that of the stage audience who only "partially approved" the play.

The problems of reception faced by Jonson and his Caroline contemporaries can be explained not in terms of some moral opposition to the court or desire to reform it, but as a response to the contradictions in the court's licensing practices. The court's willingness to license popular forms in the later Renaissance tended to undermine a distinction between aristocratic and common symbolic forms, thereby contributing to what Lawrence Stone has termed the "crisis of the aristocracy" (1967). As Stephen Orgel

(1982) has shown, the ruling elite of Renaissance England had a clear stake in keeping aristocratic forms separate from common, commercial entertainment. In the seventeenth century, however, any distinction between courtly and commercial art became progressively more difficult to establish. Just as the distinction between the landed aristocracy and the "bourgeois" gentlemen was increasingly eroded by James's policy of putting offices, monopolies, and titles up for sale, so the distinction between courtly art forms such as masques or tilts and mercenary, "common" forms of art was eroded by the court's willingness to license and patronize "bourgeois," commercial forms of entertainment.

The extent to which this crisis was exacerbated by the early Stuarts' willingness to license market forces over which they had only limited control can be underscored by putting the early Stuarts in a larger frame, contrasting their court to that of the Restoration and the early eighteenth century, when licensing became more restrictive and courtier playwrights gained the ascendancy as theater managers (White 1931). As we have seen, licensing under the early Stuarts was as much a means of allowing entertainment as a means of censoring it. Even though they licensed them, however, the Stuarts never really had an effective monopoly on entertainments; virtually the only limit on the number of theaters was economic competition among companies, and even companies that went out of business in the capital often restarted later on or toured in the provinces.

The restoration of theater licensing in 1660 was a reform intended to demarcate between legitimate and licentious forms of theater, promoting the former and restraining the latter. Only two licenses were granted (to the courtiers Killigrew and Davenant). Owing "to the Extraordinary Licentiousness that hath benn Lately used In [other plays and entertainments]," Charles II stated in these licenses, "it was his Pleasure . . . that there shall be noe more Places of Representations, nor Companies of Actors of Playes . . . in our Cities of London and Westminster . . . then the two to be now Erected by vertue of this Authority" (Adams 1917, 88). Charles II stated further that licensed plays would be reformed and thereby become a means of civilizing their audiences: "Wee are assured, that, if the Evill & Scandall in the Playes that now are or have bin acted were taken away, the same might serve as Innocent and

Harmlesse diuertisements for many of our Subiects" (Adams 1917, 87).

This restraint of so-called licentious forms of theater benefited the courtier-playwrights Davenant and Killigrew and the monarchy as well. Davenant and Killigrew were able to turn earlier attacks on the immorality of the theater against their competition. Popular entertainers were banished from the stage, as we can glimpse in Davenant's *Playhouse to Be Let* (1663), in which a number of players apply unsuccessfully for the privilege of leasing a newly available theater. The lessors, a player and a housekeeper, send two fencers off to the Red Bull and also dismiss traditional popular entertainers from Jonson's world who managed to survive the civil war:

> All the dry old fools of Bartholomew fair
> Are come to hire our house. The German fool,
> Yan Boridge of Hambrough, and numberless
> Jack puddings; the new motion men of Norwich,
> Op'ra puppets; the old gentlewoman
> That professes the galliard on the rope;
> Another rare Turk that flies without wings;
> Rich jugglers with embroidered budgets.
>
> (1872, 4:24)

That only Davenant and Killigrew were granted licenses to manage acting companies in two theaters also helped ensure that the drama would reinforce and support the monarchy that licensed it. Thus Puritan opposition to the stage and Parliamentary opposition to the monarchy were momentarily preempted. And with the passage of the Stage Licensing Act in 1737, effective censorship put an end to the kinds of drama the established authority did not want staged (Crean 1937–38; Loftis 1963, 128–53; Liesenfeld 1984). The stage was set for the recoding of Jonson's model in neoclassical terms of Augustan poetry and criticism, as Stallybrass and White have shown (1986, 27–79). This stage marked a new threshold of repression in bourgeois subjectivity, new forms of control over popular culture (Malcolmson 1973; Payne 1979), and new forms of censorship (Barker 1984; Davis 1983).

From the Brand to the Brand Name:
Censorship and Political Criticism in the
Early Modern Past and the Postmodern Present

As political critics have sought to turn Renaissance culture to political account in the present, it should not be surprising that Renaissance censorship has received increasing attention, especially inasmuch as censorship marks for many political critics who have participated in the present subversion/containment debate over the theater's politics the decisive determination of the court's politics (barbaric or enlightened). Nor should it be surprising that this attention to Renaissance censorship coincides with a much broader interest in present (and quite different) forms of censorship in the United States and Great Britain having to do with fine-arts funding, advertising regulation, television programming, performances by mass-culture icons such as Madonna and 2 Live Crew, speech codes on university campuses, President Bush's 1991 commencement address on "political correctness" at the University of Michigan, John Frohnmayer's forced resignation from the National Endowment for the Arts the day after Patrick Buchanan, running against Bush in the 1992 presidential primaries, began attacking him for funding "pornography," and Vice President Dan Quayle's attacks on the liberal "cultural elite."[1]

It remains to be considered whether a critique of early modern censorship is congruent with the larger postmodern aim of politicizing criticism to give it an "oppositional" social function. Typically, one might expect that the answer would be affirmative. In this book, historicizing Jonson in particular and the complex dynamics of early modern censorship in general would be said to serve, however indirectly, to illuminate the similarly complex dynamics of censorship in the postmodern present and thereby to expand the possibilities for a critique of its multiple forms. The present book's "payoff" would be less the readings of Jonson and his contemporaries than the way they might widen the scope of an oppositional political criticism, thus turning the past to "political account" (Cohen 1987).

While I consider ways in which a critique of postmodern forms of censorship might be expanded, I wish primarily to interrogate how "accountings" of current critiques of early modern and postmodern forms of censorship are enabled (and, to a significant degree, demanded) by the institution of criticism, an institution that presents itself as always standing unequivocally in opposition to censorship. The desire expressed by many avowedly political critics to recode the past and thereby oppose oppressive social forces and structures in the present has tended to deflect attention away from questions internal to the practices of criticism, questions involving academic freedom and the role the institution of criticism plays in legitimating and delegitimating critical discourses. Ironically, the tendency of political critics to legitimate themselves by invoking a universal, ahistorical definition of censorship has left them unprepared to deal effectively with present forms of censorship both internal to the discipline of English studies and external to it (such as the current right-wing assault on the fine arts, mass culture, and higher education and cultural studies in particular). I suggest, by contrast, that historicizing censorship means that different forms of censorship must be read in a local way rather than in terms of a theory or an ahistorical hermeneutics of censorship.[2]

This alternative involves a rethinking of criticism (both literary and cultural) and of the position of the critic with regard not to humanist notions of freedom (what Foucault terms the general-intellectual) but to post-Marxist notions of the "liberatory" and the specific-intellectual.[3] Above all, it means rethinking the widely held assumption that criticism is always institutionally constrained, hence always political. The critical profession has tended to legitimate itself by appealing to an aristocratic model of cultural distinction (see Larsen 1977, 80–103; Bourdieu 1988). Critical legitimation and professional accreditation require both the acquisition of cultural capital and the disavowal of that acquisition: in a way that generally goes without saying, the authentic critic is opposed to the self-seeking, careerist professional. As Pierre Bourdieu argues, the acquisition of cultural capital depends on a fundamental institutional, structural censorship that is misrecognized as such:

> The metaphor of censorship should not mislead: it is the structure of the field itself which governs expression, and not some legal proceeding which has been specially adapted to designate and repress the transgression of a linguistic code. This structural censorship is exercised through the medium of the sanctions of the field, functioning as a market on which the prices of different kinds of expression are formed; it is imposed on all producers of symbolic goods, including the authorized spokesperson, whose authoritative discourse is more subject to the norms of official propriety than any other, and it condemns the occupants of dominated positions either to silence or to shocking outspokenness. (1991, 138)

In following Bourdieu, I want not only to widen the scope of a critique of censorship but to critique the ways in which critique itself is implicated in censorship.

I take the reception of a moral definition of censorship in Renaissance studies as my point of departure. In historicizing the Renaissance to criticize aspects of the current social order, political critics have tended to transfer their ahistorical definition of Renaissance censorship to the present. Why, we may ask, is an ahistorical, moral definition of censorship professionally receivable? Why hasn't early modern censorship itself been historicized by political critics? The answer, I think, lies in the way an ahistorical definition helps to legitimate the institution of criticism in general and Renaissance critics in particular. This definition of censorship makes available in the Renaissance a certain essentially moral notion of critical opposition, which in practice means that when reading Renaissance texts, the political critic looks either for secret messages that escaped the censor or for criticism openly licensed and countenanced by the court. By extension, a similar kind of critical opposition becomes available in the present: the political critic can be seen to oppose at once the professionalism and the formalism of a supposedly apolitical literary criticism and the postmodern (now post-Reaganite and post-Thatcherite) state. Thus censorship and criticism become self-identical terms that can be juxtaposed in a stable opposition; the critic is "opposed" to censorship.

To begin my critique of the legitimating functions enabled by an ahistorical definition of censorship, I turn first to two influential modes of political criticism, namely, liberal humanism and Marxism. I then consider more broadly the pressure to legitimate criticism through this definition in the context of the present debate over "politically correct" criticism (see Berman 1992; Aufderheide 1992). Liberal humanist critiques of censorship assume an opposition between the resisting subject and the repressive state, and that opposition narrows the meaning of censorship in such a way that it virtually disappears from view in the Western present.

This problem can be seen clearly in the eloquent and forceful defense of liberal humanism articulated by Annabel Patterson in *Censorship and Interpretation*. In addressing the implications of her account of Renaissance censorship for criticism in the present, Patterson narrows censorship to two kinds, state censorship and self-censorship. "I suggest the members of our own profession have been guilty of a complicity in a new form of censorship," she writes, "imposed from within the academy. . . . We have handed over to others the absolute control of the public discourse of our time. We have developed the only truly effective system of censorship in the modern world—the one that is self-imposed" (1984, 23). Once censorship is defined in terms of this binary opposition, it follows almost inevitably that a critique of the present is constructed in terms of two radical oppositions, between the Western past and the Western present, on the one hand, and between twentieth-century Western liberal and non-Western totalitarian regimes, on the other. Censorship in the present is identified with non-Western totalitarian regimes, which are seen as analogous to the Renaissance absolutist state. Patterson states, for example that "a description of censorship in Russia *before the revolution*" given by Daniel Balmuth is "virtually identical with my own argument" (1984, 21). She then constructs an equivalence between early modern censorship and that of contemporary Eastern Europe and the Soviet Union: "Today's intellectuals will have to decide for themselves . . . whether we are indeed in a position to feel complacent about our freedoms, in contrast to our ancestors in early modern Europe, or our contemporaries in [Brezhnev's] Soviet Union" (1984, 23).

Philip Finkelpearl makes a similar comparison while endorsing Patterson's account of Renaissance censorship: "Rather than an errorless, mechanistic monster like Nazi Germany, Jacobean England more nearly resembles such inefficient regimes as those in present-day Hungary or (some years ago) Poland and Czechoslovakia. There, in films at least, much is allowed, and more slips by through artistic cunning and the employment of arcane codes mastered by the cognoscenti" (1986, 138). In liberal humanist accounts of Renaissance censorship, differences between forms of censorship give way to the ideological coherence of an ahistorical contrast between censorship and freedom: we are free and they weren't (or aren't). Historically, different versions of censorship are constructed in terms of a division between extremes of the Right and the Left, which is then collapsed (the Right and the Left are the same) and displaced by another opposition between free liberal societies and repressive totalitarian states.

A perceived radical discontinuity between past and present indirectly serves to legitimate the present. Because Western critics presume that censorship does not exist in the "democratic" West (supposedly having ended here in the seventeenth century), they feel free to judge all non–Western forms of censorship as medieval, premodern, unenlightened, and barbaric.[4] Yet this assumption ironically limits the force of a critique of past and present forms of censorship. The immediate problem with a critique of Renaissance censorship, as Patterson herself acknowledges, is that it will prove anachronistic: "A book about the cultural impact of censorship may be seen as both timely and peculiarly academic, a displacement of truly significant issues into memory and mental space" (1984, 3). A critique of Renaissance censorship hardly matters if no such constraints exist in the present. The critique of more recent forms of censorship is similarly problematic. The contradictions and inefficiencies of Soviet or Nazi forms of censorship are occluded, and state censorship remains virtually invisible in modern liberal societies.[5]

A related problem with the liberal humanist model of literary censorship arises with regard to censored writers. As we have seen, once censorship is defined as an opposition between the censoring state and otherwise free writers, writers and literature itself are almost automatically defined as opponents of censorship, as are political critics who rise now to defend freedom of expression. Paradoxically, however, this liberal humanist critique of censorship implicitly legitimates rather than criticizes the present liberal modern state, precisely by leaving it out of account. In this view, state censorship in the West has ended; the only remaining form of censorship is the one that is voluntarily opposed. A further problem for an oppositional humanist is that the relation between past and present can be turned to advantage by revisionists, who have legitimated the Renaissance by differentiating it from a totalitarian regime such as the Stalinist Soviet Union.[6] Revisionists make the contradictions and limitations of the pluralistic liberal humanism they affirm all the more stark: like the Renaissance absolutist state they revise, the liberal state depends on a terroristic expulsion of those who dissent from consensus and pluralism, admitting dissent only because there is a consensus that free-ranging debate is in the participants' mutual interest.

In producing a critique of the early modern past and the postmodern present, Marxists have displaced a modern liberal humanist account of a critique intentionally inscribed by producing authors with a postmodern account of a critique unintentionally inscribed by economic forces of production. Yet like liberal humanists, Marxists share the same historiography of the Renaissance and the same definition of censorship. For Marxists and liberal humanists alike, the English Revolution marked the end of censorship and the emergence of the public sphere and enlightened debate.[7] Thus Marxists do not see censorship as a problem in the present. Indeed, they do not see it at all, censorship having been displaced in the Marxist view by post-Renaissance capitalist forms of subjection. Domination by the brand has given way not to new liberated practices but to domination by the brand name. While capitalism is regularly thought to have progressive tendencies insofar as it opens up new markets among oppressed subcultures, the chief fear of Marxists is that in the present postmodern consumer capitalist regime, these new markets will only become new sites of control and colonization.

This fear is often focused on both aesthetics and criticism. Consumption of elite and mass culture helps to reproduce the status quo by elevating the literary text above history and politics, mystifying the text's ideological production and reproduction. For example, Bertolt Brecht criticizes bourgeois notions of what he calls "culinary" criticism of elite culture:

> The style of today's criticism is culinary. Our critics take a consumer attitude, which does not mean, however, that they enjoy theater and use it in the interest of the public—that is to say, they are on the side of the public, critically facing the theater as consumers; rather, together with the public and theater, they consume the works that have come down to them as so-called cultural goods of their class. One does not produce anymore, one consumes, one enjoys, and one legitimizes a given situation. According to this ritual, the final arbiter in matters of art is taste, in fact a taste that favors individualistic nuances, calling for variations. (Hohendahl 1982, 26)

In similar terms, Max Horkheimer and Theodor Adorno argue in "The Culture Industry: Enlightenment as Mass Deception" (1944) that commodified mass culture serves to incorporate dissent and to induce conformity. Carrying out this line of critique, other Marxists have criticized mass leisure or "free time" as mystified: anything but free, leisure serves the interests of capital by interpellating workers into a capitalist ideology in which freedom is exclusively equated with the choices presented to a consumer (Rojek 1985). Consumption of elite and mass culture functions as a mystified compensation for the lack of real social transformation through the proletariat's ownership and control of the means of production. In Herbert Marcuse's phrase, consumption is a form of "repressive tolerance."

Marxist critique responds by demystifying consumption as an ideological practice, subordinating it to production. In his essay "The Author as Producer," Walter Benjamin, for example, hopes to make consumers into revolutionary producers: "What matters . . . is the exemplary character of production, which is first able to induce other producers to produce, and second, to put an improved apparatus at their disposal. And this apparatus is better the more consumers it is able to turn into producers—that is, readers or spectators into collaborators" (1986, 230). Inasmuch as consumption is for Marxists always a form of repressive social legitimation, it should not be surprising that critique always takes the form of turning consumers into producers or reproducers.

Although this Marxist critique of economic forms of subjection involves an advance over humanist critiques in that it involves a critique of the Western present, the division Marxists perceive between Marxist economic and political forces in the production of culture and the priority they give to economic forces ensure that censorship is marginalized or ignored altogether. Marxists leave little room either for the possibility that consumers could be active, reactionary reproducers of culture or for the possibility that the Left might censor as well. Instead, they have assumed both that politicizing criticism will have a receptive audience, and that aesthetic consumption is always regressive. The transfer of the means of production (from the bourgeoisie either to the proletariat or to some revolutionary vanguard) or the control of cultural reproduction by a professional-managerial class is often assumed to involve the end of censorship (over cultural production) and the democratization of literary criticism. Marx defended the freedom of the press and, along with Engels, declared in a celebrated passage of *The German Ideology* that under communism everyone would be a critic. Marxists and other political critics who have chosen to intervene at the level of cultural reproduction rather than the means of production share a similar assumption: politicizing aesthetics and criticism will automatically produce progressive social change.[8] The choice is between change (assumed to be progressive) and the status quo.

The tendency of Marxists to omit a critique of censorship in the postmodern present follows in large part from their account of literary production. Though Marxists have recently argued that a particular political effect is not inscribed in production, they have nevertheless kept in place an essentialist account of literary production: the economy always has priority over politics within production, and production always has priority over consumption as a determinant of literature. Thus the economy, not politics, will necessarily be the final horizon of interpretation by which the revolutionary potential of a particular text might be gauged, and censorship will be marginalized as a narrower and hence less significant horizon.[9] As we have seen, Marxist histories of literary criticism always begin with the eighteenth century, criticism being under-

stood as the antithesis of censorship.[10] Critique will focus negatively on economic consumption (because it is always essentially
mystified) and positively on converting consumption into production (because production is always essentially the means of
liberation).

Yet the fact that aesthetics and literary criticism too are commodified, part of a culture-critique industry, introduces a certain
pessimism about the capacity of political criticism to succeed in
changing the social order. The institutions of art and criticism along
with the culture industry all neutralize the critical functions of the
public sphere with increasing effectiveness (Burger 1984; Hohendahl 1982). In what Jürgen Habermas has characterized as a transition "from a culture-debating public to a culture-consuming public" (1989, 159–74), the public sphere collapses as a feudal notion of
publicity based on conspicuous consumption, display, and pomp
returns in the form of public relations, displacing and debasing the
critical functions of an enlightened, rational public. Even cultural
critique is absorbed by the commodifying brand name as well.
Terry Eagleton complains, for example, that Fredric Jameson's
work "resembles nothing so much as some great California super-
market of the mind, in which the latest flashiest dressed commodities (Hjemslev, Barthes, Deleuze, Foucault) sit stacked upon the
shelves of some more tried and trusty household names (Hegel,
Schelling, Croce, Freud) awaiting the moment when they will all be
casually scooped into the Marxist basket" (1986, 70–71).[11] Yet Eagleton himself hardly escapes the same commodifying forces, and it
is predictable both that Marxists should arrive at the same kind of
despairing pessimism they so often attribute to post-Marxists such
as Baudrillard and Foucault and that debate between Marxists involves charges that consumption-centered critics are hedonists and
countercharges that production-centered critics are censors.[12]

In securing a distinction between the critic and the censor, these
liberal humanist and Marxist accounts of censorship come at a
significant cost. Liberal humanist critique takes the form of moralistic criticism of censorship that always occurs elsewhere (not, that
is, in political criticism). Similarly, by thinking about the possibilities for social change and the impediments to them primarily in
economic terms, Marxists tend to marginalize or altogether ignore
censorship in the past and present. More crucially, present accounts

of political critics' oppositional relation to the state and the profession leave the critics in a professionally strong position (since political accounts of "literature" are professionally receivable) but relatively impotent to defend themselves against the forces that threaten to strip them of their professional autonomy. This threat is directed not only at avowedly political critics but at any postmodern critic who thinks that all criticism is institutionally enabled and constrained. In the United States particularly, the threat comes not from the supposedly insidious, all-pervasive, and containing economic practices of late capitalism but from the neoconservative and religious Right, who accuse the Left of being, of all things, censors. Roger Kimball, the managing editor of the neoconservative journal the *New Criterion,* remarks in *Tenured Radicals,* for example: "It is a sobering irony that what began as an appeal by the Left for free speech at Berkeley in the sixties has ended with an equally fervent appeal by the Left for the imposition of censorship" (1990, 69). And in a series of editorials and op-ed pieces the *Wall Street Journal* has attacked "ivory censors" who institute a "new orthodoxy" of cultural diversity.[13]

As debates over the politics of criticism and of higher education in general proliferate and intensify, a significant contradiction emerges. While differences between critics are hardening, polarities being put in place, and sides being taken, surprising or unintelligible oppositions and alliances seem to be arising between groups whose interests one would think were opposed. The boundary separating the Right from the Left, for example, is not always clear. Stanley Fish is labeled a "tenured radical" (Kimball 1990), lumped together with the avowedly political critics he criticizes.[14] Similarly, many of the differences that made histories of criticism intelligible are now in question. Anthologies of criticism seem increasingly incoherent in their attempts to integrate an ahistorical literary theory with a history of criticism (Lodge 1988; Selden 1988). It is also surprising that the primary audience for the neoconservative critiques of higher education has been self-identified liberals in the profession itself (Wallen 1991).

A number of explanations are available to account for these contradictions. One could simply say that they are apparent rather than real: the neoconservatives have at best distorted postmodern political criticism, or at worst they've simply gotten it wrong.

Some might wish to discount the right-wing critique precisely because it is being made by the Right. On one side, the religious far Right has vigorously tried to censor 2 Live Crew, a Madonna Pepsi commercial, and other television advertising, and the neoconservatives, led by Lynn Cheney and President Bush, have steered the National Endowment for the Humanities and the National Endowment for the Arts to the right. On the other side, the Modern Language Association has lobbied its members to protest the attempts to restrict funding of the NEA, a broad spectrum of critics and journalists have protested the death sentence against Salman Rushdie, and Henry Louis Gates, Jr., has testified on behalf of 2 Live Crew. In view of these events, any critique of the academic Left's "censorious" practices may seem ludicrously off target.[15] In the face of what some political critics might take to be an instance of the Right's outrageous obscurantism, the best response, these critics would argue, is simply to restate, unequivocally and in essentially libertarian fashion, one's opposition to censorship in any form, whether practiced by the Left or the Right.[16]

Another explanation would address how market forces have driven the profession, and this generally takes two forms, one weak and the other strong. The weak, moralistic form of this critique identifies New Historicists as yuppies (Neely 1987) and claims that their focus on status competition rather than opposition belies their own political situation in the 1980s (Norbrook 1984c). In the stronger version, the present crisis of difference is seen as a function of the autocritical speed of late capitalist modes of critical production and consumption. From this perspective, one could argue that differences between critical practices have become more and more fetishized as criticism has become more and more commodified. Differences are installed in two contradictory ways: on the one hand, critics compete for the most global theory (my theory is bigger than your theory); on the other, critics eschew theory for a practice that is more nuanced, more detailed, slower in arriving at a critical payoff (or not arriving at all) than other practices (an economy of less is more).

I would not want to discount the importance of any of these explanations, nor do I seek to criticize them by measuring them in relation to some authentic materialist critical practice (since that would only inscribe a new idealist theory of materialist criticism).

Instead, I want to problematize both the way the desire to differentiate critical practices functions as a mode of institutional legitimation and the way the legitimation of literary criticism has hinged on a history of criticism that inscribes a radical difference between a modern history of literary criticism (free of institutions and history) and a postmodern theory of the institution of criticism. Instead of breaking with the early modern past, postmodern political criticism marks, in my view, a new phase of a long-standing legitimation crisis.

Various attempts to legitimate the profession by appealing either to neoliberal notions of discourse ethics such as interpretive communities, dialogue, conversation and solidarity, "healthy" debate, controversy, consensus, "teaching the conflicts," multiculturalism, cultural diversity, a public sphere of enlightened debate free of censorship, or to more radical postmodern, often antihumanist notions of "dissensus," textual heterogeneity, and so on have already been compromised to the point of breakdown. As present struggles have intensified over appointments to funding agencies such as the NEH, over who serves on tenure committees, over accreditation procedures and admissions policies—over, in short, who determines who is a critic and who is a censor, over what counts as criticism and what counts as repression—charges of censorship both against and by political critics have proliferated. The legitimation of the critical community increasingly involves the delegitimation of its would-be censors. Yet from the perspective of those who are delegitimated, whether neoconservatives or "tenured radicals," that delegitimation looks like an illegitimate attempt to censor legitimate critics, particularly when the accused "censor" is a member of the critical profession. Indeed, there is a formal symmetry in the rhetoric adopted by neoconservative critics and by the official defenders of the profession (for example, the executive council of the Modern Language Association). Both sides say they are for diversity and open debate; both sides say they are telling the truth and accuse the other of engaging in scurrilous, irresponsible misrepresentation, fraud, distortion, and of attempting to censor or otherwise restrict authentic critical inquiry and genuine dialogue.[17]

Given the present legitimation crisis, it is important that postmodern political critics (in the wide sense of "postmodern" noted earlier), rather than neoconservatives on the Right or so-called liberals within the profession, determine who is a critic, what counts as criticism, and that they oppose criticism to censorship. I do not mean to suggest that there is a pure symmetry or equivalence between political critics on the Left and both neoconservative and "liberal" antipolitical critics on the Right. It is valuable (and perhaps easy enough) to show the contradictions in right-wing arguments that ostensibly defend freedom of speech, liberal education, and liberty but clearly mask illiberal attempts to repress political criticism. And strategically, of course, a move against censorship *tout court* may sometimes be useful. "Censorship is un-American," as MTV has it.[18] And even if critique and censorship are never entirely antithetical, even if, as Donald Thomas comments, "the relevant question at any stage of human history is not 'Does censorship exist?' but rather 'Under what sort of censorship do we live?'" (1969, 318), one could argue that the contradictions of an inevitably censorious critique could still be managed in a progressive direction.

Yet the felt urgency to criticize what they take to be an intellectual fraud perpetrated by the Right should not permit political critics to ignore problems they face in deciding the difference between criticism and censorship or engaging in debate. To dismiss the present debate over political correctness as essentially without intellectual significance (as merely political in the older, modern, denigrating sense) is to continue to legitimate the profession in a way that crucially depends on the reinscription of an essentially ahistorical and monolithic definition of censorship.

Several unfortunate consequences have followed. Political critics often forget that the Left has no monopoly on change: change may be reactionary precisely because the economy, as post-Marxists have argued, has no political effect built into it. Furthermore, political critics tend to focus on book censorship and on literature— hence the attention to Rushdie—leaving other media unexamined. It is a troubling omission, inasmuch as neoconservatives and the religious Right in the United States, for example, want to censor elite and mass cultural practices in order to regulate the potentially progressive political effects of the economy, restraining the unruly vagaries of a "free" market by imposing the visible hand of market discipline. A related consequence is a certain historical amnesia with regard to past instances of censorship in the United States. Trials over the fine arts or popular music tend to come as a surprise, as instances of "new" censorship, precisely because the political norm is assumed to be the absence of censorship.[19] Attempts to reassert that norm regularly involve retaining little more than a naive essentialism in the faith of legal guarantees of academic freedom or freedom of artistic expression, as if these guarantees automatically had progressive consequences in practice.

This has of course never been the case. The principle of academic freedom was, for example, paradoxically used to deny tenure to heterodox professors in the 1950s on the grounds that they could not think independently (see Schrecker 1986). Similarly, free speech has been connected to arguments for a free market for less than progressive purposes. The Philip Morris Company (which sends out free copies of the Bill of Rights) has justified the advertising of its tobacco products in Third World countries, and George Bush has opposed regulating the minutes per hour allowed for commercials in television programming for children.[20] Similarly, the scandalous contradiction in the Right between the desires for an unregulated market and a regulated body, antiporn advocate and savings-and-loan defrauder Charles Keating being the prime example, goes unnoticed.[21]

In addition to these consequences, a narrow definition of censorship often provides antipolitical critics an entry point to argue for a depoliticized account of aesthetics and criticism: liberal and neoconservative critics appeal to aesthetic standards and differentiate them from censorship. A given artist, so this argument goes, should not be funded by the NEA because she or he is not a "good" artist; the critic bases this judgment solely on the criterion of taste.[22]

Paradoxically, then, in refusing to interrogate what goes without saying, political critics have closed down local possibilities for an oppositional critique of the Right. Again, a different understanding of censorship opens up new prospects for critique. Perhaps the greatest oppositional potential now lies in rhetorically staging the censorious tactics of the religious Right in a way that involves critically imitating them rather than differentiating them from one's own high-minded, principled stand against censorship. Book burning, for example, was to be employed in a performance piece by Survival Research Laboratories, with Bibles as the books to be burned. Artpark, the place and institution sponsoring the performance, canceled a scheduled appearance in Lewistown, New York, the reason being the group's plan to incinerate Bibles in their performance. Eighteen local artists who protested this cancellation as a form of censorship arrived at Artpark with a platform in the shape of the Bible and other props and were arrested by park police (see Licata 1990). The late David Wojnarowicz entertained similar fantasies in a program note to an exhibit at the New York city gallery Artists Space, whose initial funding by the NEA was later withdrawn: "At least in my imagination I can fuck somebody without a rubber or I can, in the privacy of my own skull, douse Helms with a bucket of gasoline and set his putrid ass on fire or throw Rep. William Dannemeyer off the empire state building. These fantasies give me some distance from my outrage for a few seconds" (*Witnesses* 1989, 10).[23] The oppositional potential of a Survival Research Laboratories performance or of Wojnarowicz's fantasies remains unactivated from within the essentially libertarian anticensorship position held by many political critics. More paradoxically, in a 1990 MTV "Rock the Vote" commercial, Madonna literally wrapped herself in the flag to encourage the practice of democracy though she herself was not registered to vote.

By suggesting that there are possibilities for a postmodern "opposition" to right-wing censorship, I mean to call attention to new paradoxes of censorship in the present rather than suggest that I have resolved the unrecognized paradoxes of an earlier criticism of censorship. Activating any oppositional potential in political criticism or in the arts is not simply a matter of inscribing in an even stronger form a distinction between censorship and political criticism or political art. While often critical of the Enlightenment, many postmodern artists invoke moral notions of artistic freedom when denied NEA grants, or they appeal to an artist's "moral rights" or legal copyright, as when Wojnarowicz successfully sued the Reverend Donald Wildmon to keep him from circulating a decontextualized version of Wojnarowicz's art.[24]

More crucial perhaps than the inability of postmodern artists to escape from modern notions of freedom and censorship is the fact that no one identifies with the censorship political critics want to oppose. One might generalize that censorship is always thought to be something others do. Even in the Stalinist Soviet Union, it did not officially exist; similarly, East German censors thought of themselves not as censors but as critics.[25] Opponents of censorship usually attempt to unmask this disavowal as bureaucratic hypocrisy. Perhaps it is as simple as that. Yet any attempt to clarify the opposition between the real critics and the real censors is open to paradoxes and reversals that seem to me most important to examine at the very moment when the pressure to assert one's opposition to censorship is felt to be most intense. The notion of "opposition" is as much a problem as a solution when one is formulating a critique of censorship in the present. The mere reassertion of the potential for opposition to censorship is rather empty, given that opposition can always be delegitimated, collapsed into political correctness and censorship and distinguished from a depoliticized notion of "creative art." Indeed, it is precisely this delegitimating move that has made the present right-wing critique of higher education in the United States so popular with campus liberals. As I have already suggested, this critique has a certain force inasmuch as the postmodern view of art as institutionally constrained has been used to authorize (what is now called) censorship.

In contrast to a unified, monolithic, libertarian definition of censorship, then, a more expansive and historicized definition opens up the possibility of a wider, more comprehensive critique of censorship, both within the critical profession and outside it, and a deeper awareness of the problematic tendency to exclude an internal critique when making an external critique and vice versa. Provisionally speaking, the internal critique must address the degree to which the autonomy of the political critic is relative, provide a metacritique of the discipline of English studies, so to speak, in terms of both research and pedagogy. As for criticism, a historical account of censorship opens up a critique of the self-censorship (often unconscious) of one's own writing required to make it professionally receivable. The same point holds for pedagogical practice. By positioning themselves as opponents of censorship (or any other equivalent form of power/repression), political critics authorize themselves as teachers. Liberal humanists, either neo-Whig or revisionist, and Marxists may disagree as to whether censorship was repressive or lenient, but they will not disagree as to whether Renaissance literature produces a critique of censorship. Thus they secure an internal realm of the imagination or an institutional space in which to be oppositional (even if that opposition is also said to be constrained).

In securing this realm, political critics indirectly do the work of the state, interpolating subjects into a capitalist economy precisely by allowing them to imagine they are oppositional within it. Yet this very notion of opposition closes off a critique of self-censorship in saying what goes without saying. Who, after all, is for censorship? To put the point another way, one cannot say one is for censorship without risk of being censored or censured by one's professional colleagues.

As a legitimating discourse, postmodern political criticism is paradoxical in relation to academic freedom in ways that conventional apologies for the contradictions of postmodern criticism have not taken into account. Political critics regularly adopt a language of resistance, subversion, and opposition which is sometimes directed at local targets on the Right such as Jesse Helms, sometimes at whole systems such as capitalism or patriarchy. Like modern critics, postmodern critics (both avowedly political critics and antifoundationalist neopragmatists) assume that criticism is wholly opposed to censorship, wholly on the side of academic freedom. However distorted or rabid neoconservative critiques of "political correctness" or the "new orthodoxy" of the Left may be, the language of opposition functions within the institution in a way that does not decisively escape these critiques. Adopting this discourse is one of the present modes, perhaps *the* central mode, of making one's criticism receivable in the profession and hence of receiving institutional accreditation. Though the language of opposition often usefully tends to demystify structures of oppression and domination outside the academy, it simultaneously often masks (intentionally or not) its implication in the disciplinary structures internal to the academy, such as the self-censorship one engages in to make one's writing professionally receivable (not only determining what one can or cannot say to avoid censure by one's colleagues but taking into account the social position of the critics with whom one differs when deciding if differing demands deference toward them or invites one to marginalize or even dismiss them). In short, the language of opposition sometimes obscures the normalizing function of that very language within the institution of criticism itself, the extent, that is, to which opposition *is* now the reigning critical orthodoxy.

If criticism is institutional and if it is therefore always regulated, always subject to different forms of censorship, then we need to think harder and longer about the strategies of legitimating and de-legitimating discourse within the institution of criticism and other institutions regulating the arts as well. This project is significant precisely because it means the present debate over political correct-ness will not disappear, however much we may wish to think that it is a mere diversion (of no intellectual moment) from our real work as critics. Though there may be no escape from a modern definition of censorship, there are at least new ways of problematizing present modes of legitimating criticism adopted both by the so-called polit-ically correct postmodern Left, which has mounted critiques of the Enlightenment, and by so called liberals, who defend Enlighten-ment versions of discourse ethics.[26] Both sides beg precisely the questions that need asking: How does one tell a "free" conversation from the inculcation of politically correct views? How does one distinguish criticism from polemic? How does one stage a debate when conservatives talk to other conservatives about political crit-ics and when political critics talk to other political critics about conservatives? How does one teach conflicts if one side walks away from the podium or the other attempts to commandeer it? And how does one distinguish between a conversation worth listening to and a meaningless dialogue one ought to ignore? How can one urge critics to address the public sphere when the public sphere is already acknowledged to be a phantom (Robbins 1990), when critical de-bate is the empty drivel of a television talk show? When the profes-sion answers back to the neoconservative Right, who speaks on its behalf? When the wagons are circled, who is in the profession and who is not? Is it any surprise that those without academic freedom, namely, untenured faculty and graduate students, are precisely the ones who have not spoken (been asked to speak? been permitted to speak?) for the humanities?

These questions may all be subsumed under a more general one: How can one legitimate criticism without reinscribing a modern definition of it? Whereas liberals have not taken into account how their critique of political correctness (defined as an attempt to im-pede genuine conversation and dialogue) is itself a delegitimating strategy, political critics face an inverse problem. If one wants to call neoconservatives or liberals "censors," one is hard pressed to defend modern notions of academic freedom without contradicting one-self. How can one mount a defense from a postmodern perspective that collapses power into knowledge and calls into question modern notions of pure autonomy or pure freedom? How can political critics avoid the charge of political correctness when the institutional hegemony of political criticism depends precisely on such prescriptions as "Always historicize," on setting up a new categorical imperative to write self-consciously political criticism? For though political critics concede that nothing is inherently subversive, the aim is to specify the conditions under which subversion or opposition has occurred, so that a counterhegemonic reading can be produced. The claim that avowedly political critics are more political than other critics involves as well a claim for the legitimate hegemony of political criticism (it is less mystified, more self-conscious, more inclusive, not sexist, racist, and so on).

Precisely because the present debate over political correctness and its meaning will expand rather than go away, the Renaissance and Jonson will continue to provide an important historical perspective, making contemporary censorship practices visible in a different way and enabling the articulation of a new range of paradoxes and problems concerning criticism as a regulatory practice: illiterate hate speech (swearing and invective); the relationship between giving offense and taking offense, or tolerating what offends you; pardon as a form of tolerance (just forget it) and as a form of historical amnesia (just forget it).[27] A genealogical history of censorship and regulation in the early modern past may potentially open up a space within the profession to problematize criticism as a regulating, contestatory activity and perhaps to mount a critique of antiintellectual, moralistic, indeed "politically correct" cultural criticism in a way that does not simply replicate the neoconservative critique of political criticism and of the profession in general, but not because the Renaissance gives us a way to oppose that critique or dispense with it. To imagine one could use the early modern past to oppose censorship as it has traditionally been defined would likely mean in practice that one would only provide more fuel for the already incendiary legitimation crisis of postmodern political criticism.

Notes

Preface

1. Annabel Patterson has noted Jonson's importance as an exemplary case: "Any account of ideology in literature that assumes a sharp divide between ruling class and opposition, between writers who legitimate and writers who subvert, will fail to deal with Jonson" (1985, 158). See also Richard Dutton 1991, 1–2 and forthcoming. My Foucauldian account of Jonson's relation to different forms of censorship bears out Patterson's point and affirms Dutton's sense of Jonson's centrality, but my account of Jonson's paradoxes differs markedly from Patterson's liberal humanist oppositional perspective and from Dutton's moderate revisionist perspective. See also Butler 1992a on *The Magnetic Lady* as a test case.

2. In speaking of "discourses" of censorship and in adopting the adjectives "Foucauldian" and "post-Marxist" (which is by no means "anti-" or "ex-" Marxist) to describe my critical perspective, I allude both to Foucault's genealogical mode of historicism (1977a–e, and 1978) and to Barthes 1970; Baudrillard 1975; 1981; 1983; Bourdieu 1977, 1979, and 1984; Kristeva 1984; Laclau 1988; Laclau and Mouffe 1985; and Marin 1972. Despite important differences, these critics all break with Marxist or humanist accounts of domination, arguing that domination works not only—not even primarily—through brute forms of repression but through mastery of a discursive or simulacral economy, that is, a semiotic system of symbolic differentiation that allows the dominant classes, as Jean Baudrillard puts it, "to transcend and to consecrate their economic privilege in a semiotic privilege" (1981, 45). Political struggle is defined here in terms of discursive rewriting and recoding, not open conflict and antagonism. Louis Marin and Julia Kristeva emphasize the crucial importance of legitimation and delegitimation in this recoding. For examples of

genealogical histories of Renaissance culture, see Tennenhouse 1986; and Halpern 1991. In its desire to differentiate the past from the present, the genealogical method has much in common with anthropological and New Historicist criticism interested in "estranging" the Renaissance.

My account of censorship as a multiple, dispersed network of practices that need to be examined locally and case by case both elaborates and revises Foucault's own work on discursive forms of power and Bourdieu 1991. Though Foucault often criticized monolithic models of power, he never historicized censorship. In criticizing the repressive hypothesis, he reinscribed an ahistorical definition of censorship as a figure for the kind of monolithic model of power he wished to criticize, making censorship synonymous, for example, with repression (see 1978, 17, 34, 84). Foucault's influential essay "What Is an Author?" (see note 23 in Chapter 1 herein) similarly reinscribes a traditional production-centered account of censorship, so that a genealogical history of early modern censorship and early modern literary criticism has gone unwritten.

3. In situating Jonson in relation to a theatrical legitimation crisis, I owe an obvious debt to Timothy Murray (1987), who uses legitimation to position ideology critique in relation to epistemology. I seek to expand the scope of the determinants of what Murray terms a "crisis of signification" to include censorship and the institution of literary criticism.

4. The OED cites Milton's *Areopagitica* as the first modern instance, but it may have entered the language much earlier. The "grand censors" of the quarto epistle of *Troilus and Cressida* evidently are the ecclesiastical licensers, the archbishops of Canterbury and London (alluded to indirectly through the reference to the "galled goose of Winchester" and "the stews licensed by the Archbishop of Winchester" [epilogue 53]). These bishops had banned satires in 1599. On censorship in ancient Greece and Rome, see Finley 1977.

5. On Freud's use of censorship as a metaphor, see Borch-Jacobsen 1988, 3–4; the entries on censorship and compromise-formation in Laplanche and Pontalis 1973, 65–66, 76; and especially Levine 1986.

6. In an essay on an exhibition titled " 'Degenerate Art': The Fate of the Avant-Garde in Nazi Germany," mounted by the Los Angeles County Museum, I further complicate the term *censorship* by calling into question the distinction between simulated or staged censorship and literal censorship. Censorship, I argue, is always staged (Burt, forthcoming a).

7. A converse problem with dissolving the distinction between criticism and censorship is apparent in the work of Sue Curry Jansen. In a wide-ranging analysis, Jansen (1988) has argued, following Foucault, that censorship is culturally constitutive. She maintains that it is possible to distinguish only between good and bad forms of censorship. Yet this very distinction reinscribes that between criticism and censorship, which she criticizes, in a new form: good censorship is critical and dialogical; bad censorship is uncritical and monological.

8. My account of Jonson is also intended to make it clear that a history of censorship will narrate not an originary moment in the Renaissance when

censorship emerged to control discourses that earlier had been freely produced and circulated but the emergence in the Renaissance of new forms of censorship, new problems of reception, and new technologies of cultural production and reproduction. I call into question histories that narrate either a triumphant end of censorship in the Renaissance (and birth of the free citizen) or its internalization by a bourgeois subject and its increasing effectiveness (external censorshp gives way to internalized self-censorship). Thus I part company with Francis Barker (1984), who forcefully argues that external state censorship over production came to an end when censorship was internalized by the consuming modern subject. Barker's focus on internalized censorship and consumption marks an advance over both liberal humanist and Marxist accounts of literary production and reception aesthetics and structuralist accounts of consumption. Barker complicates the humanist opposition between resisting subjects and a repressive state by demonstrating that the bourgeois subject's internalized resistance, neurotic self-division, may serve the interests of the bourgeois state. There is thus no opposition between a free, unfettered subject and a subjecting state.

Yet because Barker adopts the same definition of censorship as liberal humanists and Marxists, drawing the same contrasts between external repression (state censorship) and internal repression (self-censorship)—establishing the same hierarchy of production over consumption—he too is able to see only two kinds of censorship. Consequently, his account of the Renaissance overstates historical discontinuities between past and present. Like liberal humanists and Marxists, Barker makes no mention of post-Renaissance forms of state censorship such as the Stage Licensing Act of 1737. Barker's definition of censorship produces a similarly misleading historiography in its contrast between pre- and postrevolutionary England: the internalization of censorship over consumption, which Barker locates in Milton, was in place well before the English Revolution; an early version can be seen in Chaucer's prologue to "The Miller's Tale," where readers are invited to turn the page and skip the tale if they think it might be offensive. Similarly, there was plenty of state censorship afterward (on new forms of censorship during the eighteenth century, see Davis 1983). Furthermore, in addition to producing historiographical problems, Barker's limited definition of state censorship leads to another problem, namely, minimizing the extent to which these forms of censorship were negotiated. Rather than secure a clearer form of control, the Stage Licensing Act, for example, was contravened by both the Lord Chamberlain and his examiners as well as by theater managers.

Introduction

1. I refer here to what Carole Vance (1989) terms the "new" censorship in the United States and abroad, including Jesse Helms's amendment to the act refunding the NEA; the cancellation of NEA funding for the "Witnesses" exhibit at Artists Space; the cancellation of the scheduled Robert Mapplethorpe exhibit

at the Corcoran Gallery and the prosecution of the museum director of the Cincinnati exhibition; the Florida ruling that a 2 Live Crew album was obscene; the cancellation of New York's public access Channel J by Time Warner; the forced resignation of National Endowment of the Arts chair John Frohnmayer; Vice President Dan Quayle's attack on the "cultural elite"; new legislation in Great Britain and Ireland such as the Obscene Publications Act, the Cable and Broadcasting Act, and the Video Recording Act. For a more thorough analysis of these cases and others, see Burt forthcoming b, and for a usefully detailed narrative of these and other cases see Dubin 1992. On the Rushdie affair, see Rushdie 1990; Appiganesi and Maitland 1989. On 2 Live Crew, see Gates 1990; Jones 1990. On canceled commercials for Diet Coke and Diet Pepsi made, respectively, with Madonna and George Michael, see Vickers 1991. For a neoconservative view of the NEA, see "The Flag and the Community" 1990; Kimball 1990; Lipman 1990; and Kramer 1989. For Leftist responses, particularly to the Mapplethorpe controversy, see Vance 1989 ; Ross 1990; Staniszewski 1989; and Stimpson 1990. On secrecy and censorship in the United States in the 1980s, see Curry 1988, and for similarly repressive developments in England, see Cubbitt 1990. Images of book burning are more varied in their implications than most accounts of the Rushdie affair allow. See, for example, the photo of Nazi youths burning books to drive home the point that Leftist academics are "fascists" in Taylor 1991. In a contrasting use of the same tactic, Survival Research Laboratories planned to burn Bibles in Artpark in order to protest censorship (Licata 1990). For a brilliant analysis of the Rushdie affair which involves a critique of liberal notions of censorship very much in line with my own, see Webster 1990.

2. To be sure, histories of censorship have been written (see Gildersleeve 1908; Finkelpearl 1986; Clare 1990; and Dutton 1991). These, however, adopt an ahistorical definition of censorship. In addition to constructing false oppositions between censorship and liberty, traditional definitions also tend to imply false identities. Consider the strongest account to date: Patterson 1984. Although Patterson's account of court censorship is appealing for its inclusiveness, it obscures important differences between forms of censorship. In Patterson's view tact, personal inhibition, fear, and turning a blind eye all amount to the same thing.

3. As Janet Clare notes, the present debate over Renaissance theater censorship has been framed in terms of its repressiveness or leniency (1990, ix–xiii). For Whig and Marxist versions of this "old" historicist account, see Heinemann 1980; Hill 1985; Patterson 1984; Tricomi 1989; and Clare 1990. For an anthropological version, see Mullaney 1987. Postmodern Marxist (Dollimore 1989; Venuti 1989), materialist feminist (Howard 1991), and Foucauldian (Barker 1984) accounts of cultural opposition and domination in the theater, while very different both from each other and from the old historicist accounts, nevertheless adopt the same ahistorical definition of censorship.

4. For revisionist versions of this account, see Marcus 1986a, 7–9; and 1986b; Sharpe 1987, 35–39; 290–301; Worden 1988; and Dutton 1990; 1991. Kevin Sharpe goes so far as to argue that censorship virtually did not exist:

what "has now become clear is that there is little substance to the spectre of censorship that stalks [Martin] Butler's and others' pages" (1987, 23). He makes no mention at all of the censorship of the late Jonson plays. Similarly, Blair Worden (1988) views stage censorship as capricious and arbitrary, the censor being little more than an annoyance to dramatists and acting companies. From the fact that no dramatist was punished for libel, Philip Finkelpearl has concluded: "I do not propose James for honorary membership in the Civil Liberties Union, but among the many traits he displayed—along with a drunkard's indifference—was an intermittent predilection for tolerance and compassion" (1986, 133). Following Finkelpearl, Paul Yachnin contends that the theater was "powerless" because its representations "were seen to subsist in a field of discourse isolated from the real world, and . . . such representations were seen normally as incapable of intervening in the political arena" (1991, 51). Very different and, to my mind, much stronger and more sophisticated versions of the containment argument have been articulated by New Historicists (Greenblatt 1988; Goldberg 1983a; Tennenhouse 1986). For Greenblatt's response to criticism of his subversion/containment thesis, see Greenblatt 1990, 165–70.

5. These shared ahistorical assumptions help to account for an internal incoherence in the argumentation of some old historicist work on censorship. Janet Clare, for example, says that "there was very little scope for writers . . . to have formulated principles of artistic freedom" (1990, 18) but then states two pages later that "Jonson expressed his ideal of a state where artistic freedom is guaranteed by the clemency and wise judgement of the ruler" (20). The same ahistorical assumptions also help to explain why critics who oppose themselves to other critics so often seem to be in agreement, possessing a similar internal incoherence in their argumentation. After dismissing evidence of court censorship early on in *Criticism and Compliment,* Kevin Sharpe, for example, endorses Annabel Patterson's account of censorship (1987, 37–39, and see note 165, 297). For similar examples of self-contradiction, see Finkelpearl 1982; 1986; Finkelpearl is alternately a Whig and a revisionist.

I should add that the assumptions I interrogate are by no means exhaustive. Another problem with the classical definition of censorship is that it implies an account of the body inflected neither by gender nor by ethnicity. For recent attempts to correct this problem, see Barker 1984; and Boose forthcoming.

6. Jonson was different from other dramatists in many respects, but not in his assumptions about censorship. Other dramatists, such as George Chapman in *Byron,* part 1, and Thomas Heywood in *An Apology for Actors,* adopted reformist strategies similar to Jonson's, though, as we shall see, this does not mean there was anything like a consensus about the content of what should be censored or the limits of liberty. In *An Apology for Actors,* Thomas Heywood wrote he "also could wish, that such as are condemned for their licentiousnesse, might by a generall consent bee quite excluded from our society" (*ES,* 4:252). Like Jonson, Heywood justifies plays on the grounds that they have been passed by the censor, "the Office of the Revels, where our court playes have beene in late daies yearely to be rehearsed, perfected, and corrected before they come to the publike view of the prince and the nobility" (*ES,* 4:252). Further,

Heywood distinguishes on moral grounds between different kinds of entertainment: "I speake not in defense of any lascivious shewes, scurrelous jests, or scandalous invectives" (*ES*, 4:253). The dispersal of authority among dramatists often led to wars of theaters. Heywood, for example, would exclude the companies that had performed Jonson's comical satires. In his *Apology for Actors,* Heywood criticizes the boys' companies, the very ones that had performed the plays that got Jonson into trouble:

> Now to speake of some abuse lately crept into the quality, as an inveighing against the state, the court, the law, the citty, and their governement, with the particularizing of men's humors (yet alive), noble-men, and others: I know it distastes many; neither do I in any way approve it, nor dare I by any meanes excuse it. The liberty which some will arrogate to themselves, commiting their bitternesse, and liberall invectives against all estates, to the mouthes of children, supposing their juniority to be a priviledge for any rayling, be it never so violent, I could advise all such to curbe and limit this presumed liberty within the bands of discretion and governement. But wise and judiciall censurers, before whom such complaints shall at any time hereafter come, wil not (I hope) impute these abuses to any transgression in us, who have ever been carefull and provident to shun the like. (*ES*, 4:253)

It was the Children of Saint Paul's that produced Jonson's *Cynthia's Revels, Poetaster,* and *Epicoene,* as well as Chapman's *Byron* plays and Jonson, Chapman, and John Marston's *Eastward Ho!*.

7. For accounts of these cases of Jonson's subjection to dramatic censorship, see H & S, 1:190–200, 237–39, 275–415; McPherson 1974, 4, 10–12; and Clare 1990, 51–54, 83–89, 118–24, 168–70, 211–14. On *Sejanus,* see Ayres 1983. On James's censorship of *Neptune's Triumph,* see Limon 1986, 25. For the text of the warrant for the reversion of the Office of the Master of the Revels, see H & S, 1:237–39. On Jonson's attempt to secure the office under Elizabeth, see Loewenstein 1984, 78–84. On the examination by the Attorney General, see H & S, 1:242–44. On Jonson's citations for recusancy, see H & S, 1:220–23. For a brilliant analysis of Jonson as a double agent, see Archer 1993. The failure to grasp Jonson's paradoxical relation to censorship has led some critics to make rather startling claims for the progressive direction of Jonson's politics. Albert Tricomi argues, for example, that *Sejanus* is a republican play, maintaining that "the values of 'Ancient Liberty' and free speech in representative bodies were major concerns of . . . Jonson" (1989, 55). More reasonably, Janet Clare maintains that in *Poetaster* "Jonson expressed his ideal of a state where artistic freedom is guaranteed by the clemency and wise judgement of the ruler" (1990, 20). I would agree with this point provided it is clear that Jonson is willing to defend artistic freedom only because he wants to regulate and censor the public theaters.

8. Modern and postmodern critics might want to distinguish between these censors, ranking the court censor above the market censor on the grounds

that the penalties the court censor could inflict were much more severe than those of a market censor. What is striking about Jonson, however, is that he does not draw that distinction, regarding both as threats to his body. Just as he feared being consumed by Vulcan in "Execration upon Vulcan," so too he refused to "waste [him]self / On those who have no taste" ("Ode to Himself," 13–14). Jonson's negotiation between both censors is precisely what demands critical attention. In failing to draw a modern, commonsense distinction between them, Jonson is by no means exceptional. In a recent example, Salman Rushdie (1990) regards both Khomeini and Viking Press as threats. Asked whether he might consider dropping a paperback edition of *The Satanic Verses,* Rushdie says: "If you want to keep a book in print for any length of time . . . then it has to be a paperback. If the paperback doesn't exist, the book has effectively been suppressed. It's the only way it can receive the judgment of posterity. So my main reason for wanting the paperback is to prevent this book from being banned by the back door" (113). Rushdie has, of course, since twice changed his mind, first agreeing not to print the book in paperback and then arguing (successfully) that it be printed in paper.

9. The similarities between the court censor's categories and the ones Jonson adopts in the epistle have been noted in McPherson 1985. For a biographical, allegorical account of the relationship between *Volpone* and the censorship of *Eastward Ho!,* see Riggs 1988, 122–45. See also Dutton, forthcoming; and Donaldson 1984.

10. For recent old and new historicist accounts, see Orgel 1975; Knapp 1979; Newton 1979 and 1982; Goldberg 1983a; Wayne 1984; Norbrook 1984a; Cohen 1985; Loewenstein 1984; Womack 1986 and 1989; Stallybrass and White 1986; Marcus 1986b; Burt 1987; Evans 1989; Venuti 1989, and Dutton forthcoming. For very different reasons, these critics, myself included, share in a widespread consensus that Jonson's relation to the court was deeply contradictory. (An older, discredited Whig account of Jonson as an unambiguous court flatterer survives in Edwards 1979 and Finkelpearl 1987.) One of the problems with present accounts of Jonson's contradictory relation to the court is that they have tended to marginalize Jonson's experience with censorship, making it little more than a temporary obstacle Jonson overcame early in his career. For one instance of this view, see Evans 1989, 69–75. For an important corrective, see Riggs 1988, 122–45. Furthermore, because censorship has been defined in these contexts as repressive, it has been largely divorced from the questions of license that preoccupied Jonson throughout his career.

11. I draw here on Bourdieu's work on the sociology of taste (1984). Bourdieu's exclusive focus on economic, cultural, and symbolic forms of capital and his implicit assumption that cultural production has priority over consumption lead him to minimize censorship; further, they mean that his analysis of aesthetic distinction as a form of social legitimation tends to revert rather quickly to mere ideological demystification. I am indebted as well to related accounts of the emergence of the aesthetic in England: Agnew 1986 and Greenblatt 1988; in England and France: Murray 1987; and in France: Jouhaud forthcoming.

12. Even repressive acts paradoxically function positively. Book burnings

were less about blocking access to forbidden books than they were about purifying the nation-state from the corrupting influences of other nations and religions. See also note 29 to the Introduction herein.

13. The contradictions of court censorship have recently been noted by a number of critics. As Annabel Patterson observes, the authorities' response to criticism ranged "from extreme and savage reprisal to turning a blind eye" (1984, 53). See also Finkelpearl 1986; Levy 1988; Dutton 1990 and 1991; Clare 1990; and Yachnin 1991. My differences from these critics in interpreting these contradictions will become clear as my argument proceeds.

14. For examples, see Burt 1987, 556–58.

15. On the complexity of *license* and *liberty,* see Marcus 1986b, 7–9, 40; and Mullaney 1987.

16. Just as the distinction between market and court censorship begins to break down, so too does the distinction between prepublication and post-publication censorship. Consumers try to stop the production or publication of works they wish to censor. On the heterogeneity of the literary marketplace, see also Halasz 1990.

17. For a most polemical account of the priority of consumption over production, of symbolic forms of capital (prestige and status) over economic capital, see Jean Baudrillard's critique of Marx's anthropology (1981). For an analysis closer to my own of the relative determining force of these forms of capital, see Bourdieu 1984.

18. I do not mean to imply that there was no limit on censorship or that all forms of censorship were the same. Licensing and censorship were not simply flip sides of the same coin. Licensing involved other forms of regulation such as economic ones. Yet the dispersal of different forms of censorship and regulation doesn't involve an escape from censorship and regulation altogether. In saying that there was no alternative to censorship, I would not want to deny, however, that the content of legitimate liberty might be defined expansively or narrowly.

19. For a critique of New Historicism along these lines, see Holstun 1989, and for a complementary argument, see Norbrook 1991a. For other critiques, see Ferguson et al. 1986; Howard 1986; Neely 1987; Boose 1987; and Venuti 1989.

20. For these debates, see Howard 1986; and Venuti 1989, 7–12.

21. For defenses of centered subjectivity, see Marcus 1988, 29–32; and Patterson 1989, 1–12. For a defense of decentered subjectivity, see Venuti 1989, 3–14. The appeal to economic determinations of the theater as a means of saving critique takes two forms, one weak and one strong: in the weak version, a simple notion of economic interest is used to demonstrate the politics of a given writer. Thus, Shakespeare is often contrasted to Jonson on the basis of their sources of income. Jonson made more from his masques than from his plays. It follows for some critics that Jonson "sold out" to the court and that his plays are more valuable than his masques. See Finkelpearl 1987; Auberlen 1984, 117–18. The strong version of this move links economics with theatrical

representation. Drawing both on Louis Althusser's and on Ernesto Laclau and Chantal Mouffe's theory of overdetermination as well as on Fredric Jameson's conception of a political unconscious, Walter Cohen and Lawrence Venuti have usefully pointed out that the theater's mode of cultural production was mixed, neither entirely feudal nor entirely capitalist. Yet in practice, Cohen argues that the artisanal mode of production was dominant, and he derives from this hierarchical arrangement of determinations the conclusion that the public theaters were by definition subversive. Thus, both weak and strong versions of the appeal to the economy save critique by constructing an opposition between two falsely unified, monolithic terms, namely, censorship and capitalism.

22. In theorizing problems of reception specific to early Stuart theater, I do not, however, abandon the premise of extradiscursive determinations, unlike some post-Marxists, such as Laclau, for whom "everything is discourse" (1988, 83). To see politics as a matter of pure textuality is inevitably to re-inscribe an opposition between textuality and extratextual determination and, hence, only to exchange one monolithic determination for another. In practice, the court displaces capitalism as the final determination, semiotics displace History as the "real." See, for example, Francis Barker's critique of a "meta-physic of depth" (1984, 43) and Leonard Tennenhouse's Baudrillardian, post-modern account of the theater (1990). Tennenhouse criticizes what he calls the "depth model" of politics employed by Marxist and humanist political critics in favor of attention to surfaces, but he ends up reintroducing the depth model in locating the court as the determinant of the theater. Similarly, Barker rests his Foucauldian account of the body on a Marxist account of the transition from feudalism to capitalism and the end of state censorship.

23. Political critics of the Renaissance frequently derive their accounts of the theater from Marxists (Benjamin 1969 and 1986; Althusser 1970, 1971; Althusser and Balibar 1970; Macherey 1978; Eagleton 1976; Bennett 1979a; 1990) and, like these Marxists, keep in place a hierarchy of production and reproduction over consumption. It is precisely this hierarchy I mean to call into question from a post-Marxist perspective. The hierarchy has meant that censorship and capitalism have been unprofitably polarized as competing determinations of the theater. Following Foucault's account of authorship in "What Is an Author?" (1977d), Patterson (1984, 26, 48), Barker (1984, 51), and revisionists including Finkelpearl (1986) and Dutton (1990; 1991) argue that censorship was the crucial determination of literature, and consequently, they either marginal-ize capitalism or ignore it altogether. Conversely, Marxists and New Histor-icists (Knapp 1979; Newton 1979 and 1982; Goldberg 1983a; Cohen 1985; Norbrook 1984a; Wayne 1984; Marcus 1986b; Womack 1986 and 1989; Stally-brass and White 1986; Agnew 1986; Greenblatt 1988; Evans 1989; and Venuti 1989) have either marginalized or ignored censorship in arguing that the theater's capitalist mode of production inscribed a critique of the court within it. Recent Jonson criticism has been structured by the same opposition, with revisionists and New Historicists focusing on court censorship and postmod-ern Marxists focusing on capitalism.

24. The necessity for an "antiessentialist" historicist practice is now virtually critical orthodoxy. See Dollimore and Sinfield 1985; Howard and O'Connor 1987, 1–17; Kastan 1988; Marcus 1988, 233 n. 25; Venuti 1989, 7–12.

25. For a further analysis of these hermeneutic problems, see Burt 1988 and 1990; and Braunmuller 1990.

26. See also Fish 1988b. For a forceful response to these accounts, see Norbrook forthcoming. The traditional view of Milton, it may be noted, is part of a misunderstanding of the bourgeois revolution and the role aristocratic culture played in it. The significant questions are not, as revisionist and Marxist historians and critics believe, whether a revolution or civil war occurred or whether it had long- or short-term causes, but what it meant: Was it a moment of liberation? Or was it, as Francis Barker (1984, 10–11) and Richard Wilson (forthcoming) argue, a moment in which new forms of subjection displaced older ones?

27. The same argument, I hope it is clear, can easily be made against any attempt to claim that being unlicensed is evidence of the radical politics of a text. I take such arguments up directly in Chapter 2 (see Potter 1989 for an analysis that complements my own). For now, let me say that though "license" could be employed to demonize progressive texts that others would have wanted to legitimate, unlicensed texts could be conservative, as was William Prynne's *Twelve Considerable Serious Questions Touching Church Government* (1644). The argument advanced in Siebert 1952 and Hill 1985 that the 1640s saw the massive printing of previously censored radical texts has been called into question in Lambert 1987 and Potter 1989.

28. For critiques of Marxism which complement my own, see Goldberg 1983b and Greenblatt 1988. Greenblatt notes that Jameson's theory of the aesthetic "seems to depend upon a utopian vision that collapses the contradictions of history into a moral imperative. . . . This effacement of contradiction is not the consequence of an accidental lapse but rather the logical outcome of theory's search for the obstacle that blocks the realization of its eschatological vision" (1988, 5).

29. I should add that in broadening the meaning of censorship, I do not mean to conflate it with all forms of subjection. I mean, rather, to relate its dynamics more precisely to the dynamics of other forms of subjection involving ideology (Althusser 1971) and the varied disciplinary practices mapped by Foucault 1977c; Elias 1978; Bakhtin 1968; Barker 1984; and Stallybrass and White 1986.

1. Branding the Body, Burning the Book

1. For an analysis of Jonson's "corpus" which complements my own, see Loewenstein 1986, whose pun it is. On Jonson's body, see Adams 1979; and Helgerson 1983, 179–84. Ian Donaldson (1988) takes up Jonson and the thematic of book destruction from a different perspective. For similar instances where Jonson conflates the body and the book, see his reference to Fletcher's

"murdered poem" in "*The Faithful Shepherdess:* To the Worthy Author, Mr John Fletcher" (*Ungathered Verse* 8.14); Jonson's reference to Faranby's edition of Martial as *Jesuitaru castratus* (H & S, 1:216); Jonson's "The Humble Petition of Poor Ben. To the Best of Masters, Monarchs, and Men": "this so accepted sum, / Or dispensed in books, or bread / (For with both the muse was fed)" (*Underwood* 76.14–16). For another instance in which Jonson views his theater audience as censors, see the preface to *Sejanus,* where spectators who disliked the play are compared to "common torturers, that bring all wit to the rack" (25).

2. I thank Ian Donaldson for drawing my attention to the importance of "public fame" in this passage. One might try to cross-reference the book burning in *Sejanus.* There may be a critique of the decision to burn Cordus's history (since Cordus is clearly guilty of treason) but whether we are to accept Arruntius's critique is for me an open question. Even if we grant that there is a critique of Tiberius, however, the critique is not of censorship in general but of Tiberius's particular decision to burn Cordus's book. Similarly, in "*The Faithful Shepherdess:* To the Worthy Author, Mr John Fletcher," Jonson criticizes the audience that has censored or "murdered" Fletcher's poem, but his criticism takes the form of a reciprocal kind of revenge: Jonson imagines a compensatory moment of censorship "when fire / Or moths shall eat what all these fools admire" (15–16).

3. The extent to which a public performance was a mode of legitimation can be registered in the phrase that frequently appears on title pages of quarto editions: "As it has been divers times publikely acted." See also the title page of the quarto edition of *Everyman out of His Humour* ("Containing more than hath been Publickely Spoken or Acted") and the dedication to the Inns of Court ("vse-full studies to the publike," 18–19).

4. It is worth noting that Jonson's spokesman in *Cynthia's Revels* is named Crites in the folio and Criticus in the quarto. Jonson also used Criticus as his authority in his lost "Apology to *Bartholomew Fair*" (H & S, 1:134, 144).

5. The exact lines are as follows:

> Some parts there of search, and mastery in the arts.
> All the old Venusine, in poetry,
> And lighted by the Stagerite could spy.
>
> (88–90)

Herford and Simpson identify this text as "a translation of the Horace's *Ars Poetica*" (11:77 n. 90). Jonson concludes his inventory with another work of literary criticism, namely, what he calls "twice twelve years stored up humanity": according to Herford and Simpson, this store is "probably a collection on the lines of the later *Discoveries made upon Men and Matter*" (11:79 n. 101).

6. The assumption that criticism and censorship are antithetical has implicitly informed the two dominant modes of Jonson criticism at present. Revisionists redeem the court by absorbing censorship into licensed criticism. As Kevin Sharpe puts it: "Working within courtly modes, Jonson enjoyed a

freedom for political commentary proffered through criticism and compliment" (1987, 296). Similarly, Jonathan Goldberg dismisses Jonson's difficulties at court, including the court's censorship of his early plays:

> These are acts in a contained rebellion. Jonson's mode of being a "good subiect" allows him to speak out. . . . Jonson's success—pensioned by the king, patronized by his courtiers, the city, and the gentry—exhibits how well he fit within his society, how fully he contained it. His is so entirely a voice constituted by and representative of his society that he could speak out against it and yet speak within it. . . . His fantasy of rebellion is licensed by the king. And throughout his career, that fantasy was very close to the facts. His rebellions were royally countenanced. (1983a, 220, 221)

Given that the court licensed Jonson's political critique, revisionists conclude, there is no need for modern critics to criticize either Jonson for his service to the court or the court for patronizing him, and Jonson's encounters with the court censor can be either ignored or dismissed as temporary difficulties overcome early in his literary career. See also Evans 1989, 69–75.

7. The semantic instability of verbs such as *censor* or *censure* arises in part because *criticize* and *criticism* do not enter the language until the middle or later seventeenth century. The *OED* gives 1649 as the first instance of *criticize;* 1654 as the first instance of *critick* as a noun; and 1674 as the first instance of *criticism*.

8. These are the same unexamined assumptions that enabled the production of modern histories of literary criticism that appeared from the 1930s through the 1970s. See Tayler 1967; Redwine 1970; Springarn 1974.

9. For an explicit instance of this way of formulating the problem of reception, see Sharpe 1987, 297. For different accounts of the audience's composition and what its diversity meant, see Cook 1981; Butler 1984, 293–306; Cohen 1985, 168–70; Gurr 1987; and Sharpe 1987, 21–39. For an exemplary evolutionary account of taste, see Andrew Gurr 1987, 115–90. Arguing that novelty was the "chief determinant" of theatrical production, Gurr concludes: "The result was constant, pressurised evolution in the players' repertoire of plays, a kind of aesthetic Darwinism" (115).

10. I might add that criticism arises within court culture, not in some imagined oppositional space outside it. For significant work on literary criticism in this regard, see Javitch 1978; Ferguson 1979; Montrose 1983; Murray 1987; Elsky 1989; and Kegl 1990.

11. Modern editors have often been at odds in their classification of Jonson's literary criticism. *Discoveries,* for example, is regularly included in anthologies of Renaissance literary criticism. Herford and Simpson, however, place it among Jonson's prose works. Similarly, Richard C. Newton calls it an "expository prose work" (1979, 182).

12. James Redwine says, for example, that Jonson "not only expounded his theories in prologues and epilogues, he also made his characters discuss plays and play-making; his criticism appears in poems, epigrams, and dedicatory

verses. His letters, personal, dedicatory, and those addressed 'To the Reader,' usually contain interesting critical remarks, as do Drummond's notes on his informal conversation. If his criticism appears in a variety of places, it also appears in a variety of guises: as an ardent defense of poesy, an attack on contemporary audiences, an apologia pro vita sua, or an appeal to one or more of the ancients. . . . One must try to penetrate the accidental complexities of his criticism and, reducing the whole to its essential parts, present in an orderly manner what real complexity there is" (1970, xi–xii). It is precisely this essentialist reading of the dispersal of Jonson's literary criticism that my historicist account of it contests.

13. Some critics, particularly medievalists and classicists, might wish to follow a more traditional (I would say ahistorical) history of literary criticism such as that offered, for example, by William K. Wimsatt and Cleanth Brooks (1964), who begin their history of criticism with classical Greece. I am not arguing that specific critical activities began in the Renaissance but that a discourse of criticism emerged. Wimsatt and Brooks's history is typical in its index: there is no entry for "critic" or for "criticism" (presumably because these are terms without critical interest). I should add that in historicizing literary criticism, I will span Jonson's canon and censorship in the early Stuart theater, even at moments reaching back to late in Elizabeth's reign. Certain critics, especially revisionists (who tend to scrutinize the court year by year), might argue that my global perspective is itself ahistorical (or crudely historical at best). My structural, institutional history of literary criticism and censorship registers a different set of changes from those an empirical, modern one would register; that is, I do not mean to deny that significant changes occurred in the Revels Office because of court pressures having to do with an ambassador's interests, shifts in patronage factions and alliances, or changes in domestic and foreign policy. My concern, however, is with the uneven development of theater censorship. While revisionist historians have profitably examined narrow changes within censorship, the practice they call censorship remains in their accounts constant and unchanging. My postmodern history of literary criticism differs from modern histories of reception not only in determining which documents to consider as evidence (office book of Henry Herbert, statutes, theater epilogues and plays, moments in the plays themselves) but in determining how to read them. Moreover, it specifies the emergence of literary criticism as a separate prose discourse. Revisionists and Marxists locate criticism or critique in any given text; neither revisionists nor Marxists differentiate criticism in general from a specifically literary mode of criticism. See note 23 to the Introduction.

14. As Joan Landes (1988) has shown, the aristocratic public sphere of the old regime included women and was in that way more progressive than the "enlightened" sphere that accompanied the French Revolution. While Jonson's criticism was regularly misogynist, his patrons included women and men, and his club at the Apollo included the "choice ladies" (H & S, 8:4). Habermas notes that only men were admitted to the coffeehouses (1989, 33), and Eagleton concedes that "the public sphere is a notion difficult to rid of nostalgic idealiz-

ing connotations; like the organic society, it sometimes seems to have been disintegrating since its inception." Nevertheless, he remarks, "It is not my intention here, however, to enter into these theoretical contentions" (1984, 8). Marxists, including Eagleton (1984, 119–20), have often dealt with the bourgeois public sphere's problematic exclusivity by developing a notion of a counter public sphere. But that notion remains tied to hackneyed Marxist notions of which class is the most revolutionary and makes each public sphere equally monolithic. By contrast, I would argue that there are always already certain kinds of competing exclusions and that after the Renaissance different kinds of exclusion replaced others.

15. The literary marketplace was, in any case, multiple rather than single. Alexandra Halasz has significantly distinguished between the circulation of pamphlets in the literary marketplace and the circulation of theatrical productions:

> What makes the theater such a useful exemplar for the production and circulation of discourse is the finitude of its reach: the audience is contained within the walls of the theater and the maximal audience within the city and its environs. Bound by time, place and a relatively limited audience, theatrical discourse has a short diastole, making the factors and periodicity of production conscious. Yet to take the theater as *the* model for the production and consumption of discourse in the marketplace is to obscure its position in the field, for the regular, rapid production of plays depends heavily on material in print, and play texts themselves significantly occupy the pamphlet platform. (1990, 18).

I would add only that the printing of plays further complicates the generic distinction Halasz draws between the finite, enclosed theatrical performance and the more freewheeling pamphlet.

16. See Eccles 1933; Dutton 1990; Charles 1982; Streitberger 1986; and Clare 1990. For a similar view of French censors in the ancien régime as men of letters, see Roche 1989, 13.

17. From a perspective that defines literary criticism in the modern terms I am interrogating, G. E. Bentley makes a similar point based on Herbert's remarks about *The Young Admiral:* "It is easy to think of the Master of the Revels as an enemy to dramatic genius and a stern foe of the players, for most of his recorded activities are inhibitive. But he did not think of himself this way. . . . [His] comments on *The Young Admiral,* a rather foolish tragicomedy, may not place Sir Henry very high on the scale of dramatic critics—especially modern ones—but they do demonstrate that in his own mind he was not simply the watchdog for the King's prerogative, the bishops' hegemony, and the tender sensibilities of friendly foreign powers, but the promoter of the best interests of the national theatrical enterprise" (1971, 186, 187). See also Alfred Harbage's remarks on Charles's interest in court drama and Herbert's record of reception of Sir William Davenant's play *The Wits:* " 'The kinge commended the language, but dislikt the plott and characters.' Characters, plot, language:

distinguished and weighed by the king—here is refined literary criticism!" (1936, 10). Harbage characteristically adds that "Henrietta had not a jot of literary taste" (11).

18. For an ahistorical, formalist account of Jonson's poetics of imitation, see Watson 1987. For an uneven, largely thematic attempt to historicize Jonson's imitative poetics in relation to his dramatic rivals and court patronage (without regard to censorship), see Rowe 1988. On food and Jonson, in addition to a note in Cognard 1979, see the fine essays by Hedrick 1977, Schoenfeldt 1988, Loewenstein 1986, and Boehrer 1990. On food and writing, see Cave 1979, and on food and society, see Elias 1978, Mennel 1985.

19. See Jonson's own comment on education in *Discoveries:* "Children should be drawne on with exercise, and emulation" (H & S 8:1659–60). On the politics of copia, see also Goldberg 1990.

20. The reversion of the Office of the Revels in 1621 to Jonson might seem to contradict this division, since Jonson himself was a dramatist. Yet when the reversion was granted, Jonson had not written for public theaters for five years and apparently had no plans to return to it. At the time the reversion was granted, he was strictly a court poet, clearly aligned with the dominant court faction. John Lyly was strictly a courtier—poetry was part of court service— and Samuel Daniel had Queen Anne as a patron. Whether there was a division between poetry and politics in the Renaissance is now a matter of dispute. Compare the discussions of the courtier in Javitch 1978 and Montrose 1983. Javitch argues that the poet and courtier competed for priority at court. Montrose believes that no such distinction was ever made: writing poetry was part of the work of being a courtier.

21. Compare Richard Brome's delegitimation of this mode of criticism in his prologue to *Covent Garden Weeded:* "He [the author] hath no faction in a partial way, / Prepar'd to cry it up and boast the Play" (1653, 2:3–4). For other examples, see Philip Massinger's prologue to *The Guardian* (1976, 26–32) and Brome's prologue to the *Antipodes* (1653, 3:1–11). On the Apollo Room, see Riggs 1988, 285–87, 297. On Jonson's relation to the Devil Tavern, see Esdaile 1943, and on the Mermaid, see Shapiro 1950. On the regulation of alehouses, see Clark 1983.

22. The differences between the French Academy and English criticism were relative, to be sure. Even in France there were controversies (see Jouhaud 1990) and an alternative academy of belles lettres was formulated by Abbé D'Aubignac (see Murray 1987). Moreover, there were provincial academies and the gendered criticism of the *précieuses*.

23. The metaphor of copia describes the library of Sir Robert Cotton, who, in the words of an admirer, "augmented his store" (Sharpe 1979). Compare Jonson's use of "store" as a metaphor for translation, where it figures a more militant symbolic exchange close to colonial conquest: "What treasure thou hast brought us! And what store / Still, dost thou arrive with, at our shore" (H & S, 7:4–5). Jonson goes on to describe Chapman's activity as a "trade" (8).

24. Indeed, Jonson often sold the books he owned. According to Drummond, who uses a somatic metaphor apt for my purposes, Jonson often did to

his library a version of what Vulcan does once; "several times he hath devoured his books" (H & S, 1:174). And after selling his books, he sometimes bought new copies (McPherson 1974, 9).

25. As an index of this shift, Sharpe (1979, 480) notes that *Utopia* has no libraries, whereas the *New Atlantis* does.

26. For more complicated accounts of Jonson's first folio, see Murray 1987; Loewenstein 1984; and Wayne 1982.

27. Indeed, as Murray comments, "the recognizable sources of *Discoveries* are often paraphrased and intermixed in the book with Jonson's own prose musings in a fashion that resembles theatrical counterfeiting" (1987, 48).

28. See Hunter 1847, 211; and Wimsatt and Brooks 1974, 176–81.

29. Vulcan is a version of the grotesque body Jonson often associates with the market. Through a pun on fire as venereal disease—"Winchesterian goose" (142); "the nun Kate Arden [a famous prostitute] / Kindled the fire" (149)—Jonson associates Vulcan with the nondifferentiating market. His final lines confirm the association:

> I'll conclude all in a civil curse.
>
> .   .   .   .   .
>
> Pox on thee, Vulcan, thy Pandora's pox,
> And all the evils that flew out of her box
> Light on thee: or if those plagues will not do,
> Thy wife's pox on thee, and Bess Braughton's too.
> (190, 213–16)

(Bess Braughton was a costly and famous whore who died of venereal disease.) Jonson's revenge is that Vulcan will burn from the "fire" set by nondifferentiating, unruly women. In contrast to the market, the library allows Jonson to regulate the movement from prepublication to postpublication of his own writings, putting some into circulation and not others.

Cervantes' account of the burning of Don Quixote's library offers an interesting contrast to Jonson's in its formulation of a patriarchal politics of imitation. Cervantes equates the original with the father and then symmetrically opposes both to an equation between the copy and the son. A debate ensues between the curate and the barber over whether the original or the copy ought to be destroyed. The curate argues that *Amadis de Gaul* "is this first book of knighthood that ever was printed in Spain and all the others have had their beginning and original from this; and therefore methinks that we must condemn him to the fire, without all remission, as the dogmatizer and head of so bad a sect" (1612–20, 41). The barber disagrees: " 'Not so fie!' qouth the barber; 'for I have heard that it is the very best contrived book of all those of that kind; and therefore hee is to be pardoned, as the only complete one in his profession.' 'That is true,' replied the curate, 'and for that reason we do give him his life for this time.' " Saving the father (the original) becomes an infanticidal principle of censorship: the copies (or the sons) are to be destroyed, equated with bastards.

The curate and barber proceed to examine an imitation of *Amadis*, namely, *Las Sergas*, described as "Amadis's lawfully begotten son" (41). The curate says, "His father's goodness shall nothing avail him. Take this book . . . and make the foundation for the fire we mean to make" (41). The curate's defense of a patriarchal politics of imitation is subverted, however, by the woman, who during the night, throws out all the books in the library. Whereas the unruly woman figures the subversion of patriarchy for Cervantes, Jonson upholds a patriarchal model by stressing Vulcan's cuckolding and by mobilizing a misogynist image of the prostitute to figure the indifference of an illegitimate censor such as Vulcan.

30. The uncertainty is indirectly reinforced by the contradiction between Jonson's hyperbolic willingness to burn romances and his own interest in the genre (see Patterson 1984, 166). Jonson's writings include "three books not afraid / To speak the fate of the Sicilian maid" (95–96); "three books not amisse / Reveald (if one can iudge) of Argenis" among the MS texts (H & S, 11:78 n. 95–97). Jonson refers here to John Barclay's romance *Argenis*, which James I had invited him to translate late in 1622 and which was entered on the Stationers' register October 2, 1623 (11:75).

31. See also Jonson's use of the "piece" metaphor in "Inviting a Friend to Supper" (Howsoe'er, my man / Shall read a piece of Virgil, Tacitus,") and his description of his son as his "best piece of poetry" in *Epigrams* 45.10.

32. The terms "whole" and "part" had significant ramifications for literary property rights. See Herford and Simpson's account of the conflicts over the registration of Dekker's *Whole Magnificent Entertainment* for James I and Jonson's quarto edition (1604) of "Ben Jonson: His Part of King James Royal and Magnificent Entertainment" (7:77–79).

33. On Jonson's contradictory relation to spies and what Jonson terms the "trade of application" in the epistle to *Volpone*, see Eccles 1937; and Archer 1992.

34. Yet even this critique reinscribes, at least in Noam Chomsky's case, idealized notions of truth and propaganda, which can themselves be a form of censorship when it comes to formulating policy. Chomsky's model is extremely dogmatic: it allows for only a certain kind of truth to be receivable, namely, his own.

35. My point is made all the more strongly by the contrast between Eagleton's sweeping argument that "criticism was born of a struggle against the absolutist state" (1984, 9, and see 107) and Habermas's more nuanced, comparative account of literary criticism and the public sphere (1989). As Habermas argues, England was exceptional, never an absolutist state in the full sense. Marxist historians such as Perry Anderson (1974) have confirmed that Europe comprised diverse absolutist states rather a single one.

36. See also David Hume, "Of the Standard of Taste." After asserting that "the joint verdict of such [critics as Hume defines them], wherever they are to be found, is the true standard of taste and beauty," Hume confronts several "embarrassing" questions: "But where are such critics to be found? By

what marks are they known? How distinguish them from pretenders?" (1742, 278–79). Hume resolves the embarrassment in a much less rigorous fashion than Kant by appealing to a universal standard of taste.

37. See also Kant's subsequent distinction between following one's predecessors and merely imitating them (1790, 137–39).

38. For other critiques of Habermas's discourse theory as too Kantian, see Wellmer 1991, 181, and for a critique of Eagleton's Kantianism, see Bennett 1990. For a similar critique of Bennett's Kantianism, see Eagleton 1990, 382.

39. One might point out that the library continues to operate as a form of public display, as symbolic capital and badge of the scholar-owner's serious status as a patron. Similarly, the eighteenth-century libel law refigured the relationship between the author and his book by equating an attack on one's writings with an attack on one's character and person. See, for example, the note from "The Publisher to the Reader" regarding Pope's *Dunciad:* "The town has been persecuted every week . . . not only with Pamphlets, Advertisements, Letters, and Weekly Essays, not only against the Wit and Writings, but against the Character and person of Mr. Pope" (Sutherland 1943, 202).

2. Licensing Authorities

1. On dramatic professionalism, see Bentley 1971 and 1984. On non-dramatic professionalism, see Auberlen 1983; and Helgerson 1983, 1–54.

2. My focus on *Bartholomew Fair* and *The Winter's Tale* is admittedly determined by limitations of space. Had I world enough and time, I would make a similar argument about *The Tempest,* focusing on the structural contrasts between the masque (with its reapers and happy laborers) and Stephano and Trinculo's interest in taking Caliban to England to put him on stage to "fetch a doit" and between the "music of the isle" and the drum and tabor that accompany Ariel as he leads Stephano, Trinculo, and Caliban across the island. For a different, much more benign account than my own of *Bartholomew Fair* as a response to Shakespearean romance, see Cartelli 1983. The theater was controversial, of course, as early as the 1560s. No one attacked licensing per se, however, until the seventeenth century. On this difference see Gildersleeve 1908, 35–36, 71. Significantly, local authorities confiscated licenses they suspected to have been forged or illegally obtained. The extent to which these disputes over licenses reflected Puritan opposition to the theater has been a matter of dispute. Alwin Thaler (1920, 128–30) and Glynn Wickham (1981, 1:141–47) argue that the players did encounter Puritan opposition. L. G. Salingar, Gerald Harrison, and Bruce Cochrane (1968), however, contend that the primary reason permission was refused was not ideological but economic. Yet since Puritans such as Prynne opposed the theater on economic grounds (it took money from the poor), it hardly seems possible to distinguish ideological from economic forms of opposition. For other licensing controversies, see Burt 1987; Murray 1963, 2:348–50, 359–60. For similar cases, see Murray 1963, 2:6, 339–40, 341; see also Bruce and Hamilton 1858–97, 9:321, 334–35, 354–55.

3. What I describe here is generally characterized as the transition from feudalism to capitalism, itself a matter of intense debate between revisionists (see, for example, Sharpe, 1978), on the one hand, and Whigs and Marxists, on the other. For Marxist and Whig rejoinders to the revisionist critique, see Butler 1984; Ely and Hunt 1988; Tricomi 1989; and Venuti 1989. For a brilliant reinterpretation of Renaissance literature in terms of the transition from feudalism to capitalism, see Halpern 1991.

4. For an illuminating Foucauldian analysis of the theater as a disciplinary institution, see Wilson 1987. A Foucauldian perspective on the theater enables us to see more clearly how Jonson's antitheatricality paradoxically nearly coincides with radical Protestant attacks on the theater. For an analysis of this paradox, see Burt 1987, 551–54.

5. See *OED,* s.v. "hocus pocus." See also Guilding 1895, 263–64; *JCS,* 2:612–13. It is worth noting that one of Vincent's fellow travelers was in all probability a recusant: "Being searched, there was found about him 23s. 6d., in money, a paire of beades with a small crucifix at th'end thereof" (Guilding 1895, 265).

6. For a sophisticated account of the equivocal relation of this masque (as well as other masques by Jonson) to James's authority, see Goldberg 1983a, 55–65, 136–39.

7. The importance of "license" in *Bartholomew Fair* has been established from an ahistorical perspective by Ian Donaldson 1970, 46–77. For a brilliant old historicist account, see Marcus 1986b, 38–63. See also Stallybrass and White 1986.

8. There is no record of a further performance at court until 1661. See H & S, 9:245. Herford and Simpson speculate that the "rising power of Puritanism may have been a deterrent" (245). One can better appreciate the tensions between *Bartholomew Fair* and James's political authority by contrasting the play to *Cynthia's Revels.* In the earlier play, Jonson uses the court masque to affirm both Cynthia's (Elizabeth's) and Crites' (Jonson's) authority. In *Bartholomew Fair,* Jonson only has the license of the Revels Office.

9. For critics who defend the fair and the puppet show, see especially Enck 1957, 189–208; Barish 1959, 3–17, and 1972, 3–35; Waith 1963, 2–21; Sweeney 1985, 157–89; and Haynes 1984. For those who regard Jonson as a critic of the fair and the puppet show, see, among others, Levin 1965, 173–78; Cope 1967, 127–52; Barton 1984. Joel Kaplan's (1970) account of what he calls the play's moral ambiguities is closer to my own.

10. On the use of puppets in miracle plays, see Chambers 1925, 2:157–59. Also valuable is Speaight 1956, 52–72.

11. Leatherhead's assertion that he has the Master's hand for his authority (5.3.16) may be more a more precise allusion to licensed shows than may appear. In a letter dated July 16, 1619, sent to all mayors, sheriffs and other authorities in the land, Sir George Buc says that he has licensed puppet shows titled *The Conspiracy of Gunpowder Treason under the Parliament House* and the *Destruction of Sodome and Gomorha.* See Bawcutt 1984a, 329. It is worth adding that even a puppet show about the Gunpowder Rebellion would probably have

been equivocal. On the one hand, like Gunpowder Treason Day, it would have celebrated the defeat of a Catholic insurrection against King James and thus would have affirmed his authority. Yet the anti-Catholicism of Gunpowder Treason Day (or a show about the rebellion), together with other holidays such as Elizabeth's Accession Day, was attractive to Puritans, many of whom opposed James's willingness to compromise with Catholics in England and on the Continent. See Underdown 1985, 70–71, 129.

12. Ian Donaldson concludes that the play "is a comic parable upon the . . . gospel text: *Judge not, that ye be not judged*" (1970, 77).

13. On prostitution in the play, see Maus 1984, 83–84.

14. Although all women (with the exception of widows) were property in the Renaissance and thus exchanged by men, wardship was controversial in seventeenth-century England because it "allowed all tenants-in-chief of the king who inherited their lands as minors (under 21 if they were men, under 14 if they were women) to be bought and sold by people who [like Justice Overdo] had little or no interest in the welfare of the wards" (Smith 1979, 124).

15. Jonson's ambivalence toward his audience in the induction has been noticed in Kaplan 1970, 154–56. Wayne 1982 and Agnew 1986, 119–21 view the contract as a response to market pressures that eroded an earlier, feudal model of community.

16. On the importance of patronage factionalism in relation to the Master of the Revels, see Dutton 1991; and Clare 1990.

17. It is possible, of course, to argue that Pembroke might have been better able to control the censor, or consolidate his control over various factions by allowing them access to the censor. Apart from the total lack of evidence for such an argument, its force is limited by its assumption of a conspiracy theory of politics and by its projection of a modern liberal notion of consensual politics back onto the Renaissance. I thank Richard Dutton for drawing my attention to this episode.

18. For other instances, see Henry Farley's record of entertainments in Renaissance London in 1616:

> Spectators come
> To see a strange outlandish fowle,
> A quaint baboon, an ape, an owl,
> A dancing bear, a giant's bone,
> A foolish engine move alone,
> A morris-dance, a puppet play,
> Mad Tom to sing a roundelay,
> A woman dancing on a rope,
> Bull-baiting also at the Hope;
> A rhymer's jests, a juggler's cheats,
> Or players acting on the stage.
> (Altick 1978, 8)

Sir Henry Wotton's account of a fire-eater in a letter dated June 18, 1633, also bears interestingly on the nature/artifice exchange in *The Winter's Tale* (4.3):

> Let me add to these a strange thing to be seen in London for a couple of pence, which I know not whether I should call a piece of art or nature: it is an Englishman, like some swabber of a ship come from the Indies, where he hath learnt to eat fire as familiarly as ever I saw any eat cakes, even whole glowing brands, which he will crash with his teeth and swallow. I believe he hath been hard famished in the Tierra del Fuego, on the south of the Magellan strait. (Smith 1907, 2:346)

Jonson also alludes to a famous horse in *Poetaster,* when Captain Tucca says to Horace: "I'll teach thee to turne me into Bankes his horse, and to tell gentlemen I am a Iugler and shew trickes" (582–84). Alwin Thaler (1920, 498–99) also notes that marginal entertainers competed with traveling companies.

19. It is worth noting that Shakespeare legitimated play in *The Winter's Tale* precisely by combining genres Greene kept separate, namely, romance and coney-catching pamphlets. On Greene's failed strategies of self-legitimation, see Auberlen 1983, 157–78.

20. On Shakespeare and textiles, see Richard Wilson 1986.

3. Th'Only Catos of This Critick Age

1. On the differences between Charles and James as Jonson's patrons, see especially Marcus 1986b, 10–19.

2. For a further examination of Massinger, see Burt 1988; and Venuti 1989.

3. I am not denying that there were significant historical differences (or the possibility of change) between the Jacobean and Caroline courts. As we will see, the Caroline court reformed the Jacobean court and introduced theatrical innovations of its own. My point is that the tastes of the Jacobean and Caroline courts were contradictory, whatever the specificity of each court's tastes and practices.

4. On the new office, see Gildersleeve 1908, 46. For two accounts of lion baiting in the Tower, see G. B. Harrison 1966, 110, 207; and for an account of a bearbaiting to which Jonson alludes in *Love Restored,* see Nichols 1828, 2:259, also 1:517, 2:307–8.

5. On the court's reception of *Pleasure Reconciled,* see Marcus, 1979, 290, and on its reception of *Time Vindicated,* see Pearl 1984, 69.

6. For similar instances of Jonson's problems in earlier masques, see Fischer 1977; and Burt 1987.

7. My thinking about the body and court censorship is indebted to Leonard Tennenhouse. I depart from his view, however, that the monarch's body determined the semiotics (and hence politics) of theatrical representation.

8. Old historicist accounts of censorship tend to focus narrowly on politics

and have thus ignored how censorship regulated presentations of the monarch's and the aristocratic body. See, for example, Margot Heinemann's remarks on censorship: "It was, of course almost exclusively a political censorship. Except for the specific ban on oaths and profane language introduced in 1606, the censor was scarcely concerned with questions of morality or good taste. At incest, adultery, rape, sexual invective and innuendo, or Rabelaisian sex-and-lavatory clowning he seems not to have a turned a hair" (1980, 37). Censorship of depictions of the monarch's body has gone unremarked in discussions of particular censored plays, or its significance has been dismissed when noted (see, for example, Dutton 1991, on *A Game at Chess*). Modern assumptions about sexuality and about taste determine this rather ahistorical account of the drama to which, in an equally ahistorical manner, revisionists appeal when they assert the good taste of the court. The censor did in fact turn a hair in a number of instances. As Anne Lancashire points out in her edition of *The Second Maiden's Tragedy* (1611), "under Elizabeth I and James I dramatic censorship was above all political rather than moral. . . . Some censorship of obscenities, however, also occurred" (1978, 275). See also Bald 1938 and 1937–38.

9. I am indebted for the material in this paragraph to Kim Walker 1991. See also Veevers 1989; Tomlinson 1992.

10. On the reception of *The Triumph of Peace,* see Orgel and Strong 1973; Butler 1989; and Venuti 1989.

11. On *The Court Beggar* and theater licensing, see Freehafer 1969.

12. On these topical allusions, see Freehafer 1969, 369–70.

Conclusion

1. On these cases, see note 1, Introduction. In linking these examples, I do not mean to suggest that they are all forms of the same kind of censorship. On the contrary, I wish to move away from a monolithic definition of censorship precisely in order to account for the differences between these examples.

2. For an example of the kind of theory I am opposing, see Jansen 1988 especially "The Semantics of Censorship and Resistance," 192–201. For an example of the sort of multiplicity I am interested in, see Suleiman et al. 1990; Webster 1990; and Bourdieu 1991.

3. On the distinction between the general-intellectual and the specific-intellectual, see Foucault 1977b, 205–17. For similar antihumanist accounts of freedom and the intellectual, see Andrew Ross's discussion of what he calls the "liberatory" in relation to pornography censorship (1989, 171–208). See also Rajchman 1985, 77–93; and Bové 1990.

4. This equivalence has been played out in relation to Islam in the Rushdie affair in an often orientalist manner. Western critics describe Islam as medieval, and Rushdie is chastised for having been critical of Margaret Thatcher. See Ignatieff 1989, 254–56. For a critique of this kind of view, see Webster 1990.

5. For the contradictions in censorship under Stalin, see Jansen 1988, 114–30. On the peculiarities of Nazi censorship in occupied France, see Davis 1990.

6. In "Tolerant Repression," Blair Worden (1990) argues that the court of Henry VIII, for example, was not like Stalin's.

7. Jürgen Habermas states, for example: "The elimination of censorship marked a new stage in the development of the public sphere. . . . Censorship came to an end with the Licensing Act of 1695" (1962, 58, 59). For a similar account of England, see Hill 1985.

8. See Howard 1986; Sinfield 1985; Ferguson 1987.

9. To be sure, a Marxist critique of censorship can be made. Marx (1842, 109–31) himself argued against censorship. See Trotsky 1924, however, for a sophisticated defense of censorship. For a more recent neo-Marxist example, see Herman and Chomsky 1988. This critique, however, produces the same kind of problems I have identified in Marxist accounts of the economy. Chomsky and Herman focus only on economic production, adopting what they call a propaganda model. Were market censorship over production to disappear and the truth be printed or shown on television, they assume that the public would automatically react to it in a progressive manner. In fact, the public interest has regularly been constructed to legitimate repression.

10. See, for example, the Habermasian account in Eagleton 1984 or the similar account in Hohendahl 1982.

11. Edward Said (1983, 146–49) criticizes both Jameson and Eagleton on precisely the same grounds as Eagleton criticizes Jameson. Lawrence Venuti, to his credit, recognizes the problem: "The commodification of scholarly criticism goes on apace, absorbing even those activities which seek to interrogate and change the very economic process of commodification" (1989, 271). Recognition of the problem does not neutralize it, however.

12. For this debate, see Holub 1984, 121–34. Holub points to a contradiction in the critique of classical Marxists offered by reception aestheticians: "Neither Iser, nor Jauss, nor any West German reception theorist is willing to dispense with all constraints on the production of meaning from the side of the text" (133). According to Hans Robert Jauss, "The producing of a socialist manner of reading demands the internalization of the correct social norms so that the subject can adapt to the society." In Jauss's view, Marxists adopt a conformist model of reading and act as censors, negating the genuinely emancipatory role of literature (see Holub 1984, 132). Yet Jauss's reception aesthetics reverts to an apolitical humanist notion of the literary as beyond all historical and ideological determination, and often feeds back into a romantic conception of artistic expression. A similar kind of problem can be found in structuralist versions of reader-response criticism. Roland Barthes (1989) has celebrated the death of the producing author and the birth of the consuming reader, a shift that in his view opens the text to a free play of interpretation. Structuralists like Barthes do not allow for the fact that a constraint such as the author-function could be progressive, and their account of the reader as a producer reinscribes the Marxist account of consumption as a form of reproduction. In licensing the

reader as the active producer of the text instead of its passive consumer, both reception-aesthetics and structuralist accounts of reading and textuality assume that censorship does not exist or that it would be possible to move beyond it. They ignore the fact that there are always constraints on discursive production and reproduction, as Foucault has argued.

13. "The Ivory Censor" 1990. See also Sykes 1988, 133–50.

14. In discounting this position, political critics would be denying it a hearing, effectively censoring it and thereby playing into the hands of the Right.

15. On the MLA's response to recent NEA controversies, see Brombert 1989, 1–2; Franklin 1989, 3–4; and Stimpson 1990, 3. *PMLA* will also publish a special issue on censorship in 1993. For similar academic responses, see Warren 1991, 1. For left-wing academic censorship, see Mari J. Matsuda's influential essay (1989). For a related case against casting Jonathan Pryce as a Vietnamese pimp in the New York production of *Miss Saigon,* see Lisa Yoffee 1991.

16. Stanley Fish takes Milton's assertion in *Areopagitica* that some things must be censored as paradigmatic rather than as an aberrant moment in Milton's account of censorship. Fish moves away from his usually cheerful assessment of the profession, arguing that there is no such thing as free speech and concluding "there is no safe place" (1992, 245). While I agree with Fish that free speech is always bounded and thus never free, I do not agree that we should stop making appeals to free speech or shouting "censorship" in a crowded room. Precisely because, as Fish points out, any battle against censorship will be a battle to let the voices one wants to hear (including, and above all, one's own) be heard, appeals to free speech and attacks on one's opponents as censors are crucial, indispensable weapons in one's arsenal. Indeed, they may be the only weapons one has. For a related critique of Fish's neopragmatist account of political criticism, see Burt 1990.

17. I am thinking here in particular of the session "Answering Back: the Future of the Profession" at the 1991 meeting of the Modern Language Association organized by the executive council.

18. This slogan was printed on the program cover of the 1990 MTV Music and Video Awards; 1990 also involved a "Fight Censorship" campaign of MTV advertisements. MTV itself has acted, of course, as censor of Neil Young, black artists, and most recently, of Madonna's video, "Justify My Love."

19. For an analysis of the contradictions in the right-wing view of the market which complements my own, see Ross 1990.

20. On Philip Morris and television advertising, see Schiller 1989, 56–63.

21. On Keating's involvement with a right-wing antiporn movement in Cincinnati, see Carr 1990, 22; and Kendrick 1987, 218.

22. For examples of this argument, see Kramer 1989, 1–2. Robert Brustein, in typical liberal fashion, equates present would-be theater censors on the Left and Right and advises both to "lighten up" (1990, 35–37). For a more insidious version of this "liberal" strategy, see Taylor 1991, 32–40. Taylor equates the religious Right's attacks of the 1970s with the new fundamentalism of political

critics in the 1980s. (He is completely oblivious to the Right's attacks on the fine arts and mass culture in the 1980s.) See also Adler et al. 1990.

23. This passage and a similar one endorsing the death penalty for "fascists" such as Cardinal John O'Connor initially caused former NEA director John Frohnmayer to withdraw the funding for the program. Frohnmayer then backpedaled and withdrew funding only for the program notes, ironically keeping his actions open to further criticism from the arts community for his willingness to cave in to would-be censors of the arts.

24. On Wojnarowicz's case, see Hess 1990; Dubin 1992, 208–20. On moral rights, see Buskirk 1991.

25. On Soviet censorship, see Jansen 1988, 225–50; on East German censorship, see Darnton 1991; on Europe, see Schöpflin 1983.

26. A perfect example of this problem is the controversy over two exhibits at the Smithsonian Institution. The Right accused the Smithsonian of having a leftist "political agenda" in mounting an exhibit titled "The West as America." In another instance, the curator Laurie Braun came under fire from the Left when she attempted to withdraw from the exhibit "Eadweard Muybridge and Contemporary American Photography" (which she had not organized) a piece by Sol Lewitt which she found degrading and offensive to women. On "The West as America," see Foner and Weiner 1991; on the Muybridge exhibition, see Kimmelman 1991; Livingston 1991.

27. I am pursuing these topics in a book in progress tentatively titled *Once More unto the Breach: Handling Offense in the Theaters of Shakespeare*. On hate speech in the Renaissance, see Hughes 1991. On pardon in Shakespeare, see Natalie Davis's tantalizingly brief remarks (1987, 113–14). For broader examinations of tolerance, civility, and pardon, see, respectively, Abel 1991; Dhoquois 1991; Sabel 1991.

Works Cited

Abel, Oliver, ed. 1991. *Le pardon: Briser la dette et l'oubli*. Serie Morales no. 4. Paris: Autrement.

Adams, Joseph Quincy, ed. 1917. *The Dramatic Records of Sir Henry Herbert, Master of the Revels, 1574–1673*. New Haven: Yale University Press.

Adams, Robert M. 1979. "On the Bulk of Ben." In *Ben Jonson's Plays and Masques*, ed. Robert M. Adams, 482–92. New York: Norton.

Adler, Jerry, et al. 1990. "Taking Offense: Is This the New Enlightenment or the New McCarthyism?" *Newsweek,* December 24, pp. 48–54.

Agnew, Jean-Christophe. 1986. *Worlds Apart: The Theater and the Market in Anglo-American Thought*. Chicago: University of Chicago Press.

Althusser, Louis. 1970. "Contradiction and Overdetermination." In *For Marx,* pp. 87–128. Trans. Ben Brewster. New York: Vintage Books.

———. 1971. "Ideology and the Ideological State Apparatus." In *Lenin and Philosophy and Other Essays*. Trans. Ben Brewster. London: New Left Books.

Althusser, Louis, and Etienne Balibar. 1970. *Reading Capital*. 2d ed. Trans. Allen Lane. London: New Left Books.

Altick, Richard D. 1978. *The Shows of London*. Cambridge: Harvard University Press.

Anderson, Perry. 1974. *Lineages of the Absolutist State*. London: Verso.

Appiganesi, Lisa, and Sara Maitland, eds. 1989. *The Rushdie File*. Syracuse: Syracuse University Press.

Archer, John Michael. 1993. *Sovereignty and Intelligence: Spying and Court Culture in English Renaissance Writing*. Stanford: Stanford University Press.

Ashton, Robert. 1965. *The City and the Court, 1603–1643*. Cambridge: Cambridge University Press.

———. 1983. "Popular Entertainment and Social Control in Later Elizabethan and Early Stuart England." *London Journal* 9:1–11.

Atkinson, J. T., ed. 1893. *Quarter Sessions Records.* 4 vols. York: North Riding Record Society.

Auberlen, Eckhard. 1983. *The Commonwealth of Wit: The Writer's Image and His Strategies of Self-Representation in Elizabethan Literature.* Tübingen: Gunter Narr.

Aufderheide, Patricia, ed. 1992. *Beyond PC: Toward a Politics of Understanding.* Saint Paul, Minn.: Graywolf Press.

Ayres, Philip J. 1983. "Jonson, Northampton, and the Treason in *Sejanus.*" *Modern Philology* 80 (May): 356–63.

Bakhtin, Mikhail. 1968. *Rabelais and His World.* Trans. Helene Iswolsky. Cambridge: MIT Press.

Bald, R. C. 1937–38. "Arthur Wilson's *The Inconstant Lady.*" *Library* n.s. 4:18.

———. 1938. "*Bonducca, The Humourous Lieutenant,* and *The Woman's Prize,*" *Bibliographical Studies in the Beaumont and Fletcher Folio of 1647* (supplement to the Bibliographical Society's *Transactions,* no. 13), pp. 66–68.

Barish, Jonas. 1959. "*Bartholomew Fair* and Its Puppets." *Modern Language Quarterly* 20:3–17. Revised in *Ben Jonson and the Language of Prose Comedy,* pp. 187–239. New York: Norton, 1960.

———. 1972. "Feasting and Judging in Jonsonian Comedy." *Renaissance Drama* n.s. 5:3–35.

———. 1981. "Jonson and the Loathèd Stage." In *The Anti-theatrical Prejudice,* pp. 132–54. Berkeley: University of California Press.

Barker, Francis. 1984. *The Tremulous Private Body: Essays on Subjection.* New York: Methuen.

Barnes, Thomas G. 1959. "County Politics and a Puritan Cause Célébre: Somerset Church Ales, 1633." *Transactions of the Royal Historical Society.* 5th ser. 9:103–22.

Barroll, Leeds. 1988. "A New History for Shakespeare and Our Time." *Shakespeare Quarterly* 39 (Winter): 441–64.

Barthes, Roland. 1970. *Writing Degree Zero and Elements of Semiology.* Trans. Annette Lavers and Colin Smith. Boston: Beacon.

———. 1989. "The Death of the Author." In *The Rustle of Language,* pp. 49–55. Trans. Richard Howard. Berkeley: University of California Press.

Barton, Anne. 1984. *Ben Jonson, Dramatist.* Cambridge: Cambridge University Press.

Bas, George. 1963. "James Shirley et 'th'untuned kennel': Une petite guerre des théâtres vers 1630." *Etudes Anglaise* 16, no. 1:11–22.

Baudrillard, Jean. 1975. *The Mirror of Production.* Trans. Mark Poster. St. Louis: Telos Press.

———. 1981. *For a Critique of the Political Economy of the Sign.* Trans. Charles Levin. St. Louis: Telos Press.

———. 1983. *Simulations.* Trans. Paul Foss et al. New York: Semiotext(e).

Bawcutt, N. W. 1984a. "Craven Ord Transcripts of Sir Henry Herbert's Office-Book in the Folger Library." *English Literary Renaissance* 14, no. 1:83–94.

——. 1984b. "New Revels Documents of Sir George Buc and Sir Henry Herbert, 1619–1662," *Review of English Studies,* n.s. 35:316–31.

Beal, Peter. 1980. "Massinger at Bay: Unpublished Verses." *Yearbook of English Studies* 10:190–203.

Beaumont, Francis, and John Fletcher. 1979. *The Dramatic Works in the Beaumont and Fletcher Canon.* ed. Fredson Bowers. Cambridge: Cambridge University Press.

Beier, A. L. 1985. *Masterless Men: The Vagrancy Problem in England, 1500–1660.* London: Methuen.

Belsey, Catherine, 1985. *The Subject of Tragedy.* London: Methuen.

Benjamin, Walter. 1969. "The Work of Art in the Age of Mechanical Reproduction." In *Illuminations,* pp. 217–52. Trans. Harry Zohn. New York: Schocken Books.

——. 1986. "The Author as Producer." In *Reflections,* pp. 220–38. Trans. Edmund Jephcott. New York: Schocken Books.

Bennett, Tony. 1979a. *Formalism and Marxism.* London: Verso.

——. 1979b. "Popular Culture and the Turn to Gramsci." In *Popular Culture and Social Relations,* ed. Tony Bennett et al., pp. xi–xix. Philadelphia: Open University Press.

——. 1979c. "The Politics of the 'Popular' and Popular Culture." In *Popular Culture and Social Relations,* ed. Tony Bennett et al., pp. 6–21. Philadelphia: Open University Press.

——. 1979d. "Texts in History: The Determinations of Readings and Their Texts." In *Post-structuralism and the Question of Theory,* ed. Derek Attridge, Geoff Bennington, and Robert C. Young, pp. 63–81. Cambridge: Cambridge University Press.

——. 1990. *Outside Literature.* London: Routledge.

Bentley, G. E. 1941–68. *The Jacobean and Caroline Stage.* 7 vols. Oxford: Clarendon Press.

——. 1971. *The Profession of Dramatist in Shakespeare's Time, 1590–1642.* Princeton: Princeton University Press.

——. 1977. "The Salisbury Court Theater and Its Boy Players." *Huntington Library Quarterly* 60, no. 2:127–49.

——. 1978. "The Troubles of a Caroline Acting Troupe: Prince Charles's Company." *Huntington Library Quarterly* 61, no. 3:217–49.

——. 1984. *The Profession of Player in Shakespeare's Time, 1590–1642.* Princeton: Princeton University Press.

Bergeron, David M. 1986. *Shakespeare's Romances and the Royal Family.* Kansas: University of Kansas Press.

——. 1988. "Patronage of Dramatists: The Case of Thomas Heywood." *English Literary Renaissance* 18, no. 2:294–304.

Berman, Paul, ed. 1992. *Debating PC: The Controversy over Political Correctness on College Campuses.* New York: Bantam Books.

Blagden, Cyprian. 1960. *The Stationers' Company: A History, 1403–1959.* Cambridge: Harvard University Press.

Boehrer, Bruce. 1990. "Renaissance Overeating: The Sad Case of Ben Jonson." *Publications of the Modern Language Association* 105 (October): 1071–82.

Boose, Lynda. 1987. "The Family in Shakespeare Studies, or Studies in the Family of Shakespeareans, or The Politics of Politics." *Renaissance Quarterly* 60 (Winter): 707–42.

——. Forthcoming. "The Bishops' Ban, Elizabethan Pornography, and the Sexualization of the Jacobean Stage." In *Enclosure Acts: Sexuality, Property, and Culture in Early Modern England,* ed. Richard Burt and John Archer. Ithaca: Cornell University Press.

Borch-Jacobsen, Mikkel. 1988. *The Freudian Subject.* Trans. Catherine Porter. Stanford: Stanford University Press.

Bourdieu, Pierre. 1968. "Outline of a Sociological Theory of Art." *International Social Science Journal* 20:589–612.

——. 1977. *Outline of a Theory of Practice.* Trans. Richard Nice. Cambridge: Cambridge University Press.

——. 1979. "Symbolic Power." *Critique of Anthropology* 4 (Summer): 77–85.

——. 1984. *Distinction: A Social Critique of the Judgement of Taste.* Trans. Richard Nice. Cambridge: Harvard University Press.

——. 1988. *Homo Academicus.* Trans. Peter Collier. Stanford: Stanford University Press.

——. 1991. "Censorship and the Imposition of Form." In *Language and Symbolic Power,* ed. John B. Thompson, trans. Gino Raymond and Matthew Adamson, pp. 137–59. Cambridge: Harvard University Press.

Bové, Paul A. 1990. "Power and Freedom: Opposition and the Humanities." *October* 53:78–92.

Bradbrook, Muriel. 1976. *The Living Monument: Shakespeare and the Theater of His Time.* Cambridge: Cambridge University Press.

Braunmuller, Al. 1990. " 'To the Globe I Rowed': John Holles Sees *A Game at Chess.*" *English Literary Renaissance* 20, no. 2:340–56.

Brennan, Michael G. 1988. *Literary Patronage in the English Renaissance: The Pembroke Family.* London: Routledge.

Bristol, Michael. 1985. *Carnival and Theater: Plebeian Culture and Renaissance Authority.* New York: Methuen.

——. 1991. "In Search of the Bear: Spatio-temporal Form and the Heterogeneity of Economies of *The Winter's Tale.*" *Shakespeare Quarterly* 42, no. 2:145–67.

Brombert, Victor. 1989. "President's Column." *Modern Language Association Newsletter* (Winter): 1–2.

Brome, Richard. 1653. *The Dramatic Works of Richard Brome.* 3 vols. Rpt. New York: AMS Press, 1966.

Brown, Laura. 1985. *Alexander Pope.* Oxford: Basil Blackwell.

Bruce, J., and W. D. Hamilton, eds. 1858–97. *Calendar of State Papers: Domestic Series of the Reign of Charles I,* vol. 9: *1635–36.* London: Longman, Green, Longman, and Roberts.

Brustein, Robert. 1990. "Lighten up America." *New Republic,* September 22, pp. 35–37.

Burger, Peter. 1984. *Theory of the Avante-Garde.* Trans. Michael Shaw. Minneapolis: University of Minnesota Press.

Burke, Peter. 1977. "Popular Culture in Seventeenth-Century London," *London Journal* 3:143–62. Rpt. in *Popular Culture in Seventeenth-Century England,* ed. Barry Reay, pp. 31–90. New York: St. Martin's Press, 1985.

———. 1978. *Popular Culture in Early Modern Europe.* London: Temple Smith.

Burt, Richard A. 1987. " 'Licensed by Authority': Ben Jonson and the Politics of Early Stuart Theater." *English Literary History* 54 (Fall): 529–60.

———. 1988. " ' 'Tis Writ by Me': Massinger's *The Roman Actor* and the Politics of Reception in the Renaissance Theater." *Theatre Journal* 40 (October): 332–47.

———. 1990. " 'A Dangerous Rome': Shakespeare's *Julius Caesar* and the Discursive Determinism of Cultural Politics." In *Contending Kingdoms: Historical, Psychological, and Feminist Approaches to the Literature of Sixteenth-Century England and France,* ed. Marie-Rose Logan and Peter Rudnytsky, pp. 109–27. Detroit: Wayne State University Press.

———. Forthcoming a. " 'Degenerate "Art" ': the Simulation of Censorship and Public Aesthetics in Post-Liberal Los Angeles and Berlin." In *The Administration of Aesthetics: Censorship, Political Criticism, and the Public Sphere,* ed. Richard Burt. Minneapolis: University of Minnesota Press.

———. Forthcoming b. "Introduction: the 'New' Censorship." In *The Administration of Aesthetics: Censorship, Political Criticism, and the Public Sphere,* ed. Richard Burt and John Archer. Minneapolis: University of Minnesota Press.

Buskirk, Martha. 1991. "Moral Rights: First Step or False Start?" *Art in America* 79 (November): 37–45.

Butler, Martin. 1984. *Theatre and Crisis, 1632–1642.* Cambridge: Cambridge University Press.

———. 1988. "*Love's Sacrifice:* Ford's Metatheatrical Tragedy." In *John Ford: Critical Re-Visions,* ed. Michael Neill, pp. 201–32. Cambridge: Cambridge University Press.

———. ed. 1989. *The Selected Plays of Ben Jonson.* Vol. 2. Cambridge: Cambridge University Press.

———. 1990. "Stuart Politics in Jonson's *Tale of a Tub.*" *Modern Language Review* 85 (January): 12–28.

———. 1991. " 'We Are One Mans All': Jonson's *Gypsies Metamorphosed.*" *Yearbook of English Studies* 21:253–73.

———. 1992a. "Ecclesiastical Censorship or Early Stuart Drama: The Case of Jonson's *The Magnetic Lady.*" *Modern Philology* 89 (May): 469–81.

———. 1992b. "Late Jonson." In *The Politics of Tragicomedy,* ed. Gordon McMullan and Jonathan Hope, pp. 166–88. London: Routledge.

Carr, C. 1990. "Robert Mapplethorpe Trial." *LA Weekly,* October 26, pp. 20–28.

Cartelli, Thomas. 1983. "*Bartholomew Fair* as Urban Arcadia: Jonson Responds to Shakespeare." *Renaissance Drama* n.s. 14:151–72.

Cartwright, William. 1951. *The Plays and Poems of William Cartwright.* Ed. G. Blakemore Evans. Madison: University of Wisconsin Press.

Cave, Terence. 1979. *The Cornucopian Text: Problems of Writing in the French Renaissance.* Oxford: Clarendon Press.

Cervantes, Miguel de. 1612–20. *Don Quixote of the Mancha.* 4 vols. Trans. Robert Shelton. Rpt. London: Gibbons, 1895.

Chambers, E. K. 1923. *The Elizabethan Stage.* 4 vols. Oxford: Clarendon Press.

——. 1925. *The Medieval Stage.* 2 vols. London: Oxford University Press.

Charles, Amy M. 1977. *A Life of George Herbert.* Ithaca: Cornell University Press.

——. 1982. "Sir Henry Herbert: The Master of the Revels as a Man of Letters." *Modern Philology* 80: 1–12.

Chassinon, Jean. 1604. *The merchandise of popish priests. Laying Open to the World, how cunningly they cheate and abuse poor people, with theyr false, deceitfull, and counterfeit wares.* London.

Clare, Janet. 1990. *Art Made Tongue-Tied by Authority: Elizabethan and Jacobean Censorship.* Manchester: Manchester University Press.

Clark, Peter. 1983. *The English Alehouse: A Social History, 1200–1830.* London: Longman.

Cognard, Roger. 1979. "Jonson's 'Inviting a Friend to Supper.'" *Explicator* 37, no. 3:4–5.

Cohen, Walter. 1985. *Drama of a Nation: Public Theater in Renaissance England and Spain.* Ithaca: Cornell University Press.

——. 1987. "Political Criticism of Shakespeare." In *Shakespeare Reproduced: The Text in History and Ideology,* ed. Jean R. Howard and Marion O'Connor, pp. 18–46. New York: Methuen.

Cook, Ann Jennalie. 1981. *The Privileged Playgoer of Shakespeare's London, 1574–1642.* Princeton: Princeton University Press.

Cope, Jackson. 1967. "*Bartholomew Fair* as Blasphemy." *Renaissance Drama* n.s. 8:127–52.

Cox, Lee Sheridan. 1969. "The Role of Autolycus in *The Winter's Tale,*" *Studies in English Literature* 9:283–301.

Crean, P. J. 1937–38. "The Stage Licensing Act of 1737," *Modern Philology* 35:239–55.

Cubitt, Sean. 1990. "Innocence and Manipulation: Censorship, Consumption, and Freedom in 1980s Britain." In *Consumption, Identity, and Style: Marketing, Meanings, and the Packaging of Pleasure,* ed. Alan Tomlinson, pp. 102–20. London: Routledge.

Curry, Richard O., ed. 1988. *Freedom at Risk: Secrecy, Censorship, and Repression in the 1980s.* Philadelphia: Open University Press.

Darnton, Robert. 1991. "The Good Old Days." *New York Review of Books,* May 16, pp. 44–48.

Davenant, William. 1872. *The Dramatic Works of Sir William D'Avenant.* Ed. James Maidment and W. H. Logan. 5 vols. Rpt. New York: Russell and Russell, 1964.

Davis, Lennard J. 1983. *Factual Fictions: The Origins of the Novel*. New York: Columbia University Press.

Davis, Natalie Zemon. 1987. *Fiction in the Archives: Pardon Tales and Their Tellers in Sixteenth-Century France*. Stanford: Stanford University Press.

———. 1990. "Rabelais among the Censors: 1940s, 1540s." *Representations* 32 (Fall): 1–26.

Dhoquois, Regine, ed. 1991. *La politesse: Vertu des apparences*. Serie Morales no. 2. Paris: Autrement.

Dollimore, Jonathan. 1986. "Subjectivity, Sexuality, and Transgression: The Jacobean Connection." *Renaissance Drama* n.s. 17:53–82.

———. 1989. *Radical Tragedy: Religion, Ideology, and Power in the Drama of Shakespeare and His Contemporaries*. 2d edition. Chicago: University of Chicago Press.

Dollimore, Jonathan, and Alan Sinfield. 1985. "Introduction: Shakespeare, Cultural Materialism and the New Historicism." In *Political Shakespeare: Essays on Cultural Materialism,* ed. Dollimore and Sinfield, pp. 2–17. Ithaca: Cornell University Press.

Donaldson, Ian. 1970. *The World Turned Upside Down: Comedy from Jonson to Fielding*. Oxford: Clarendon Press.

———. 1984. "Jonson and Anger." In *English Satire and the Satiric Tradition,* ed. Claude Rawson, pp. 56–71. Oxford: Basil Blackwell.

———. 1988. "Jonson and the Destruction of the Book." Unpublished paper presented at the Folger Shakespeare Library, Washington, D.C.

Dubin, Steven C. 1992. *Arresting Images: Impolitic Art and Uncivil Actions*. New York: Routledge.

Dutton, Richard. 1983. *Ben Jonson: To the First Folio*. Cambridge: Cambridge University Press.

———. 1990. "Politics, Patronage, and the Master of the Revels, 1622–1640: The Case of Sir John Astley." *English Literary Renaissance* 20, no. 2:287–319.

———. 1991. *Mastering the Revels: The Regulation and Censorship of English Renaissance Drama*. Iowa City: University of Iowa Press.

———. Forthcoming. "Ben Jonson and the Master of the Revels." In *Theatre and Government under the Early Stuarts,* ed. Martin Butler. Cambridge: Cambridge University Press.

Eagleton, Terry. 1976. *Ideology and Criticism*. London: Verso.

———. 1983. "Political Criticism." In *Literary Theory*, pp. 194–217. Oxford: Oxford University Press.

———. 1984. *The Function of Criticism: From the "Spectator" to Post-structuralism*. London: Verso.

———. 1986. "Fredric Jameson: The Politics of Style." In *Against the Grain*, pp. 65–78. London: Verso.

———. 1990. *The Ideology of the Aesthetic*. Oxford: Basil Blackwell.

Eccles, Marc. 1933. "Sir George Buc, Master of the Revels." In *Thomas Lodge and Other Elizabethans,* ed. C. J. Sisson, pp. 409–506. Cambridge: Harvard University Press.

———. 1937. "Jonson and the Spies." *Review of English Studies* 13:285–89.

Edwards, Edward. 1864. *Libraries and Founders of Libraries*. London. Rpt. Amsterdam: Gerard Th. Van Heusdan, 1968.

Edwards, Philip. 1979. *Threshold of a Nation: A Study in English and Irish Drama*. Cambridge: Cambridge University Press.

Eisenstein, Elizabeth. 1979. *The Printing Press as an Agent of Change: Communications and Cultural Transformations in Early Modern Europe*. Cambridge: Cambridge University Press.

Elias, Norbert. 1978. *The Civilizing Process: The Development of Manners: Changes in the Code of Conduct and Feeling in Early Modern Times*. Trans. Edmund Jephcott. New York: Urizen Books.

Elsky, Martin. 1989. *Authorizing Words: Speech, Writing, and Print in the English Renaissance*. Ithaca: Cornell University Press.

Ely, Geoff, and William Hunt, eds. 1988. *Reviving the English Revolution: Reflections and Elaborations on the Work of Christopher Hill*. London: Verso.

Enck, John J. 1957. *Jonson and the Comic Truth*. Madison: University of Wisconsin Press.

Esdaile, Katherine A. 1943. "Ben Jonson and the Devil Tavern." *Essays and Studies* 29:93–100.

Evans, Robert C. 1989. *Ben Jonson and the Poetics of Patronage*. Lewisburg, Pa.: Bucknell University Press.

Ferguson, Margaret W. 1979. *Trials of Desire: Renaissance Defenses of Poetry*. New Haven: Yale University Press.

———. 1987. Afterword to *Shakespeare Reproduced: The Text in History and Ideology*, ed. Jean Howard and Marion O'Connor. London: Methuen.

Ferguson, Margaret W., et al., eds. 1986. *Rewriting the Renaissance: The Discourses of Early Modern Europe*. Chicago: University of Chicago Press.

Finkelpearl, Philip J. 1982. "The Role of the Court in the Development of Jacobean Drama." *Criticism* 24 (Spring): 138–58.

———. 1986. " 'The Comedian's Liberty': Jacobean Censorship Reconsidered." *English Literary Renaissance* 16, no. 1:123–38.

———. 1987. "The Bard and the Barbarians: The Present of Absence." Unpublished paper delivered at the Folger Shakespeare Library, Washington, D.C.

Finley, M. I. 1977. "Censorship in Classical Antiquity." *Times Literary Supplement*, July 29, pp. 755–56.

Firth, C. H., and R. S. Rait, eds. 1911. *Acts and Ordinances of the Interregnum, 1642–1660*. 2 vols. London: Wyman and Sons.

Fischer, Jeffrey. 1977. "*Love Restored*: A Defense of Masquing." *Renaissance Drama* n.s. 8:233–53.

Fish, Stanley. 1984. "Authors-Readers: Jonson's Community of the Same." *Representations* 7:26–58.

———. 1988a. "Commentary: The Young and the Restless." In *The New Historicism*, ed. H. Aram Vesser, pp. 303–16. New York: Routledge.

———. 1988b. "Driving from the Letter: Truth and Indeterminacy in Milton's *Areopagitica*." In *Re-membering Milton: Essays on Texts and Traditions*, ed. Mary Nyquist and Margaret W. Ferguson, pp. 234–54. New York: Methuen.

———. 1992. "There's No Such Thing as Free Speech, and It's a Good Thing

Too." In *Debating PC: The Controversy over Political Correctness on College Campuses*, ed. Paul Berman, pp. 231–49. New York: Bantam Books.

"The Flag and the Community." 1990. *Wall Street Journal*, June 18, p. A10.

Foner, Eric, and Jon Weiner. 1991. "Fighting for the West." *Nation*, July 29, pp. 163–64.

Ford, John. 1887. *Dramatic Works*. 2 vols. Ed. John Gifford. London: John Murray.

Foster, Elizabeth Read. 1960. "The Procedure of the House of Commons against Patents and Monopolies, 1621–1624." In *Conflict in Stuart England: Essays in Honor of Wallace Notestein*, ed. William Aiken, pp. 70–94. London: J. Cape.

Foucault, Michel. 1977a. *Discipline and Punish: The Birth of the Prison*. Trans. Alan Sheridan. New York: Pantheon.

———. 1977b. "Intellectuals and Power." In *Language, Counter-Memory, Practice: Selected Essays and Interviews*, ed. Donald F. Bouchard, trans. Sherry Simon, pp. 205–17. Ithaca: Cornell University Press.

———. 1977c. "Nietzsche, Genealogy, and History." In *Language, Counter-Memory, Practice: Selected Essays and Interviews*, ed. Donald F. Bouchard, trans. Sherry Simon, pp. 113–38. Ithaca: Cornell University Press.

———. 1977d. "What Is an Author?" In *Language, Counter-Memory, Practice: Selected Essays and Interviews*, ed. Donald F. Bouchard, trans. Sherry Simon, pp. 139–64. Ithaca: Cornell University Press.

———. 1977e. *Power/Knowledge: Selected Interviews and Other Writings, 1972–77*. Ed. Colin Gibson. New York: Vintage.

———. 1978. *The History of Sexuality*, vol. 1: *An Introduction*. Trans. Robert Hurley, New York: Pantheon Books.

Fox, Harold G. 1947. *Monopolies and Patents: A Study of the History and Future of the Patent Monopoly*. Toronto: University of Toronto Press.

Franklin, Phyllis. 1989. "From the Editor." *Modern Language Association Newsletter* (Winter): 3–4.

Freehafer, John T. 1969. "Brome, Suckling, and Davenant's Theater Project of 1639." *Texas Studies in Language and Literature* 10:367–83.

Freud, Sigmund. 1964. *Moses and Monotheism*. In *The Standard Edition of the Complete Psychological Works of Sigmund Freud*, ed. and trans. James Strachey et al. Vol. 23. London: Hogarth Press.

Gardiner, Samuel R., ed. 1906. *The Constitutional Documents of the Puritan Revolution, 1625–1660*. 3d ed. Oxford: Clarendon Press.

Gates, Henry Louis, Jr. 1990. "2 Live Crew Decoded." *New York Times*, June 19, p. A26.

Gildersleeve, Virginia. 1908. *Government Regulation of the Elizabethan Drama*. Rpt. Westport, Conn.: Greenwood Press, 1975.

Goldberg, Jonathan. 1983a. *James I and the Politics of Literature: Jonson, Shakespeare, Donne, and Their Contemporaries*. Baltimore: Johns Hopkins University Press.

———. 1983b. "The Politics of English Renaissance Literature: A Review Essay." *English Literary History* 49, no. 4:153–82.

————. 1990. *Writing Matter: From the Hands of the English Renaissance.* Stanford: Stanford University Press.

Gossett, Suzanne. 1988. " 'Man-Maid Begone!': Women in Masques." *English Literary Renaissance* 18, no. 1:96–113.

Govett, L. A. 1890. *The King's Book of Sports.* London.

Green, Mary Anne Everett. 1872. *Calendar of State Papers: Domestic Series of the Reigns of Edward VI, Mary, Elizabeth, and James I, 1547–1625.* Vol. 12. Rpt. Nendelen, Lichtenstein: Klaus Reprints, 1967.

Greenblatt, Stephen. 1980. *Renaissance Self-Fashioning: From More to Shakespeare.* Chicago: University of Chicago Press.

————. 1988. *Shakespearean Negotiations: The Circulation of Social Energy in Renaissance England.* Berkeley: University of California Press.

————. 1990. *Learning to Curse: Essays in Early Modern Culture.* New York: Routledge.

Greene, Thomas. 1982. *The Light in Troy: Imitation and Discovery in Renaissance Poetry.* New Haven: Yale University Press.

Grivelet, Michel. 1954. "Notes sur Thomas Heywood et le théâtre sous Charles Ier." *Etudes Anglaise* 8, no. 1:101–6.

Guicharnaud, Jacques. 1989. "The Comédie Française." In *A New History of French Literature,* ed. Denis Hollier, pp. 345–58. Cambridge: Harvard University Press.

Guilding, J. M. 1895. *Reading Records: Diary of a Corporation, James I to Charles I.* Vol. 2. London: James Parker.

Gurr, Andrew. 1970. *The Shakespearean Stage, 1574–1642.* Cambridge: Cambridge University Press.

————. 1987. *Playgoing in Shakespeare's London.* Cambridge: Cambridge University Press.

————. 1988. "Singing through the Chatter: Ford and Contemporary Theatrical Fashion." In *John Ford: Critical Re-Visions,* ed. Michael Neill, pp. 81–96. Cambridge: Cambridge University Press.

Habermas, Jürgen. 1972. *Knowledge and Human Interests.* Trans. Jeremy Shapiro. Boston: Beacon Press.

————. 1989. *The Structural Transformation of the Public Sphere: An Inquiry into a Category of Bourgeois Society.* Trans. Thomas Burger. Cambridge: MIT Press.

Halasz, Alexandra. 1990. "Mapping Pamphlets." Unpublished paper delivered at the Shakespeare Association of America meeting, Vancouver.

Hall, Stuart. 1981. "Notes on Deconstructing the 'Popular.' " In *People's History and Socialist Theory,* ed. Raphael Samuel, pp. 227–43. London: Routledge and Kegan Paul.

————. 1986. "Popular Culture and the State." In *Popular Culture and Social Relations,* ed. Tony Bennett et al., pp. 22–49. Philadelphia: Open University Press.

Halpern, Richard. 1991. *The Poetics of Primitive Accumulation: Studies in the English Renaissance.* Ithaca: Cornell University Press.

Harbage, Alfred. 1936. *Cavalier Drama: An Historical Study and Critical Supplement to the Study of the Elizabethan and Restoration Stage.* Rpt. New York: Russell and Russell, 1964.

———. 1967. *Shakespeare and the Rival Traditions*. Bloomington: Indiana University Press.

Harrison, G. B., ed. 1966. *A Jacobean Journal: Being a Record of Those Things Most Talked of during the Years 1603–1606*. New York: Macmillan.

Harsnett, Samuel. 1603. *The Declaration of egregious Popish Impostures, to withdraw the harts of her Maiesties Subiects from their allegeance, and from the Christian Religion professed in England, vnder the pretence of casting out deuils*. London: James Roberts.

Haynes, Jonathan. 1984. "Festivity and the Dramatic Economy of Jonson's *Bartholomew Fair*." *English Literary History* 51, no. 4:645–68.

Hedrick, Don K. 1977. "Cooking for the Anthropophagi: Jonson and His Audience." *Studies in English Literature* 17:233–45.

Heinemann, Margot. 1980. "Puritanism, Censorship, and Opposition to the Theatre." In *Puritanism and Theatre: Thomas Middleton and Opposition Drama under the Early Stuarts*, pp. 18–47. Cambridge: Past and Present.

Helgerson, Richard. 1983. *Self-Crowned Laureates: Spenser, Jonson, Milton, and the Literary System*. Berkeley: University of California Press.

Herman, Edward S., and Noam Chomsky. 1988. *Manufacturing Consent: The Political Economy of the Mass Media*. New York: Pantheon.

Hertz, Neil. 1985. *The End of the Line: Essays on Psychoanalysis and the Sublime*. New York: Columbia University Press.

Hess, Elizabeth. 1990. "Artist Doesn't Turn the Other Cheek." *Village Voice* September 9, pp. 98–99.

Hill, Christopher. 1961. *The Century of Revolution, 1603–1714*. New York: Norton.

———. 1964. "The Uses of Sabbatarianism." In *Society and Puritanism in Prerevolutionary England*, pp. 145–218. Rpt. New York: Schocken Books, 1972.

———. 1985. "Censorship and English Literature." In *The Collected Works of Christopher Hill*, 1:32–72. Amherst: University of Massachusetts Press.

———. 1986. "Literature and the English Revolution." *Seventeenth Century* 1, no. 1:15–30.

Hohendahl, Peter Uwe. 1982. *The Institution of Criticism*. Ithaca: Cornell University Press.

Holstun, James. 1989. "Ranting at the New Historicism." *English Literary Renaissance* 19, no. 2:189–225.

Holub, Robert C. 1984. *Reception Theory: A Critical Introduction*. London: Methuen.

Horkheimer, Max, and Theodor Adorno. 1944. *The Dialectic of Enlightenment*. New York: Seabury, 1969.

Howard, Jean R. 1986. "The New Historicism and Renaissance Studies." *English Literary Renaissance*. 16, no. 1:26–46.

———. 1991. "Script and/versus Playhouses: Ideological Production and the Renaissance Stage." In *The Matter of Difference: Materialist Feminist Criticism of Shakespeare*, ed. Valerie Wayne, pp. 211–36. Ithaca: Cornell University Press.

Howard, Jean R., and Marion O'Connor. 1987. Introduction to *Shakespeare*

Reproduced: The Text in History and Ideology, ed. Howard and O'Connor. London: Methuen.

Hughes, Geoffrey. 1991. *Swearing: A Social History of Foul Language, Oaths, and Profanity in English.* Oxford: Blackwell.

Hulme, E. Wyndam. 1896. "The History of the Patent System under the Prerogative and at Common Law." *Law Quarterly Review* 12:141–54.

———. 1900. "The History of the Patent System under the Prerogative and at Common Law: A Sequel." *Law Quarterly Review* 16:44–56.

Hume, David. 1742. "Of the Standard of Taste." In *Essays, Moral, Political and Literary,* pp. 253–77. London.

Hunter, J. 1847. "An Account of the Scheme for Erecting a Royal Academy in England in the Reign of James I." *Archaeologia* 32:132–49.

Hyde, William. 1913. *The English Patents of Monopoly.* Cambridge: Harvard University Press.

Ignatieff, Michael. 1989. "The Value of Toleration." In *The Rushdie File,* ed. Lisa Appiganesi and Sara Maitland, pp. 254–56. Syracuse: Syracuse University Press.

Irwin, R. 1958. *The Origins of the English Library.* London: George Allen and Unwin.

———. 1964. *The Heritage of the English Library.* London: George Allen and Unwin.

"The Ivory Censor." 1990. *Wall Street Journal,* April 23, p. A14.

Jackson, Sidney L. 1974. *Libraries and Librarianship in the West.* New York: McGraw-Hill.

Jameson, Fredric. 1981. *The Political Unconscious: Narrative as a Socially Symbolic Act.* Ithaca: Cornell University Press.

Jansen, Sue Curry. 1988. *Censorship: The Knot That Binds Power and Knowledge.* Oxford: Oxford University Press.

Javitch, Daniel. 1978. *Poetry and Courtliness in Renaissance England.* Princeton: Princeton University Press.

Jayne, Sears. 1956. *Library Catalogues of the English Renaissance.* Berkeley: University of California Press.

Johnson, Samuel. 1801. "An Account of the Harleian Library." In *The Works of Samuel Johnson, LL.D,* ed. Arthur Murphy, 2:171–83. London: Nichols and Son.

Jones, Lisa. 1990. "The Signifying Monkees: 2 Live Crew's Nasty-Boy Rap on Trial in South Florida." *Village Voice,* November 6, pp. 43–47.

Jonson, Ben. 1925–52. *Ben Jonson.* Ed. C. H. Herford, Percy Simpson, and Evelyn Simpson. 11 vols. Oxford: Clarendon Press.

———. 1969. *The Complete Masques.* Ed. Stephen Orgel. New Haven: Yale University Press.

———. 1975a. *The Complete Poems.* Ed. Robert Hunter. New Haven: Yale University Press.

———. 1975b. *Poems.* Ed. Ian Donaldson. London: Oxford University Press.

———. 1981. *The Complete Plays of Ben Jonson.* Ed. G. A. Wilkes. 4 vols. Oxford: Clarendon Press.

Jouhaud, Christian. Forthcoming. "Power and Literature: The Terms of the

Exchange in France, 1620–1640." In *The Administration of Aesthetics: Censorship, Political Criticism, and the Public Sphere,* ed. Richard Burt. Minneapolis: University of Minnesota Press.

Kant, Immanuel. 1790. *The Critique of Judgement.* Trans. James Creed Meredith. Oxford: Clarendon Press, 1925.

Kaplan, Joel. 1970. "Moral and Dramatic Energy in *Bartholomew Fair.*" *Renaissance Drama* n.s. 3:137–56.

Kastan, David Scott. 1988. "The Summer of '42: the Closing of the Theaters." Unpublished paper delivered at the Renaissance Society of America meeting, Columbia University.

Kaufman, Ralph J. 1961. *Richard Brome: Caroline Playwright.* New York: Columbia University Press.

Kaula, David. 1976. "Autolycus's Trumpery." *Studies in English Literature* 16:287–303.

Kay, David W. 1970. "The Shaping of Ben Jonson's Career: A Reexamination of Facts and Problems." *Modern Philology* 67:224–37.

Kegl, Rosemary. 1990. "Those Terrible Approaches: Sexuality, Social Mobility, and Resisting Courtliness in Puttenham's *The Arte of English Poesie.*" *English Literary Renaissance* 20, no. 2:179–208.

Kendrick, Walter. 1987. *The Secret Museum: Pornography and Modern Culture.* New York: Viking.

Kernan, Alvin. 1987. *Samuel Johnson and the Impact of Print.* Princeton: Princeton University Press.

Kimball, Roger. 1990. *Tenured Radicals: How Politics Has Corrupted Our Higher Education.* New York: Harper & Row.

Kimmelman, Michael. "Peeping into Peepholes and Finding Politics." *New York Times,* July 21, pp. E1, 29.

Kinney, Arthur F., ed. 1990. *Rogues, Vagabonds, and Sturdy Beggars.* Rpt. Amherst: University of Massachusetts Press.

Knapp, Peggy. 1979. "Ben Jonson and the Publicke Riot." *English Literary History* 46, no. 4:577–94.

Knights, L. C. 1937. *Drama and Society in the Age of Jonson.* Rpt. New York: W. W. Norton, 1968.

Kramer, Hilton. 1989. "Notes and Comments." *New Criterion* 8, no. 1:1–2.

Kristeva, Julia. 1984. *Revolution in Poetic Language.* Trans. Margaret Waller. New York: Columbia University Press.

Laclau, Ernesto. 1988. "Metaphor and Social Antagonism." In *Marxism and the Interpretation of Culture,* ed. Cary Nelson and Lawrence Grossberg, pp. 249–58. Urbana: University of Illinois Press.

Laclau, Ernesto, and Chantal Mouffe. 1985. *Hegemony and Socialist Strategy: Towards a Radical Democratic Politics.* Trans. Winston Moore and Paul Commack. London: Verso.

Lambert, Shiela. 1987. "The Printers and the Government, 1604–1637." In *Aspects of Printing from 1600,* ed. Robin Meyers and Michael Harris, pp. 1–29. Oxford: Oxford Polylecture Press.

Lancashire, Anne, ed. 1978. *The Second Maiden's Tragedy.* Baltimore: Johns Hopkins University Press.

Landes, Joan B. 1988. *Women and the Public Sphere in the Age of the French Revolution*. Ithaca: Cornell University Press.

Langbein, John. 1977. *Torture and the Law of Proof*. Chicago: University of Chicago Press.

Laplanche, Jean, and J.B. Pontalis. 1973. *The Language of Psychoanalysis*. Trans. Donald Nicholson-Smith. New York: W. W. Norton.

Larkin James F., and Paul L. Hughes, eds. 1973. *Stuart Royal Proclamations*. 2 vols. Oxford: Clarendon Press.

Larsen, Magali Sarfatti. 1977. *The Rise of Professionalism: A Sociological Analysis*. Berkeley: University of California Press.

Levin, Richard. 1965. "The Structure of *Bartholomew Fair*," *Publications of the Modern Language Association* 80:173–78.

Levine, Michael. 1986. "Censorship's Self-Administration." *Psychoanalysis and Contemporary Thought*. 9, no. 4:605–40.

Levy, F. J. 1988. "Review of *Dangerous Matter: English Drama and Politics in 1623–24, Renaissance Drama in England and Spain, and Theatre and Crisis, 1632–1642*." *Shakespeare Studies* 20:294–306.

Licata, Elizabeth. 1990. "Bibles Not for Burning." *Art News* (November): 49–51.

Liesenfeld, Vincent J. 1984. *The Licensing Act of 1737*. Madison: University of Wisconsin Press.

Limon, Jerzy. 1986. *Dangerous Matter: English Drama and Politics in 1623–24*. Cambridge: Cambridge University Press.

Limoze, Henry Winter. 1980. " 'The Surest Suppressing': Writer and Censor in Milton's *Areopagitica*." *Centennial Review* 24, no. 1:103–17.

Lindley, David. 1986. "Embarrassing Ben: The Masques for Frances Howard." *English Literary Renaissance* 16, no. 2:343–59.

Lipman, Samuel. 1990. "Backward and Downward with the Arts." *Commentary* 89, no. 5:23–26.

Livingston, Jane. 1991. "When Museums Run Scared: Beware the Tyranny of Public Opinion." *Washington Post,* July 21, pp. G1, 9.

Lodge, David, ed. 1988. *Modern Criticism and Theory: A Reader*. London: Longman.

Loewenstein, Joseph. 1984. *Responsive Readings: Versions of Echo in Pastoral, Epic, and the Jonsonian Masque*. Yale Studies in English no. 192. New Haven: Yale University Press.

——. 1985. "The Script in the Marketplace." *Representations* 12:101–14.

——. 1986. "The Jonsonian Corpulence, or The Poet as Mouthpiece." *English Literary History* 53, no. 3:491–518.

——. 1990. "Printing and 'the Multitudinous Presse': The Contentious Texts of Jonson's Masques." In *Ben Jonson's 1616 Folio,* ed. Jennifer Brady and W. H. Henrendeen, pp. 168–91. Newark: University of Delaware Press.

Loftis, John T. 1963. *The Politics of Drama in Augustan England*. Oxford: Clarendon Press.

Loomie, Albert, S.J. 1987. *Ceremonies at the Court of Charles I: The Note Books of John Finet, 1628–1641*. New York: Fordham University Press.

Macherey, Pierre. 1978. *A Theory of Literary Production.* Trans. Geoffrey Wall. London: Routledge and Kegan Paul.

McIlwain, Charles, ed. 1965. *The Political Works of James I.* New York: Russell and Russell.

Mack, Maynard. 1987. *Alexander Pope: A Biography.* New Haven: Yale University Press.

McMullan, John L. 1984. *The Canting Crew: London's Criminal Underworld, 1550–1700.* New Brunswick, N.J.: Rutgers University Press.

McPherson, David. 1974. "Ben Jonson's Library and Marginalia." *Studies in Philology* 71, no. 5:v–106.

———. 1985. "Three Charges against Sixteenth- and Seventeenth-Century Playwrights: Libel, Bawdry, and Blasphemy." *Medieval and Renaissance Drama* 2:269–83.

Malcolmson, Robert W. 1973. *Popular Recreation in English Society, 1700–1850.* Cambridge: Cambridge University Press.

Marcus, Leah S. 1979. "The Occasion of *Pleasure Reconciled to Virtue.*" *Studies in English Literature* 19:271–93.

———. 1986a. "Defining Opposition Drama: The Court against the Court." Unpublished paper delivered at the MLA meeting, New York.

———. 1986b. *The Politics of Mirth: Jonson, Herrick, Milton and the Defense of Old Holiday Pastimes.* Chicago: University of Chicago Press.

———. 1988. *Puzzling Shakespeare: Local Reading and Its Discontents.* Berkeley: University of California Press.

Marin, Louis. 1972. *Etudes sémiologiques.* Paris: Klincksieck.

Marmion, Shakerly. 1979. *A Fine Companion by Shakerly Marmion: A Critical Edition.* Ed. Richard Sonnenshein. New York: Garland.

Marx, Karl. 1842. "Comments on the Latest Prussian Censorship Instruction." In Karl Marx and Frederick Engels, *Collected Works*, vol. 1: *Marx, 1835–1843*, pp. 109–31. Rpt. Moscow: Progress, 1970.

Massinger, Philip. 1976. *The Plays and Poems of Philip Massinger.* Ed. Philip Edwards and Colin Gibson. 4 vols. Oxford: Clarendon Press.

Matsuda, Mari J. 1989. "Public Response to Racist Speech: Considering the Victim's Story." *Michigan Law Review* 87, no. 8:2320–81.

Maus, Katharine Eisaman. 1984. *Ben Jonson and the Roman Frame of Mind.* Princeton: Princeton University Press.

———. 1989. "Ideal and Satiric Economies in the Jonsonian Imagination." *English Literary Renaissance* 19, no. 1:42–64.

Mennel, Stephen. 1985. *All Manner of Food: Eating and Taste in England and France from the Middle Ages to the Present.* London: Basil Blackwell.

Middleton, Thomas. 1964. *The Works of Thomas Middleton.* Ed. Andrew Bullen. 8 vols. New York: AMS Press.

Montrose, Louis Adrian. 1980. "The Purpose of Playing: Reflections on a Shakespearean Anthropology." *Helios* n.s. 7:51–74.

———. 1983. "Of Gentlemen and Shepherds: The Politics of Elizabethan Pastoral Form." *English Literary History* 50:415–59.

——. 1986. "Renaissance Literary Studies and the Subject of History." *English Literary Renaissance* 16, no. 1:5–12.

Moretti, Franco. 1983. "The Great Eclipse: Tragic Form as the Deconsecration of Tragedy." In *Signs Taken for Wonders: Essays in the Sociology of Literary Forms*, pp. 42–82. London: New Left Books.

Mullaney, Steven. 1987. *The Place of the Stage: License, Play, and Power in Renaissance England*. Chicago: University of Chicago Press.

Murray, John T. 1963. *English Dramatic Companies, 1558–1642*. 2 vols. New York: Russell and Russell.

Murray, Timothy J. 1987. *Theatrical Legitimation: Allegories of Genius in Seventeenth-Century England and France*. Oxford: Oxford University Press.

——. 1989. "The Academy Française." In *A New History of French Literature*, ed. Denis Hollier, pp. 267–73. Cambridge: Harvard University Press.

Nabbes, Thomas. 1882–89. *The Works of Thomas Nabbes*. Ed. A. H. Bullen. New York: Benjamin Bloom, 1968.

Neely, Carol T. 1987. "Constructing the Subject: Feminist Practice and the New Renaissance Discourses." *English Literary Renaissance* 18, no. 3:3–19.

Newton, Richard C. 1979. " 'Ben. / Jonson': The Poet in the Poems." In *Two Renaissance Mythmakers: Christopher Marlowe and Ben Jonson*, ed. Alvin Kernan, pp. 145–69. Baltimore: Johns Hopkins University Press.

——. 1982. "Jonson and the (Re)-invention of the Book." In *Classic and Cavalier: Essays on Jonson and the Sons of Ben*, ed. Claude J. Summers and Ted Larry Pebworth, pp. 31–55. Pittsburgh: University of Pittsburgh Press.

Nichols, John. 1828. *The Progresses, Processions, and Magnificent Festivities of King James the First*. 4 vols. London.

Norbrook, David. 1984a. *Poetry and Politics in the English Renaissance*. London: Routledge and Kegan Paul.

——. 1984b. "The Reformation of the Court Masque." In *The Court Masque*, ed. David Lindley, pp. 94–110. Manchester: Manchester University Press.

——. 1984c. "Absolute Revision." *English* 33:251–63.

——. 1991. "Levelling Poetry: George Wither and the English Revolution, 1642–1649." *English Literary Renaissance* 21, no. 2:217–56.

——. Forthcoming. "*Areopagitica*, Censorship, and the Early Modern Public Sphere." In *The Administration of Aesthetics: Censorship, Political Criticism, and the Public Sphere*, ed. Richard Burt. Minneapolis: University of Minnesota Press.

O'Connell, Michael. 1985. "The Idolatrous Eye: Iconoclasm, Antitheatricalism, and the Image of the Elizabethan Theater." *English Literary History* 52, no. 2:279–310.

Orgel, Stephen. 1975. *The Illusion of Power: Political Theater in the English Renaissance*. Berkeley: University of California Press.

——. 1981. "The Royal Theatre and the Role of the King." In *Patronage in the Renaissance*, ed. Guy Fitch Lytle and Stephen Orgel, pp. 261–73. Princeton: Princeton University Press.

——. 1982. "Making Greatness Familiar." In *The Power of Forms*, ed. Stephen Greenblatt, pp. 41–46. Norman: University of Oklahoma Press.

———. 1988. "The Authentic Shakespeare." *Representations* 21:1–26.

———. 1989a. "The Boys in the Backroom: Shakespeare's Apprentices and the Economy of Theater." Unpublished paper presented at the MLA meeting, New Orleans.

———. 1989b. "'Nobody's Perfect,' or Why Did the English Stage Take Boys for Women." *South Atlantic Quarterly* 88, no. 1:7–30.

Orgel, Stephen, and Roy Strong, eds. 1973. *Inigo Jones: The Theater of the Early Stuart Court*. 2 vols. Berkeley: University of California Press.

Parry, L. A. 1975. *The History of Torture in England*. Montclair, N.J.: Patterson Smith.

Patterson, Annabel. 1982. "'Roman Cast Similitude': Ben Jonson and the English Use of Roman History." In *Rome in the Renaissance: The City and the Myth*, ed. Peter A. Ramsay, pp. 381–94. Binghamton, N.Y.: Center for Medieval and Early Renaissance Studies.

———. 1984. *Censorship and Interpretation: The Conditions of Reading and Writing in Early Modern England*. Madison: University of Wisconsin Press.

———. 1985. "Lyric and Society in Jonson's *Underwood*." In *Lyric Poetry: Beyond New Criticism*, ed. Chaviva Hosek and Patricia Parker, pp. 148–67. Ithaca: Cornell University Press.

———. 1989. *Shakespeare and the Popular Voice*. London: Basil Blackwell.

———. 1990. "Censorship." In *The Encyclopedia of Literature and Criticism*, ed. Matthew Coyle et al., pp. 901–14. London: Routledge.

Payne, Harry. 1979. "Elite *versus* Popular Mentality in the Eighteenth Century." *Studies in Eighteenth-Century Culture* 8:11–35.

Pearl, Sara. 1984. "Sounding to Present Occasions: Jonson's Masques of 1620–25." In *The Court Masque*, ed. David Lindley, pp. 60–77. Manchester: Manchester University Press.

Portal, E. M. 1915–16. "The Academy Roial of James I." *Proceedings of the British Academy* 7:189–208.

Porter, Carolyn. 1988. "Are We Being Historical Yet?" *South Atlantic Quarterly* 87, no. 4:743–86.

Potter, Lois. 1989. *Secret Rites: Secret Writing*. Cambridge: Cambridge University Press.

Prynne, William. 1632. *Histromastix: The Players Scourge, or Actors Tragedie*. London: A. E. and W. I. for Michael Sparke.

Putnam, G. H. 1906. *The Censorship of the Church of Rome and Its Influence upon the Production and Distribution of Literature*. 2 vols. New York: Benjamin Bloom.

Rajchman, John. 1985. *Michel Foucault: The Freedom of Philosophy*. New York: Columbia University Press.

Randall, Dale. 1975. *Jonson's Gypsies Unmasked*. Durham: Duke University Press.

Redwine, James D., ed. 1970. *Ben Jonson's Literary Criticism*. Lincoln: University of Nebraska Press.

Reeve, L. J. 1989. *Charles I and the Road to Personal Rule*. Cambridge: Cambridge University Press.

Riggs, David. 1988. *Ben Jonson: A Life*. Cambridge: Harvard University Press.

Robbins, Bruce, ed. 1990. "The Phantom Public Sphere." *Social Text* 25/26:3–7.

Robertson, Duncan Maclaren. 1910. *A History of the French Academy, 1635–1910*. New York: D. W. Dillingham.

Roche, Daniel. 1989. "Censorship and the Publishing Industry." In *Revolution in Print: The Press in France, 1775–1800*, ed. Robert Darnton and Daniel Roche, pp. 3–26. Princeton: Princeton University Press.

Rojek, Chris. 1985. *Capitalism and Leisure Theory*. New York: Tavistock.

Ross, Andrew. 1989. *No Respect: Intellectuals and Popular Culture*. London: Routledge.

———. 1990. "The Fine Art of Regulation." Unpublished paper presented at MLA meeting, San Francisco.

Rowe, George E. 1988. *Distinguishing Jonson: Imitation, Rivalry, and the Direction of a Dramatic Career*. Lincoln: University of Nebraska Press.

Rowse, A. L., ed. 1976. *The Case Books of Simon Forman*. London: Picador.

Rushdie, Salman. 1990. "An Interview with Salman Rushdie." *Granta* 10:27–36.

Sabel, Claude, ed. 1991. *La tolérance: Pour un humanisme hérétique*. Serie Morales no. 5. Paris: Autrement.

Said, Edward. 1983. "Opponents, Audiences, Constituencies, and Community." In *The Anti-Aesthetic: Essays on Postmodern Culture*, ed. Hal Foster, pp. 135–59. Port Townsend, Wash.: Bay Press.

Salingar, L. G., Gerald Harrison, and Bruce Cochrane, eds. 1968. "Les comédiens et leur publique en Angleterre de 1520 à 1640." In *Dramaturgie et société: Rapports entre l'oeuvre théâtrale, son interprétation, et son public aux XVIe et XVIIe siècles*, ed. Jean Jacquot, Elie Konigson, and Marcel Oddon, 2:569–73. Paris: Centre National de la Recherche Scientifique.

Saunders, J. W. 1964. *The Profession of English Letters*. London: Routledge and Kegan Paul.

Schiller, Herbert I. 1989. *Culture Inc.: The Corporate Takeover of Public Expression*. Oxford: Oxford University Press.

Schoenfeldt, Michael. 1988. "'The Mysteries of Manners, Armes, and Arts,' 'Inviting a Friend to Supper,' and 'To Penshurst.'" In *The Muses' Commonweal: Poetry and Politics in the Seventeenth Century*, ed. Claude J. Summers and Ted Larry Pebworth, pp. 62–79. Columbia: University of Missouri Press.

Schöpflin, George. 1983. *Censorship and Political Communication in Europe*. New York: St. Martin's Press.

Schrecker, Ellen. 1986. *No Ivory Tower: McCarthyism and the Universities*. Oxford: Oxford University Press.

Scot, Reginald. 1576. *The Discoverie of Witchcraft*. Rpt. Carbondale: Southern Illinois University Press, 1964.

Scott, William Robert. 1912. *The Constitution and Finance of English, Scottish, and Irish Joint Stock Companies to 1720*. 3 vols. Cambridge: Cambridge University Press.

Selden, Raman. 1988. *The Theory of Criticism: From Plato to the Present*. London: Longman.

Senescu, Frances, ed. 1980. *James Shirley's "The Bird in a Cage:" A Critical Edition*. New York: Garland.

Shakespeare, William. 1980. *The Complete Works of Shakespeare*. Ed. David Bevington. 3d ed. Glendale, Ill.: Scott, Foresman.

Shapiro, I. A. 1950. "The Mermaid Club." *Modern Language Review* 45:6–17.

Sharpe, Kevin, ed. 1978. *Faction and Parliament: Essays on Early Stuart History*. London: Methuen.

Sharpe, Kevin. 1979. *Sir Robert Cotton, 1586–1631: History and Politics in Early Modern England*. Oxford: Oxford University Press.

———. 1987. *Criticism and Compliment: The Politics of Literature in the England of Charles I*. Cambridge: Cambridge University Press.

Shirley, James. 1833. *Dramatic Works of James Shirley*. Ed. William Gifford. 7 vols. Rpt. New York: Russell and Russell, 1966.

Siebert, Frederick. 1952. *Freedom of the Press in England, 1476–1776: The Rise and Decline of Government Controls*. Urbana: University of Illinois Press.

Sinfield, Alan. 1985. "Reproductions, Interventions." In *Political Shakespeare: New Essays in Cultural Materialism*, ed. Jonathan Dollimore and Sinfield, pp. 130–33. Ithaca: Cornell University Press.

Slack, Paul. 1974. "Vagrants and Vagrancy in England, 1558–1664." *Economic History Review*, 2d series, 28, no. 3:360–79.

Smith, Alan G. R. 1979. "Crown, Parliament, and Finance: The Great Contract of 1610," *The English Commonwealth, 1547–60: Essays on Politics and Society*. Peter Clark, Smith, and Nicholas Tyacke, eds. New York: Barnes and Noble.

Smith, Logan, ed. 1907. *The Life and Letters of Sir Henry Wotton to Sir Edmund Bacon*. 2 vols. Oxford: Clarendon Press.

Smuts, R. Malcolm. 1987. *Court Culture and the Origins of a Royalist Tradition in Early Stuart England*. Philadelphia: University of Pennsylvania Press.

———. 1991. "Cultural Diversity and Cultural Change at the Court of James I." In *The Mental World of the Jacobean Court*, ed. Linda Levy Peck, pp. 99–112. Cambridge: Cambridge University Press.

Speaight, George. 1956. *The History of the English Puppet Theater*. New York: John de Graff.

Springarn, J. E. 1974. *Critical Essays of the Seventeenth Century*, vol. 1: *1605–1650*. Bloomington: Indiana University Press.

Stallybrass, Peter. 1986. " 'Wee Feaste in Our Defense': Patrician Carnival in Early Modern England and Robert Herrick's *Hesperides*." *English Literary Renaissance* 16 (Winter): 234–52.

———. 1991. "The World Turned Upside Down." In *The Matter of Difference: Materialist Feminist Criticism of Shakespeare*, ed. Valerie Wayne, pp. 201–20. Ithaca: Cornell University Press.

Stallybrass, Peter, and Allon White. 1986. *The Poetics and Politics of Transgression*. Ithaca: Cornell University Press.

Staniszewski, Mary Ann. 1989. "Photo Opportunities." *Art and Auction* 12, no. 1:20–22.

Stephen, Leslie. 1963. *English Literature and Society in the Eighteenth Century*. London.

Stimpson, Catharine R. 1990. "President's Column." *Modern Language Association Newsletter* (Summer): 2–3.

Stone, Lawrence. 1967. *The Crisis of the Aristocracy, 1558–1641*. Oxford: Oxford University Press.

Streitberger, W. R. 1986. *Edmund Tyllney, Master of the Revels and Censor of Plays: A Descriptive Index to His Manual on Europe*. New York: AMS Press.

Stubbes, Philip. 1583. *Anatomy of Abuse*. New York: Johnson Reprint, 1972.

Suleiman, Susan, et al., eds. 1990. *Social Control and the Arts: An International Perspective*. Cambridge, Mass.: New Cambridge Press.

Sutherland, James. 1943. *The Poems of Alexander Pope*. Vol. 5. New Haven: Yale University Press.

Sweeney, John Gordon, III. 1985. *Jonson and the Psychology of Public Theater: To Coin the Spirit, Spend the Soul*. Princeton: Princeton University Press.

Sykes, Charles J. 1988. *Profscam: Professors and the Demise of Higher Education*. New York: St. Martin's Press.

Tait, James. 1917. "The Declaration of the *Book of Sports*, 1617." *English Historical Review* 32:561–68.

Tanner, J. R., ed. 1960. *Constitutional Documents of the Reign of James I, 1603–1625, with an Historical Commentary*. Cambridge: Cambridge University Press.

Tayler, Edward W. 1967. *Literary Criticism of Seventeenth-Century England*. New York: Knopf.

Taylor, John. 1991. "Are You Politically Correct?" *New York Magazine*, January 21, pp. 32–40.

Tennenhouse, Leonard. 1986. *Power on Display: The Politics of Shakespeare's Genres*. London: Methuen.

——. 1990. "Simulating History: A Cockfight for Our Times." *Drama Review*, 34, no. 4:137–55.

Thaler, Alwin. 1920. "The Travelling Players in Shakespeare's England." *Modern Philology* 17:128–30.

Thirsk, Joan. 1978. *Economic Policy and Projects: The Development of a Consumer Society in Early Modern England*. Oxford: Oxford University Press.

Thomas, Donald. 1969. *A Long Time Burning: The History of Literary Censorship in England*. New York: Frederick A. Praeger.

Tomlinson, Sophie. 1992. "She That Plays the King: Henrietta Maria and the Threat of the Actress in Caroline Culture." In *The Politics of Tragicomedy*, ed. Gordon McMullan and Jonathan Hope, pp. 189–207. London: Routledge.

Tricomi, A. H. 1986. "Philip, Earl of Pembroke, and the Analogical Way of Reading Political Tragedy." *Journal of English and Germanic Philology* 85:332–45.

——. 1989. *Anti-court Drama in England, 1603–1642*. Charlottesville: University Press of Virginia.

Trotsky, Leon S. 1924. *Literature and Revolution*. Ann Arbor: University of Michigan Press, 1960.

Underdown, David. 1985. *Revel, Riot, and Rebellion: Popular Politics and Culture, 1603–1660*. Oxford: Clarendon Press.

Vance, Carole S. 1989. "The War on Culture." *Art in America* 77, no. 9:39–45.

Veevers, Erica. 1989. *Images of Love and Religion: Queen Henrietta Maria and Court Entertainments.* Cambridge: Cambridge University Press.

Venuti, Lawrence. 1989. *Our Halcyon Dayes: Pre-revolutionary Texts and Post-modern Culture.* Madison: University of Wisconsin.

Vickers, Nancy. 1991. "The Art of the Double Cross." Unpublished paper presented at the MLA meeting, San Francisco.

Waith, Eugene M., ed. 1963. *Ben Jonson: "Bartholomew Fair."* New Haven: Yale University Press, 1963.

Walker, Kim. 1991. *"New Prison:* Representing the Female Actor in Shirley's *The Bird in a Cage." English Literary Renaissance* 21, no. 3:385–400.

Wallen, Jeffrey. 1991. "Political Correctness: The Revenge of the Liberals, or The University and Its (Dis)contents." Unpublished paper delivered at UCLA.

Warren, Michael. 1991. "President's Letter." *Bulletin of the Shakespeare Association of America* 14, no. 1:1.

Watson, Robert C. 1987. *Ben Jonson's Parodic Style: Literary Imperialism in the Comedies.* Cambridge: Harvard University Press.

Wayne, Don E. 1982. "Drama and Society in the Age of Jonson: An Alternative View." *Renaissance Drama* n.s. 13:103–9.

———. 1984. *"To Penshurst": The Semiotics of Place and the Poetics of History.* Madison: University of Wisconsin Press.

Webster, Richard. 1990. *A Brief History of Blasphemy: Liberalism, Censorship, and "The Satanic Verses."* Southwold, Suffolk, England: Orwell Press.

Weimann, Robert. 1968. "Le déclin de la scène 'indivisible' elisabéthaine: Beaumont, Fletcher, et Heywood." In *Dramaturgie et société: Rapports entre l'oeuvre théâtrale, son interprétation, et son public aux XVIe et XVIIe siècles,* ed. Jean Jacquot, Elie Konigson, and Marcel Oddon, 2:829–45. Paris: Centre National de la Recherche Scientifique.

———. 1978. *Shakespeare and the Popular Tradition: Essays on the Social Function of Shakespeare's Dramatic Form.* Trans. Robert Schwartz. Baltimore: Johns Hopkins University Press.

Wellmer, Albrecht. 1991. *The Persistence of Modernity.* Cambridge: MIT Press.

Wheeler, G. W., ed. 1926. *Letters of Sir Thomas Bodley to Thomas James, First Keeper of the Bodleian Library.* Oxford: Clarendon Press.

White, Arthur F. 1931. "The Office of Revels and Dramatic Censorship during the Restoration." *Western Reserve University Bulletin* 34:5–45.

Whitfield, Christopher, ed. 1962. *Robert Dover and the Cotswold Games: Annalia Dubrensia.* London: Henry Sotheran.

Wickham, Glynn. 1981. *Early English Stages.* 3 vols. London: Routledge and Kegan Paul.

Wiles, David. 1987. *Shakespeare's Clown: Actor and Text in the Elizabethan Playhouse.* Cambridge: Cambridge University Press.

Williams, Raymond. 1980. *Marxism and Literature.* Oxford: Oxford University Press.

Wilson, Edmund. 1938. "Morose Ben Jonson." Rpt. in *Ben Jonson: A Collection of Critical Essays,* ed. Jonas Barish, pp. 60–74. Englewood Cliffs, N.J.: Prentice-Hall, 1963.

Wilson, Richard. 1986. "'A Mingled Yarn': Shakespeare and the Clothworkers." *Literature and History* 12:65–85.

———. 1987. "'Is This a Holiday?': Shakespeare's Roman Holiday." *English Literary History,* 54, no. 3:31–44.

———. Forthcoming. *Will Power: Essays on Shakespearean Authority.* London: Harvester Press.

Wimsatt, William K., and Cleanth Brooks. 1964. *Literary Criticism: A Short History.* New York: Alfred A. Knopf.

Witnesses: Against Our Vanishing. 1989. New York: Artists Space.

Womack, Peter. 1986. *Ben Jonson.* Oxford: Basil Blackwell.

———. 1989. "The Sign of the Light Heart: Jonson's *New Inn* 1629 and 1987." *New Theatre Quarterly* 5:18, 162–70.

Worden, Blair. 1988. "Literature and Political Censorship in Early Modern England." In *Too Mighty to Be Free: Censorship and the Press in Britain and the Netherlands,* pp. 45–62. Zutphen: De Walburg Press.

———. 1990. "Tolerant Repression." *London Review of Books,* May 10, pp. 14–17.

Wormald, Francis, and C. E. Wright, eds. 1958. *The English Library before 1700: Studies in Its History.* London: Athlone Press.

Wright, C. E. 1958. "The Elizabethan Society of Antiquaries and the Formation of the Cottonian Library." In *The English Library before 1700: Studies in Its History,* ed. Francis Wormald and Wright, pp. 176–212. London: Athlone Press.

Yachnin, Paul. 1991. "The Powerless Theater." *English Literary Renaissance* 21, no. 1:49–74.

Yoffee, Lisa. 1991. "Ethnic Casting Issues Get Soapbox Treatment." *American Theatre* 7, no. 11:34–35.

Young, Richard B. W., Todd Furniss, and G. William Mardsen, eds. 1958. *Three Studies in the Renaissance: Sidney, Jonson, and Milton.* New Haven: Yale University Press.

Index